Corruption and Lokpal

O.P. Dhiman
and
C.P. Sharma

KALPAZ

Corruption and Lokpal

O.P. Dhiman, C.P. Sharma

ISBN : 978-81-7835-951-9

Published in 2013 in India by
Kalpaz Publications
C-30, Satyawati Nagar,
Delhi - 110052
E-mail: kalpaz@hotmail.com

Laser Type Setting : Sanya Computers, Delhi
Printed at : G. Print Process.Delhi

Dedicated

To

The Crusaders

Against Corruption

And

Black Money

Contents

Preface

The year 2011 will go down in India's political history as the year of revelation of political corruption at its peak and indifferent and repressive Government attitude to the public upsurge against it. The public waited for more than half a century for an ombudsman who could act as a watch dog over misappropriation and loot of public funds by those in the Government. But the Governments could not get through the Lokpal bill on one or the other pretext reflecting that those in power were never seriously interested in it. But the public patience had exhausted with the corruption and black money increasing by leaps and bounds. The simmering public wrath needed torch bearers who could lead them in giving expression to their impotent rage against it. Baba Ramdev and Anna Hazare emerged from the Gandhian ashes to organize their wrath in a peaceful and disciplined manner, the like of which was never seen in the world history. It is unfortunate that the authoritarian attitude of the government and party in power, instead of taking a leaf out of it, completely drunk with power, did not only try to repress their voice but abused, rebuked and ridiculed them. In turn, it challenged the fundamental rights of the people, forgot their written promises, flouted the 'sense of the House' and tried to carry through a dummy Lokpal and Lokayukta Bill, 2011 that still stands suspended in the Upper House of our parliament as per the designs of the government.

Anna Hazare's agitation and the reaction of the Government against it inspired us to author this book. In the preparation of the book we did not interview Anna Hazare or any person associated with the drafting of Jan Lokpal Bill or Government Lokpal Bills. Rather the data for this book has been mainly collected from various websites and books by different authors and arranged in a logical way to give worth to the present book 'Corruption and Lokpal'.

This comprehensive but comprehensible book discusses the history of corruption and Lokpal Bills since Nehru era. It also discusses how the fate off this bill hangs in fire by the evil designs of some of the corrupt politicians. This book is not about the facts alone, but also with the arguments that go with these facts. We are neither enthusiast of Anna Hazare's Jan Lokpal Bill nor of the Government Lokpal Bill.

We do not claim any originality, we have only examined, analyzed and presented the subject matter related to corruption, black money and Lokpal Bills in a simple, lucid and intelligible way in the light of present day socio-politico-economic conditions in India.

We have tried to evaluate the recent developments in the backdrop of Gandhian thoughts on governance and action that can provide a total solution to the problems of teeming millions in India. We feel that India did not need a British model of constitution from which all the current problems have cropped up. What India needs is a Gandhian style in governance and planning that strikes at the root of all its present problems and can serve as a panacea to remedy them all. No doubt the Jan Lokpal Bill will serve as a stepping stone but Anna's Civil society will have to struggle for Gandhian constitution and Gandhian planning to carry this movement to its logical conclusion.

We have tried to provide enough material in this book to represent the views of both sides along with our own assessment. The readers who do not agree with us are free to draw their own conclusions. The book provides them with sufficient material to form their own opinion.

This book might not have seen the light of the day in such a short period in the pre-internet era. The growing keenness of the Government and its agencies as well as the civil society groups to place their records in e-form has been a boon for us. We are really thankful to such websites, media channels and e-books that helped us in bringing out this book.

We express our most sincere and heart felt gratitude to the authors of various books, periodicals, newspapers from the treasure of which we have drawn extensively in preparing this book. This will ever remain our irredeemable debt. At the same time we tender an advance apology for any mistake that might have cropped up or any misstatement inadvertently made in this book.

We express our gratitude to Kalpaz Publications, New Delhi for extending us full cooperation to publish this book in an elegant manner.

In veneration, we dedicate this book to 'The Crusaders against Corruption and Black Money.'

We will be happy to receive comments and suggestions, if any, from readers for the improvement of this book.

O.P. Dhiman
49, Raghbir Nagar
Patiala-147001

C.P. Sharma
53, New Lal Bagh Colony
Patiala-147001

1

Prologue

August 15, 1947 was the most auspicious day in the history of India when it got freedom under the leadership of Mahatma Gandhi. The crowd of millions of people witnessed the hoisting of the tricolour at the Red Fort on that day. The crowd was unimaginably big and jubilant, throwing the first Independence Day parade into a thrilling pandemonium, which prompted Lord Mountbatten to describe it as the best parade of his life. The millions of people all over India who were part of such exciting scenes dreamed that now the *Gandian swaraj* is not far off.

But, on this day, Mahatma Gandhi declined to join the festivities in New Delhi. While his follower, Jawaharlal Nehru, spoke in the council hall about India's tryst with destiny and the crowds danced in the streets outside, Gandhi was in Calcutta, seeking to restore peace between Hindus and Muslims. His refusal to join his colleagues in New Delhi has been interpreted by some commentators as a sign that he was in mourning. This interpretation is not entirely tenable. While Gandhi was distressed by the religious rioting that accompanied Independence and Partition, he did not deny the value and achievement of political freedom. But he remained concerned with what his fellow Indians would make of their hard-won, and somewhat belated, Swaraj!

GANDHIJI'S CAUTIONS

Gandhiji felt that the so called Independence on 14th August, 1947 midnight was not the true independence, but mere transfer of power agreement between Nehru and Lord Mountbatten. He could see shadows of the coming events and realized what the country had achieved was not the real independence but the scramble for the power and pelf in which the feudal, the crooks, the corrupt might join. He also released a press statement, addressed to all the Indians, that the so called freedom was not the dream of his making.

When the Bengal ministers sought his blessings on that day, Gandhi told them, "Today, you have worn on your heads a crown of thorns. The seat of power is a nasty thing. You have to remain ever wakeful on that seat. You have to be more truthful, more non-violent, more humble and more forbearing. You had been put to test during the British regime. But in a way it was no test at all. But now there will be no end to your being tested. Do not fall a prey to the lure of wealth. May God help you! You are there to serve the villages and the poor."

After independence, Mahatma Gandhi dreamt of a new society and a new man who wouldn't be interested in exploiting others and would not allow others to exploit him. Their goal of life should be to promote their own happiness and to keep others happier. The mad craze for material progress beyond all reasonable limits should no longer attract the new man and the society. Gandhiji firmly believed that this dream of new man and new society could be achieved with the help of education and new surroundings. He, therefore, came out with a scheme of socio-politico-economic set up and a new educational system.

Gandhiji wanted to reconstruct new India based on high moral values and free from illiteracy, poverty, inequality, untouchability, communalism, exploitation, corruption and other ills which our country was facing at that time. But in order to achieve this goal, he did not assume any government office as that of President or Prime Minister.

How ungrateful we are! We never allowed him to make his dream come true and assassinated him just five and a half months after India won freedom.

It is a paradox of history that the empire builders of foreign land who started with naked corruption ended up handing over a remarkably clean administration to the leaders of independent India. It looks equally paradoxical that although our own nation builders started off with the highest standards of probity and purity, we find ourselves trapped in the cesspool of corruption. The slide down started almost from the first taste of power in 1937 when the Congress ministries were formed in several provinces under the scheme of limited provincial autonomy.

The Congress ministries remained in power for 28 months which was long enough to expose the chinks in the armour. "The practice of bogus membership made its appearance and began to grow. There was a scramble for jobs and positions of personal advantage." The venerable Mahatma was seriously concerned about growing corruption in Congress ranks and lashed out at it in the columns of Harijan. In May 1939 he told the Gandhi Seva Sangh workers, "I would go to the length of giving the whole congress a decent burial, rather than put up with the corruption that is rampant". Nehru felt more or less the same way. In a letter to Gandhiji on April 28,1938, he lamented, "What is far worse is that we are losing the high position that we have built up with so much labour in the hearts of the people. We are sinking to the level of ordinary politicians who have no principles to stand by and whose work is governed by a day to day opportunism."

Gandhiji was much relieved when the Congress ministries resigned in October 1939 on political issues arising out of Britain's entry in World War-II in September.

TRIBUTES AND PLEDGES BY OUR LEADERS

On the death of Bapu, our leaders, specially the Congressmen like Nehru, Patel, Dr. Rajendra Prasad, Sarojni Naidu and many others paid rich tributes to him and took many pledges to follow his principles and teachings.

Quoting a few, Nehru said, "Bapu has done giant's work for India and the world, and even for our poor selves , and he has done it astonishingly well. And now it is our term not to fail him or his memory but to carry on the work to the best of our ability and to fulfill the pledges we have so often taken." Sardar Patel also said the same, "Let us all solemnly pledge ourselves afresh to Gandhiji's teachings and ideals."

On the first death anniversary of Gandhiji, Dr. Rajendra Prasad said, "Twelve months have passed away since the assassination of Mahatma Gandhi, the first death anniversary is going to be observed on January 30, 1949...It will be a tragedy greater than the one which was enacted on January 30, 1948 if we also are to reduce this observance to a mere form or ceremony. We must utilize this occasion for bringing to our mind great virtues which the Mahatma embodied and for strengthening our resolve to adopt them in our individual and national life."

BETRAYAL OF GANDHI

Though rich tributes were paid to Gandhiji on his martyrdom day and pledges were made by our leaders, especially Congressmen to follow his principles and actions, yet gradually we started deviating from his teachings and ultimately bid adieu to his philosophy. We Indians, especially the Congressmen, have forgotten him. We rather betrayed him.

In November 1947 Gandhiji suggested that the political objective of the Congress having been realized, it should voluntarily dissolve itself. What he wanted was that the progressive and patriotic elements in the Congress should devote themselves to the task of nation building. Gandhiji had foreseen that the Congress would eventually degenerate into a corrupt and timid organization, and he felt worried over the "scramble for loaves and fishes in the Congress and discord and personal rivalries among members of the Congress High Command." Gandhiji, seeing a rapid deterioration among the Congress workers advised the Congress leaders to dissolve the Congress Party. But the wholly uncompromising attitude of Nehru and some others on this issue greatly disappointed Gandhiji and in a painful but helpless tone he once said, "I can carry no one with me in this."

Though Nehru said about Gandhi more than once, "We were but small men. He picked us up, made us part of a great movement and something of its greatness passed in to us." But he did not listen to his advice of dissolving the Congress. The Congress was not dissolved and thus Gandhiji was betrayed.

After independence Gandhiji felt that freedom had been achieved by the combined efforts of all nationalist forces in the country and not by the Congress alone. He wanted the first Government of free India to be a National Government capable of inspiring confidence and creating enthusiasm in the whole nation. He, therefore, insisted that the first cabinet should be broad based. It was on his insistence that a number of distinguished non-Congress men were also invited to join the cabinet. They included Sir John Mathai, the noted economist and business magnet, Sir Shaumukham Chatty, the well known financial expert, Dr. B.R. Ambedkar, a celebrated jurist and leader of the Scheduled Castes, Dr. Shyama Prasad Mookerji of Hindu Maha Sabha and Sardar Baldev Singh of Akali Dal. But the leaders of integrity—both the Congress and the non-Congress—left the Government.

After independence, India has been ruled by the Congress party till today except for two brief spans by Janta Party and National Democratic Alliance. Corruption started during Nehru's regime and continued increasing with every passing day, and at present it is touching the skies. There is long sequence of scams and every scam after the previous one is bigger and alarming. There is no strong opposition party to act as a watchdog.

The Congress has been trying to shield the corrupt since independence. They should remember the words of Gandhiji who prophetically stated, "Corruption will be out one day, however much one may try to conceal it; and the public can, as it is its right and duty in every case of justifiable suspicion, call its servants to strict account, dismiss them, sue them in a law court or appoint an arbitrator or inspector to scrutinize their conduct as it likes."

Had Gandhiji's advice to dissolve Congress been accepted, automatically two-party system would have evolved and such situation would not have risen. This clearly indicates that Gandhiji's apprehensions about the Congress party have come true.

APPREHENSIONS HAVE COME TRUE

Looking back just a few months, there was the Chief Minister who helped his cronies obtain apartments in a building reserved for war widows and veterans' families. And then, there was the other Chief Minister who presided over an illicit mining ring, depriving his state of $3 billion in revenue over the past four years. There was the infamous Commonwealth Games debacle in which gross irregularities surrounding massive infrastructure projects turned what should have been a shining moment for the emerging superpower into a national embarrassment. There was the Telecom Minister who distributed spectrum licenses to the handpicked firms at a loss of $39 billion to the exchequer (of course, there is also the previous Telecom Minister who resigned after allegations of gross impropriety emerged regarding his tenure). The recent cases of corruption against ministers in Uttar Pradesh, Rajasthan and several other states show that the corruption and black money are at their peak. This is only a passing reference to the state of affairs in this regard. The next chapter of the book deals with it at little greater length that shows that far sighted Gandhi had genuinely visualized the course of coming events.

Gandhiji's words made sense in the past, and they make sense even now. At a time when many of the ministers in state and central governments are consumed by arrogance and self-love, they need to be reminded that as elected representatives of the people, they should be motivated rather by truth, humility and service. In a deeply divided polity, the political parties must recognize that in times of crisis, they should set aside their differences and work together for social peace. When populist notions of democracy stress exclusively on rights and encourage a cavalier attitude to state property, it is well to be told that citizens also have responsibilities. Finally, in 2009 as in 1947, a special role devolves on students, who, with their lives in front of them, can do more than the middle-aged or elderly in building an India worthy of the nation's founders and of their ideals.

Gandhiji's words and warnings have a strikingly contemporary ring. Since they were uttered in Calcutta, those who live in that city, and in the state of which it is part, may read into them a special meaning. In the recent past, West Bengal has been peculiarly prone to political partisanship, State apathy and populist violence. However, these tendencies are manifest, in lesser or greater degree, in other states as well. On August 15 every year, we would do well to remember, and take heed of, what a very wise Indian said and did on this day 65 years ago.

The Congress should not forget that during the British rule that it was of the genre of the social organization like the Civil Society of today but with a different objective. The people of diverse shades of opinion had come together under its umbrella to work for a common objective to free India from the foreign rule. They had different approaches, they spoke in dissenting voices and they adopted different ways ranging from revolutionaries like Bhagat Singh, Netaji Subhash Chandra Bose etc. to moderates like Gandhiji, but we regard them all as National Heroes today and pay them our tribute.

SOCIAL UNREST

Looking at the level of political deprivation and corruption in India today, Gandhiji's fears about the governance of the country, if the Congress continued as a political party after independence, seem to have come true. After 64 years of Independence, the poverty, the inequalities, corruption and black money are at their peak. How long the people could tolerate this misrule against which Anna Hazare declared the second war of independence, first at his village level, then at the state level and now at the national level by forming Civil Society to fight them out?

What is painful in the present scenario is that instead of taking it as a public support in rooting out corruption and delivery of social justice our own elected government is behaving like the foreign colonial ruler trying to crush and disintegrate the Civil Society terming its protests as anti-social, smelling foreign hand in them and alleged backing by RSS and BJP as if they are social and political untouchables.

Anna Hazare's and Baba Ram Dev's protests against putting off a strong Lokpal Bill to check corruption and Black Money in the recent past have been two most peaceful and most disciplined public protests in the history of the world that were dealt unconstitutionally and with violence by a socially responsible Government in the most irresponsible manner. Such a situation has arisen in governance in the post Independence era not for the first time. During the Congress rule earlier also Indira became India and the constitution was put on hold by declaring emergency when her election was declared null and void by the Supreme Court of India.

The matter doesn't end here. The Government and the Congress Party spokespersons have been raising a bogie of frivolous accusations to scuttle the voice of the Civil Society as if loyalty to the country means loyalty to the Congress party. They forget that the Nation exists beyond the Congress party and Nehru family too.

Briefing both the Houses about Anna's arrest, the PM said, "We are emerging as one of the important players on the world stage. There are many forces that would not like to see India realize its true place in the comity of nations. We must not play into their hands."

But while Manmohan Singh only hinted at the possibility of foreign hand in Lokpal movement, Rashid Alvi went a step further. The Congress spokesperson said the sophisticated nature of the orchestrated campaign called for urgent attention to the hidden hand while recalling in the same breath the surprise statement from the US State Department urging the Indian government to respect democratic protests.

Digvijay Singh's blurts against Anna Hazare also reveal that so long as national interests are concerned these revolve around Sonia Gandhi and the Congress Party and all the rest of the politics is anti-national. It is strange that he divides the citizens as voters of political parties and regards those who are the voters of parties and organizations other than the Congress as untouchables. His posers to Anna Hazare are the proof of this kind of thinking in the Congress.

"If you want to take part in political process, you should participate openly... You have never raised your voice against the BJP,"

"The talk is that the BJP wants to make you a candidate in the Presidential election next year. You become a candidate, but beware of the lofty promises of the BJP, which is in the habit of leading people up the garden path... You have refused, but RSS has always come out in open support of your campaigns."

Our politicians and policy makers in the last 64 years have built a system which is utterly disappointing for the people. Dynasty and neo-feudalism has arisen out of power, lying in the hands of a few families through electoral policies. Our politicians have developed monarchy through democratic electoral system. Today, in politics there is very little space or no space for common man or common party workers to climb the ladder of power and reach the top. But, Anna Hazare and his team against corruption deserve credit for raising the conscience of the people providing it conviction and strength, though a few may have doubts about its justification and validity on the following grounds:

- Anna and his team are harnessing the frustrations and disenchantment of millions of Indians who bear the cost of the country's corruption day in and day out. While many people like to speak of deep-seated "cultures of corruption," it is clear that there is now a significant segment of the Indian population that is willing to speak out on how corruption is eating away at the country's core.

- Despite the movement's good intentions, Hazare's tactics raise difficult questions about the role of hunger strikes, the legitimacy of Civil Society, and his movement's "my way or the highway" approach to encouraging reform. In the words of Pratap Bhanu Mehta: "The Anna Hazare movement...continues to propagate the tyranny of virtue. It has eluded the distinction between protest and fast-unto-death. The former is legitimate. The latter is blackmail." As Mehta points out, Team Anna rails against the tyranny of the government, but it too is displaying authoritarian tendencies. Furthermore, can Team Anna speak for Indian Civil Society as a whole? On that score, the answer appears to be no. And what about the necessity of compromise in a democratic society? Team Anna seems to think that it is the one with all the right answers.

- One danger of Team Anna's singular focus on the Lok Pal bill is that it cannot help but depict the creation of a national ombudsman as a silver bullet—which it clearly will not be. The creation of the Lok Pal can no doubt aid the fight against graft (indeed, it was a state-level ombudsman who uncovered the aforementioned illegal mining racket, leading to the resignation of the Chief Minister) but it is insufficient. The police, the judiciary, and even the media, to name a few of the country's institutions, are in dire need of reform. The state apparatus, in nearly every sector, is woefully ill equipped to address the challenges a vibrant, growing India is facing in the 21st century.

• Finally, all sides would be well advised to tone down their righteousness dial several notches. This includes members of India's growing middle class, which has helped fuel Hazare's latest social agitation. As Manu Joseph wrote last week in a withering column in the *New York Times,* "Indians have a deep and complicated relationship with corruption. As in any long marriage, it is not clear whether they are happily or unhappily married. The country's economic system is fused with many strands of corruption and organized systems of tax evasion. The middle class is very much a part of this." Senior government leaders, on the other hand, have often demonstrated a holier than thou attitude towards Civil Society groups that is frankly laughable as shown during the recent events.

But the Government should understand that the prologue to the present situation had already been written by Mahatma Gandhi's advice to the Congress on the eve of independence, the present situation is its climax. The wheel seems to have come full circle. It is high time now that good sense prevails on the Congress Party to make amends for its overtures and by passing an all equipped strong Lok Pal provide a catharsis to the burning issue of corruption, although a lot more needs to be done socially and politically after its passage.

The Government should know that people are the ultimate arbiters of any political system. They may be under confusion of one kind or another, for sometime or longer, but not for very long. Once they wake up, no amount of gimmicks drawn from the past or present can prevent them from wiping off a tormenting system. Once the iceberg of resentment and discontent melts and starts moving, it can polish off all fortresses of corruption and criminalization. It may not happen today or tomorrow, but it will definitely happen one day.

2

Corruption and Black Money

Power and corruption go together and it needs some restraining authority to check it. For a long time religion played a disciplining role, but with the increasing plea for rationality of the scientific temper and the growing orthodoxy and rigidity in religion and the neo secularism has driven it out.

Man is a social animal. He is born with a free spirit, but as he grows, his loyalties go on narrowing down to self. As an individual he is weak and vulnerable to all sorts of risks from all around, and to protect his interests he enters into contract with his surroundings and the people around, first at the level of the family, later extending it to the tribe, the nation and the world.

Different forms of social contracts have prevailed from absolute monarchy to democracy over time and places all over the world with their typical style of governance and their strength and weaknesses. The bipartite contracts have persistently evolved between the governor and the governed and the reference point has been the protection of the weaker sections of the society.

So long as the lifestyle remained simple, Hobbes' absolute

monarchy with divine right concept seemed to be serving its purpose of protecting the life of the weaker without much costs to them and it continued without any challenge. But the expanding economic activities in the societies added new dimensions to social sharing leading to Locke's limited monarchy. But, Rousseau propagated a new form of governance with its thrust on individual freedom and the world seemed to have grabbed this idea so fast that many variants of democracy are working in a large number of countries today. But the survival of the fittest ultimately seems to dominate the scene for which the weak and the poor are exploited in the name of welfare, finally resulting into corrupt governance.

MEANING AND NATURE OF CORRUPTION

Before we initiate a discussion on corruption it would be proper to understand the meaning, the nature and type of corruption. Britannica Concise Encyclopedia defines it "as improper and usually unlawful conduct intended to secure a benefit for oneself or another. Its forms include bribery, extortion, and the misuse of inside information. It exists where there is community indifference or a lack of enforcement policies. In societies with a culture of ritualized gift giving, the line between acceptable and unacceptable gifts is often hard to draw."

Corruption is a multilateral and systematic deficiency in a society. In common speech, corruption is the phenomenon involving the act of something that is debased, impute and anti ethical.

Corruption is the lack of integrity. This could be intellectual integrity, financial integrity or moral integrity. But, when it comes to public life, it is financial integrity that dominates.

"Corruption is any course of action or failure to act by individuals or organizations, public or private, in violation of law or trust for profit or gain." **INTERPOL.**

According to the World Bank, "...a corrupt practice is offering, giving and receiving or soliciting of anything of values to influence the action of a public official in the procurement or in the extract or execution."

Corruption is all pervading in the sense that not a single country in the world can be described as non-corrupt and not a single department in any government is free from corrupt practices.

Corruption is like cancer in the blood. It needs major operation and lengthy treatment. Prof. Syed Hussain called it 'tidal corruption'. Like a tide this practice grows to immerse everything in its path. The tidal corruption multiplies the number of perpetrators of illegal practices more rapidly than any other type of criminal behaviour. A question is raised as to who are prone to corrupt practices? It can be safely answered that normally the less salaried, highly greedy officers and politicians are the main stream of corruption.

CAUSES OF CORRUPTION

There are certainly some causes at the root of this malady and many scholars, academicians and ethnologists have made efforts to find out causes of corruption. Some of them have been stated below.

Moral and Ethical Causes

- Non-following of religious and ethical teachings.
- Degeneration and deterioration of values.

Historical Causes

- Colonialism leading to poverty due to extraction of resources by empirical powers.

Social Causes

- Illiteracy and poor standards of education.
- Absence of positive socio-economic environment conducive to corruption-free society.
- Lack of urge to come out of mental make up tolerating corrupt practices,.
- Social structure and government system that generates and supports corruption.

Legal Causes

- Absence of severe punitive measures to curb corruption based upon inequality.

Economic Causes

- Poverty and unemployment.
- Over population.
- Low level of per-capita and national income.

Administrative Causes

- Delay, red-tapism, officialdom, rigidity, hierarchy, indifferent and non-sensible working of administrative system, lack of integrity, inefficiency among functionaries etc.

Political Causes

- The absence or weakness of leadership in key positions capable of inspiring and influencing conduct mitigating corruption.
- Nexus between politicians and bureaucrats.

Besides these there are many more causes of corruption. This list is exhaustive and unending. More and more new causes are added to it with the passage of time.

CORRUPTION IN INDIA

Corruption has been rampant in India since times immemorial. The malady prevailed in ancient, medieval and modern times.

Corruption in Ancient Times

In the ancient times too, corruption existed and was discussed, but it was not as high and as frequent as it is today. Therefore, there was a feeling of fear in olden days among people involved in corruption. Therefore, corruption was looked upon as a sin and criminal deed which could invite divine wrath and social condemnation. Kautilya, in his 'Arthashashtra' (4B.C.) gives exhaustive list of practices and facts that can be termed as corrupt, "...causing loss of government, misuse of government property, misappropriation of revenue, falsification of documents, obstruction in lawful process, exploiting the public, corrupting the officials, embezzlement, failure of supervision in work, false measurement, allocating expenditure under wrong heads, cheating with weight, etc..." Today all these acts and many more exist in our society.

Aligarh Muslim University historian S. Chandni Bi, who has specialized in epigraphy, the study of inscriptions, says around 1,000 years ago, there was zero tolerance towards financial bungling. According to him, inscriptions in the southern state of Tamil Nadu clearly indicate how intolerant civil society was against corrupt practices and the violators of ethical framework.

"While murder of even Brahmins was considered pardonable, crimes like cheating or swindling public funds were unpardonable even by gods. Political crime was not pardonable, but other crimes could be punished with penalties or performance of penance and charitable deeds to become eligible for elections again."

Corruption in Modern Times

In the modern days corruption is an economic, social, political, administrative, cultural and religious phenomenon. There is hardly any segment of Indian life which has not been affected by corruption today. It starts from the top, *i.e.,* politicians, bureaucracy, police and even judiciary. In the past, corruption was considered as a sin and crime where as in modern days it is considered as fashion.

POLITICIANS-BUREAUCRATS NEXUS

The main cause of corruption is a nexus between politicians and bureaucrats.

Corruption in India is a dysfunctional outcome of the interaction between the public and the private. The action includes corruption, bribery, nepotism etc. Corruption in India is a product of the way of life of an acquisitive society where 'money talks', where what 'works' is justified and where people are judged by what they have, rather than what they are. Corruption is unending and mind boggling in India that is multi-caste, multi-religion and multi-linguistic state. During pre-independence days according to drain theory of Dadabhai Naroji, British were responsible for exploitation of India. After independence the British were replaced by our own officials and politicians with no change so far as exploitation was concerned. The helpless and the voiceless are governed by the arbitrary law and use of force, injustice and unrighteousness. People find them helpless against politician-administration nexus responsible for corruption.

The founding fathers of democracy in India subscribed to the Weberian ideal of neutral civil services with impersonal, strictly rule bound, neutral bureaucracy to provide the necessary administrative objectivity and also enhance the democratic principles of equality and provide protection from arbitrary rule.

Mrs. Indira Gandhi, the then Prime Minister advocated the concept of committed bureaucracy. Not only did she express her dissatisfaction with the performance of bureaucracy, she expressed doubt about relevance of the basic assumptions of neutrality, impartiality, anonymity etc. underlying the Indian bureaucracy and she alleged that bureaucrats lacked commitment. She disgustingly referred to the administrative machinery as 'the stumbling block in the country's progress' and reiterated the necessity of creating an administrative cadre committed to the national objectives and responsive to India's social needs. She found 'committed bureaucracy' as an answer to the ills of neutrality that crippled the development process in India. She had an earnest belief that only a committed bureaucracy can bring about the desired changes.

This concept was much contested in the political and administrative circles. It was alleged that it would permanently damage the fabric of the services. But she was bent upon creating a brand of civil servants who would always say, "Yes Minister" and would be ready to crawl when asked to bend by their political masters.

The following joke in the official circles highlights how the relationship between ministers and the bureaucrats changed with times.

A newly appointed Minister of a State called the secretary of his Department to discuss the modality of running the Department. The conversation went on something like this:

Minister: How do we divide the work of the Department between us?

Secretary: Sir, you are the Minister-in-Charge. You may lay down the policy, guidelines and take decisions about all important matters. I will deal with routine affairs so as not to bother you with details.

Minister: What are the routine matters that you will handle?

Secretary: Like transfers and postings and other day-to-day matters of administration.

Minister: You are clever Mr. Secretary. You want to take the cream and leave me with the left over. That won't do. You better deal with the policy and guidelines and I will decide postings and transfers.

The Minister knew better that transfers and postings of the personnel is one of the biggest money spinners in Govt. departments today.

It was also alleged that in the name of commitment, the ruling party was seeking bureaucracy's alignment with the party's ideology in order to perpetuate its rule.

If committed bureaucracy stands for nonpartisan, socially sensitive, genuinely interested in progress and development of the country, then it is more appropriate for a developing nation than having an insensitive neutral one.

In practice, however, commitment has assumed the perverted form of politicisation and sycophancy. Commitment to social objective is one thing and dancing to the tune of the political party is another. Very often it is seen that bureaucracy simply acts to the dictates of political executives without any rational examination of the issues. This trend can be attributed to the ever growing political interference in the affairs of administration. Political interference and impartial administration can not coexist.

While administrators do not perceive their role in policy making as subservient to politicians because of their knowledge and expertise; yet they have to conform to the prerequisites of the representative politics. The political leaders claim to be the true representative of the people knowing what is good for them and because of their superior position succeed in dictating terms to the bureaucrats. The bureaucrats who are not obliging enough soon find themselves in trouble. The political masters have many means of coercion - both overt and covert. Political interference in all matters, including those where the statutory powers are vested in the civil servants, is a constant phenomenon. There are numerous instances of use of transfer, promotion, supersession, compulsory retirement from service by the elected politicians as tool to silence the voice of dissent and expression of difference of opinion.

Well, politicisation works the other way round also. Many administrators use political influence or forge alliance with the politicians to brighten their own career prospects. They take advantage of the politicians; exploit their weaknesses, particularly in times of a fluid political situation and turn out to be autonomous and irresponsible. This is an equally grim scenario.

What emerges out of the analysis is whether there is collision or collusion between the political executive and bureaucracy, in both cases it leads to organisational imbalance and ultimately the governance suffers.

Expressing concern over deteriorating administrative standards, the government appointed the Administrative Reforms Commission (ARC) in 1966 to conduct a comprehensive study of working of the administrative machinery and suggest remedies. In spite of the valuable suggestions made by ARC to streamline relationship between ministers and civil servants, nothing much seems to have changed because of political and administrative apathy. Making the matters worse is the growth of the nexus between the politicians, criminals, police and civil servants rooted in the system.

Widening Bureaucracy and Growing Corruption

The phenomenon of corruption cannot be understood without reference to the bureaucracy. Bureaucrats are responsible for mismanagement, frauds and pilferages. Bureaucracy actually fails to perform its duty in an accountable manner. It was so in the past, it is so in the present.

The Committee on Prevention of Corruption observed, "...in the primitive and medieval societies scope of public authority was small; man of the matters that were looked after by the community have now become a function of the state."

This is how the Committee explains widening role of bureaucracy.

In his 'Indian Panorama: Triumphs and Tragedies' Mr. S.K. Ghosh indicates that bribery is common for import licenses, building permissions, government employment, agricultural aids, liquor permits, bank employment and loans, admission to educational institutions, etc. In rural areas, land records can be manipulated by bribing revenue officials.

The village Sarpanch is often bribed by the landlords to decide cases in their favour. As most of the villagers are poor, the officials exploit, especially the tribal people, for advancing loans and marketing their agricultural products. During land settlements the concerned staff operating in villages is heavily bribed for manipulating records.

Nationalized banks officials are also involved in frauds amassing money by illegal means. Smuggling is a big business in India. In Mumbai, the annual profit earned from smuggling is estimated to be Rs. 8,000 crores a year. Political leaders always have a strong link with smugglers. A smuggler provides money and muscle power to the political leaders during elections and naturally expects protection from them in return.

'Pay the price and the job is yours' is an all pervasive condition for Government jobs. Every appointment, assignment and transfer carries a price tag. The merit hardly matters. The employment exchanges take bribes for registration and recommendation of names to various departments and employers. In the state Public Service Commissions corruption and bribery is rampant. Corrupt and communal persons are appointed as members of the Commissions. In some states, members are used as agents to collect money from candidates.

Our judiciary appears to be indifferent and passive towards corruption. We quote Mr. Arvind Bobde, the late Advocate General of Maharashtra:

> "...judiciary is the only institution in the country which has no public accountability. Judges are paid poorly, their status, dignity and independence is not assured."

On the impeachment of Justice V. Ram Swami of the Supreme Court, the first ever impeachment motion against a Supreme Court Judge, Krishana Ayer observed,

> "...corruption inside the institution is mounting; even judicial officers are slowly coming into the suspect class."

Corruption exists not only in villages, but in urban areas too. Usually the Income Tax Inspectors are responsible for departmental corruption as the lawyers, doctors, film stars, proprietors of coaching institutes, businessmen etc. evade taxes.

The police authorities take bribe for verification of character antecedent report, which is a must before issuing passports and arms licenses and before joining permanent jobs. In an interview to 'One India, One People' Francis Ribero, the then Police Commissioner of Mumbai pointed out how Ministers extract money from the police officials to be transferred. The concerned Ministers send a list of persons of their choice for appointments as well as promotion with the monetary consideration. Private residences of several Director Generals and Inspector Generals of Police have been raided by the CBI in different parts of our country and unaccounted wealth was recovered from them. Police administrators often have the relationship with criminals, gangsters, mafias, shooters etc. The guardians become the promoters of crimes.

The Indian railway is also known for its corruption that has promoted traveling without ticket causing huge loss of revenues to the department. Thefts of goods from coaches, railway yards and brake-vans in connivance with railway staff and RPF run into crores of rupees.

In the government hospitals scams like NHRM run into millions what to talk of smaller scams at the hospital level.

Even judiciary, the custodian of the constitution, is not free from corruption. According to Transparency International judicial corruption in India is attributable to factors such as "delays in the disposal of cases, shortage of judges and complex procedures, all of which are exacerbated by a preponderance of new laws".

Indian armed forces, protector of sovereignty and integrity of our nation are not free from this evil. The Indian Armed Forces have witnessed corruption involving senior armed forces officers from the Indian Army, Indian Navy and Indian Air Force. A number of scandals in the 2000-2010 period damaged the military's reputation; such scandals included skimming of armed forces money, re-selling of government property and faking combat missions.

The following diagrammatic display of facts gives a statistical analysis of the dimensions of corruption in India.

DIMENSIONS OF CORRUPTION

The TII-CMS India Corruption Study shows that below poverty line households paid more than 883 crore rupees to avail basic services like public distribution systems, hospitals, school education, electricity and water supply.

Ranking of top corrupt services:

Table 1. Ranking of Services

Services	*Rank*
Police	1
Land Records/Registration	2
Housing	3
Water Supply Service	4
NREGS	5
Forest	6
Electricity	7
Health	8
PDS	9
Banking	10
School Education (up to class XII)	11

TII-CMS India Corruption Study - 2007.

Levels of corruption ranked by states:

Table 2. Level of Overall Corruption in States (involving BPL households)

(arranged in alphabetical order)

State by size	*Levels of Corruption*			
	Alarming	*Very High*	*High*	*Moderate*
Big	Assam	Karnataka	Chhattisgarh	Andhra Pradesh
	Bihar	Rajasthan	Delhi	Haryana
	Jammu Kashmir	Tamil Nadu	Gujarat	Himachal Pradesh
	Madhya Pradesh		Jharkhand	Maharashtra
	Uttar Pradesh		Kerala	Punjab
			Orissa	Uttarakhand West Bengal
Small/ UTs	Goa	Meghalaya	Arunachal Pradesh	Chandigarh
	Nagaland	Sikkim	Manipur	Mizoram Pondichery Tripura

It was felt that Maharashtra had very high levels of corruption, but according to the study, it is one of the states that have corruption in moderation. It shudders to think about the situation in Uttar Pradesh and Bihar!

Even judiciary is not free from corruption.

- Thirty-six per cent of Indians paid bribes to the legal system in 2006.
- Estimated the amount paid by Indians as bribes to the legal system at about Rs 2,630 crore (Rs 26.30 billion).
- Majority of the bribes went to lawyers (61 per cent) followed by court officials (29 per cent) and middlemen (five per cent).

Nature of Bribe Demands in India

The pie chart given below highlights the nature of bribe demands in India.

Figure 1. Nature of Bribe Demands in India (N = 96)

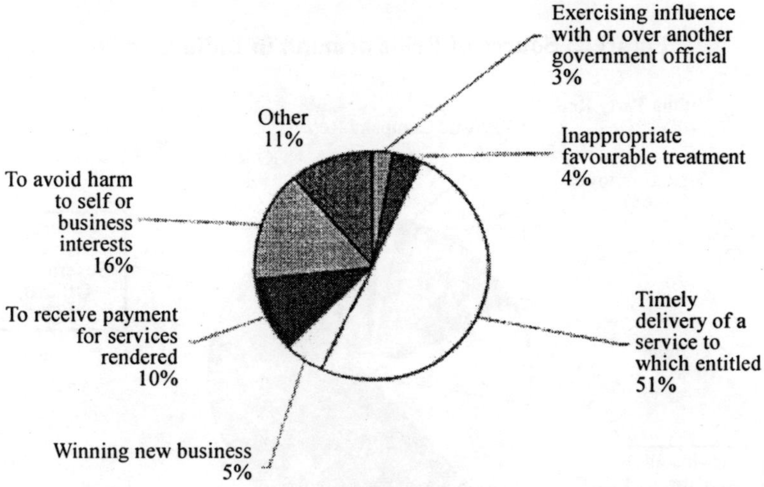

'No guesses here—if you want to get your work done, bribe them!' that is what is quite clear and in line with the notion we have.

More than half of all the bribes were paid to get the work done in time!

77% of all reported bribe demands in India are related to the avoidance of harm, including securing the timely delivery of a service - which is actually a right of a person (such as clearing customs or having a telephone line installed) and receiving payment for services already rendered.

Only 12% of the bribe demands were for gaining a personal or business advantage (including exercising influence with or over another government official, receiving inappropriate favourable treatment or winning new business).

One thing is sure, we are now used to this corrupt system and take it in our stride as part and parcel. We do not want to go extra lengths and take the easy way out. But this easy way out is actually the root of corruption in India.

Sources of Bribe Demand in India

The following figure shows sources of bribe demand in India:

Figure 2. Source of Bribe demand in India (N = 96)

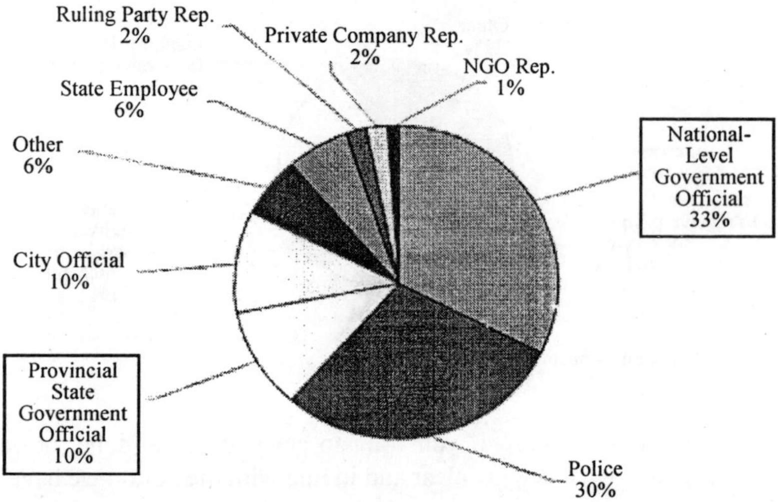

Whooping 91% of reported bribe demands originate from government officials in India. The greatest sources of bribe demands were from national level Government officials (33%), the police (30%), state/provincial officials and employees (16%), and city officials (10%) respectively.

Do you know which of the two Indian ministries ask for bribe more than others?—They are Customs Office (13%), Taxation and Water (9%).

China fares slightly well when it comes to Government officials taking bribe (85%)—Another major difference is that India Police (30%) are far more corrupt than their Chinese counterparts (only 11%).

Figure 3. Frequency of Recuring Bribe Demands (N = 45)

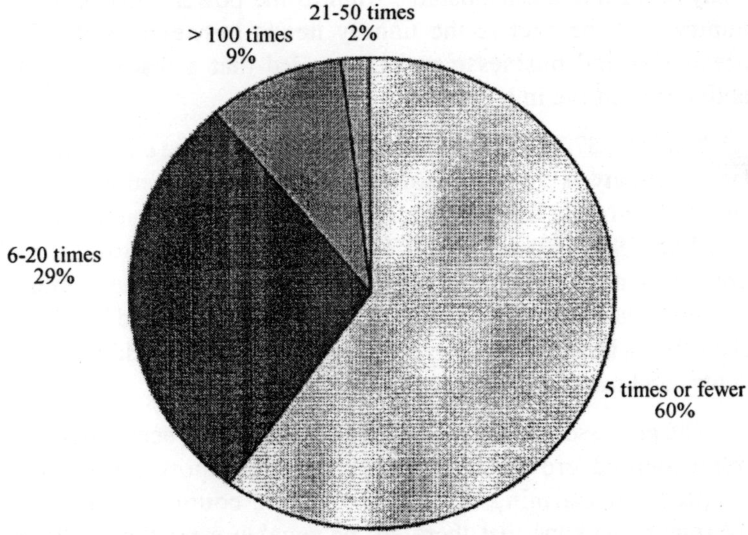

Frequency of Bribe Demands in India

Nearly 90% indicated being solicited for a bribe between two and 20 times. Overall 60% people reported bribe demands of 5 times or lower from the same individual. However, 9% asked for bribes more than 100 times. Compared to China, it differs significantly with 73% people indicating that they had received multiple bribe requests. Almost 20% of those individuals reported receiving more than 100 bribe demands in China.

Forms of Bribe

Do you want any tips on how to give bribes? Here is what our corrupt officials prefer. If in doubt, give cash, as 92% of all bribes are preferred to be 'cash or cash equivalent,' The next best thing is a 'gift,' (5%) including requests for company products, jewelry and similar items. Less common still, at approx. 1% each, were requests for hospitality or entertainment items; travel for other than business purposes; and other assistance, such as help with a visa, medical care, or scholarships.

BLACK MONEY

It may seem like an unpalatable truth to the powers that be in the country, but the fact is the unholy nexus between politicians, bureaucrats and businessmen has ensured that a black economy continues to thrive in India.

"At least $70-80 billion goes out every year. The cost of India's black economy is 5 per cent of GDP growth sacrificed every year since the mid-70s. But for this, India's size of the economy would have been $ 9 trillion," says Prof. Arun Kumar, Professor of Economics at the Jawaharlal Nehru University (JNU) and author of the book 'Black Money in India'. Per capita income could have been seven times larger; India would then have been a middle-income country and not one of the poorest, he argues.

The professor says that over the years, India has been witnessing unprecedented growth in its black economy, now estimated to constitute an alarming 50 per cent of the country's GDP. The government reckons that there are no reliable estimates of 'Black Money' inside or outside the country. "As much as Rs. 32 to 35 lakh crore is generated in this parallel economy every year," Kumar says.

WHAT HAVE WE LOST IN BLACK MONEY?

All our plans and policies failed because more than 75% of our resources were siphoned off the economy as black money.

Economic Policies Failed

Because of the existence of a substantial parallel economy, planning, monetary and fiscal policies frequently do not achieve the desired results, both at the macro and micro level. "The economy does not lack resources but faces resource shortage," he adds. A large portion of investments goes into wasteful and unproductive channels, like holding gold or real estate abroad. Targets for education, health and drinking water are, therefore, not achieved.

Parallel Economy and Inflation

The parallel economy also results in higher-than-required costs for the economy -raising the rate of inflation. If capital is over-invoiced by a project to earn more profits, the cost of setting up industry is higher. If poor-quality grain is sold in the public distribution system, people tend to buy it from the market, where the price is higher. If children need tuitions because of poor teaching, the family's cost of education increases.

Slow GDP Growth

The black economy, which has caused India to lose 5 per cent of its GDP over the last 30 years, is also the opportunity cost of not having India become the world's second-largest economy, just after the US.

Backward Infrastructure

With the additional money, India could have provided enhanced social infrastructure with better health care services, larger educational facilities and employment opportunities.

Increasing Inequality and Poverty

The black economy is largely responsible for the inequality in the country. Although black income is concentrated in 3 per cent of Indian households, Kumar estimates that 97 per cent of people have been affected.

We could have had the potential to feed 90 per cent of the hungry mouths in the country. It means every family could have had a home, and we probably wouldn't have to witness the distressing sight of a half-clothed child getting drenched in the rain.

WHAT IS ACHIEVABLE IF BLACK MONEY IS BROUGHT BACK?

According to several economists and financial experts, bank deposits in the territory of Switzerland by nationals of India total upwards of $ 1.4 billion. That is close to the nominal GDP of India today. Speaking accurately, it is believed that $1.456 trillion of Indian money is parked in Swiss bank vaults. India can transform its economy with it as follows:

Repaying External Debt

India, as of December 2010, had external debt amounting to $ 237 billion, according to the CIA World Fact Book numbers. The first step should be to pay this debt off. Assuming that with interest, the figure rises to even $275 billion, the country would be left with $ 1.181 trillion after paying off all its foreign debt.

Building Social Infrastructure

A Goldman Sachs study in 2010 has reported that India would need to invest $1 trillion in economic and social infrastructure to sustain an 8 to 9 per cent growth momentum and to overcome its problems. However, in the report, the investment banker clearly mentions that this $1 trillion includes government funding, private enterprise as well as foreign investment.

The suggestions of the report have been corroborated by Rahul Saraogi, Managing Director at Atyant Capital in a 2011 interview with Value Investing Letter. Infrastructure in India, unlike in the case of China, will be built only using a public-private partnership model. In certain sectors like telecom, airports and power, the model has been successfully working. In case of developments of ports, roads, railways and urban transportation, the models are evolving. Assuming up to 70 per cent of the funding comes from the government and the rest from other players. India would invest $ 700 billion in this sector. The bulk of the government's investment should be in water treatment, sanitation, waste management, renewable energy, health, education, urban infrastructure and allied fields.

The 8 to 9 per cent YoY (year on year) growth will ensure that the government has more than enough funds to pay for maintenance and salary of work force needed to maintain and run the expanded services.

Food Security for All

Now, left with $ 481 billion, we can meet India's challenge of one of the hungriest nations in the world. It is ranked 67th out of 84 countries listed and ranked on the Global Hunger Index Report, 2010. India accounts for 42 per cent of the world's underweight children. Unless India ensures food security for all its people, its claim for greater role in the world will be taken with a pinch, if not a lump, of salt. In that regard, universalisation of PDS is the simplest and surest way to ensure food security.

In that regard, Dr. Abhijit Sen of the Planning Commission had proposed a minimum support price-linked PDS scheme, excluding 25 per cent of the population who are not the target group. But this was shot down by C. Rangarajan, Chairman of the Rangarajan Committee, who thought that streamlining the present PDS system would be enough. Though the government has made up its mind on the proposed Food Security Bill, it is not too sure if universalization of PDS would be a viable measure.

A study by Praveen Jha, Associate Professor at Jawaharlal Nehru University (JNU) and Nilachal Acharya of the Delhi-based Centre for Budget Governance and Accountability (CBGA), shows that Universalization of PDS is even possible without the help of this magic money we are talking about. Their study shows that an additional amount of Rs. 94,419 crore per annum will be required to supplement the present provisions of food subsidy which translates to roughly $21 billion.

Taking into account inflation over the next ten years, a figure of $ 300 billion will be enough to take all Indians out of the hunger trap. With quality healthcare and social infrastructure, India can then start looking like a developed nation.

Strengthening Defense

Out of the remaining $181 billion, $60 billion should go in strengthening our defense capabilities, over and above the already-approved $100 billion procurement plan, that should give us one of the meanest fighting forces in the world.

Scientific and Social Research

The remaining $ 121 billion money should be used to fund higher education, cutting-edge scientific and social research institutes and exclusive scientific projects.

All this is only possible if the money is available. The Swiss Banking Association has already said that it might hand over to the Indian Government a list of names of individuals who have accounts there if New Delhi so requested. However, unlike the German Government, the Congress-led UPA seems to be dragging its feet. Even Wikileaks founder Julian Assange has criticized New Delhi for giving all the wrong excuses for not acting. Political observers feel that the government is worried that names of account holders coming into the public domain might haunt the various parties that make up the UPA. The grapevine has it that several prominent political leaders and their family members, apart from prominent businessmen and public figures, have money parked there.

So, till the Government actually swings into action, which is highly unlikely, all this is entirely in the realm of speculative fantasy. But just because our Government fails to fulfill our wishes, we should not stop having them.

CONCLUSION

Political corruption has become the order of the day. Corruption in political life has achieved almost criminal proportion. The virus of corruption has infested from the highest to the lowest in the hierarchy and it is salvaged by political bosses. The wide-spread corruption has eroded the entire administrative apparatus and people experience that their daily life legitimate and lawful work cannot be done in any office without greasing the palms of the dealing incumbent. This complete and abhorable erosion of honesty has greatly affected the national and individual ethics of morality. It is all because congressmen have betrayed Gandhiji, by replacing his basic principle. 'Means justify the End' by the Machiavellian principle, Nothing succeeds like Success. In a craze for power and pelf they have forgotten all moral values.

3

Corruption and Congress Rule

Seeds of corruption in India were sown by our great first Prime Minister, Jawahar Lal Nehru by patronizing corrupt Chief Ministers and colleagues. These seeds sprouted in his time and later during Dr. Manmohan Singh's regime grew into huge trees of corruption and black money under which nothing grows but incredibility and corruption.

JAWAHAR LAL NEHRU ERA

The history of corruption in post-Independence India starts with the Jeep scandal in 1948, when a transaction concerning purchase of jeeps for the army needed for Kashmir operation was entered into by V.K. Krishna Menon, the then High Commissioner for India in London with a foreign firm without observing normal procedure. Contrary to the demand of the opposition for judicial inquiry as suggested by the Inquiry Committee led by Ananthsayanam Ayyangar, the then Government announced on September 30, 1955 that the Jeep scandal case was closed. Union Minister G.B.Pant declared "that as far as Government was concerned it has made up its mind to close the matter. If the opposition was not satisfied they can make it an election issue."

Soon after on February 3,1956 Krishna Menon was inducted into the Nehru cabinet as minister without portfolio.

In 1950, AD Gorwala, an eminent civil servant was asked by Government of India to recommend improvements in the system of governance. In his report submitted in 1951 he made two observations: "One, quite a few of Nehru's ministers were corrupt and this was common knowledge. Two, even a highly responsible civil servant in an official report as early as 1951 maintained that the Government went out of its way to shield its ministers" (Report on Public Administration, Planning Commission, Government of India 1951). Corruption charges in cases like Mudgal case (1951), Mundra deals (1957-58), Malaviya-Sirajuddin scandal (1963), and Pratap Singh Kairon case (1963) were levelled against the Congress Ministers and Chief Ministers but neither Prime Minister nor any minister resigned.

The Santhanam Committee, which was appointed by the Government in 1962 to examine the issue of corruption in its report submitted in 1964 observed: "There is widespread impression that failure of integrity is not uncommon among ministers and that some ministers, who have held office during the last sixteen years have enriched themselves illegitimately, obtained good jobs for their sons and relations through nepotism and have reaped other advantages inconsistent with any notion of purity in public life."

The following comments of Nehru on the memorandum of charges against Pratap Singh Kairon submitted to the President of India by the non-Communist opposition in Punjab suggest his approach on corruption. "The question thus arises as to whether the chief minister is compelled to resign because of adverse findings on some questions of fact by Supreme Court. The ministers are collectively responsible to the legislature. Therefore, the matter was one, which concerned the assembly. As a rule, therefore, the question of removing a minister would not arise unless the legislature expressed its wish by a majority vote."

Thus, we find that Nehru's tolerance of corruption among his ministers legalized this malady and he had sown the seeds of corruption in India.

LAL BAHADUR SHASTRI ERA

After the death of Nehru then Congress Party President K. Kamaraj was instrumental in making Shastri the Prime Minister on June 9. Shastri, though mild-mannered and soft-spoken, was a Nehruvian socialist and thus held appeal to those wishing to prevent the ascent of conservative right-winger Morarji Desai.

Shstri's era is free from any sort of corruption. The Das Commission appointed during Nehru regime submitted its report against corruption charges on Pratap Singh Kairon, submitted its report on June 11, 1964 just three days after Shastri took over. It concluded as follows:

"The Commission is free to concede that a father can not legally or morally prevent his sons from carrying on business, but exploitation of the influence of his father who happens to be the Chief Minister of the state can not be permitted to be made a business of... There is no getting away from the fact that Sardar Pratap Singh Kairon knew or had more than ample reason to think or suspect that his sons and relatives were allegedly exploiting his influence and powers...In view of his inaction in the face of the circumstances wherein before alluded to, he must be held to have connived at the doings of his sons and relatives, his colleagues and the government officers."

Kairon's initial reaction was to stick to his office inspite of the adverse verdict but Shstri made him go. Kairon had no option but to relinquish his office. Had this report been submitted during Nehru Era perhaps no action would have been taken.

While the Indian politicians are fighting fiercely with each other to establish their 'Corruption Supremacy' by indulging in one scam after another and trying their best to make it to the Guinness Book in the corruption category, a revelation about our former Prime Minister Lal Bahadur Shastri came to us as a breadth of fresh air.

The incident has been captured in the book 'Lal Bahadur Shastri: Past Forward' by his son Sunil Shastri, a Congress politician and a former minister in Uttar Pradesh. Sunil Shastri says he used to imagine having a big luxury car commensurate with the status of his 'babuji' (father) and Lal Bahadur Shastri did get a Chevrolet for official use. 'One day I told babuji's personal secretary to ask the driver to bring the Chevrolet to the residence. We asked the driver for the keys and went for a drive,' he says in the book. Lal Bahadur Shastri later confronted the driver, saying, 'Do you keep a logbook with you?' 'When he nodded, babuji asked him to note the distance the car had run the previous day. When the driver said 14 km, he advised him to note it 'for private use' and then asked amma to give his personal secretary the amount applicable to be deposited in the government account.

There are many interesting anecdotes on Shastri in the book.

When Lal Bahadur Shastri's wife decided to learn Hindi, she paid the tuition fees by dispensing with the domestic maid and doing the household chores herself.

Lal Bahadur Shastri often handed over to his wife his khadi kurtas when they became unusable and asked her to make handkerchiefs out of them. "He lived on the simple philosophy of waste not, want not."

In true Gandhian style, Lal Bahadur Shastri travelled like a commoner in trains even when he was the Railway Minister. He lived according to his principles.

After the declaration of ceasefire, Shastri and Pakistani President Muhammad Ayub Khan attended a summit in Tashkent (former USSR, now in modern Uzbekistan), organised by Alexei Kosygin. On January 10, 1966, Shastri and Khan signed the Tashkent Declaration.

The next day Shastri, who had suffered two heart attacks earlier, died supposedly of a heart attack at 1:32 a.m.. He is the only Indian Prime Minister to have died in office overseas.

Although Shastri had been a cabinet minister for many years in the 1950s, he was poor when he died. All he owned at the end was an old car, which he had bought in instalments from the government and for which he still owed money. He was the first Railway Minister who resigned from office following a major train accident as he felt moral responsibility.

INDIRA GANDHI ERA

Indira Gandhi, daughter of Jawahar Lal Nehru served as the third Prime Minister of India for three consecutive terms (1966-77) and a fourth term (1980-84).

On June 12, 1975 the High Court of Allahabad declared Indira Gandhi's election to the Lok Sabha void on grounds of electoral malpractice. In an election petition filed by Raj Narain (who later on defeated her in 1977 parliamentary election from Rae Bareily), he had alleged several major as well as minor instances of using government resources for campaigning. The court thus ordered her to be removed from her seat in Parliament and banned from contesting in elections for six years.

But Indira rejected calls to resign and announced plans to appeal to the Supreme Court. Indira insisted the conviction did not undermine her position, despite having been unseated from the lower house of parliament, Lok Sabha, by order of the High Court. She said: "There is a lot of talk about our government not being clean, but from our experience the situation was very much worse when [opposition] parties were forming governments". And she dismissed criticism of the way her Congress Party raised election campaign money, saying all parties used the same methods. The Prime Minister retained the support of her party, which issued a statement backing her.

State of Emergency (1975-1977)

Indira Gandhi moved to restore order by ordering the arrest of most of the opposition participating in the unrest. Her Cabinet and government then recommended that President Fakhruddin Ali Ahmed declare a state of emergency, because of the disorder and lawlessness following the Allahabad High Court decision. Accordingly, Ahmed declared a State of Emergency caused by internal disorder, based on the provisions of Article 352 of the Constitution, on June 26, 1975.

Rule by Decree

Within a few months, President's Rule was imposed on the two opposition party ruled states of Gujarat and Tamil Nadu thereby bringing the entire country under direct Central rule or by governments led by the ruling Congress party. Police were granted powers to impose curfews and indefinitely detain citizens and all publications were subjected to substantial censorship by the Ministry of Information and Broadcasting. Inder Kumar Gujral, a future Prime Minister himself, resigned as Minister for Information and Broadcasting to protest Sanjay Gandhi's interference in his work. Finally, impending legislative assembly elections were indefinitely postponed, with all opposition-controlled state governments being removed by virtue of the constitutional provision allowing for a dismissal of a state government on recommendation of the state's governor.

Indira Gandhi used the emergency provisions to grant herself extraordinary powers.

"Unlike her father Jawaharlal Nehru, who preferred to deal with strong chief ministers in control of their legislative parties and state party organizations, Mrs. Gandhi set out to remove every Congress chief minister who had an independent base and to replace each of them with ministers personally loyal to her... Even so, stability could not be maintained in the states..."

It is alleged that she pressured President F.A. Ahmed to issue ordinances that did not need to be debated in the Parliament, allowing her to rule by decree.

Simultaneously, Indira Gandhi's government undertook a campaign to crush dissent, including the arrest and detention of thousands of political activists; Sanjay Gandhi was instrumental in initiating the clearing of slums around Delhi's Jama Masjid under the supervision of Jagmohan, who was later appointed as Lt. Governor of Delhi, which allegedly left thousands of people homeless and hundreds killed, and led to communal embitterment in those parts of the nation's capital; and the family planning program which forcibly imposed vasectomy on thousands of fathers and was often poorly administered.

Intolerant to Opposition

B.N. Tandon, who was joint secretary in the Prime Minister's Office from 1969 to 1976 kept a meticulous diary during his years with

Gandhi, wrote in his book 'PMO-Diary I: Prelude to the Emergency' published by Konark, that the former Prime Minister—described by admirers as an Iron Lady—was proud and arrogant.

"By various acts of omissions and commissions, she encouraged corruption and protected it," says the author, who sought voluntary retirement from government service in 1983. "Her political belief," Tandon writes, "was that any kind of means are permissible in a fight for power."

Tandon reveals that Indira Gandhi rarely trusted reports prepared by the Intelligence Bureau and was passionately opposed to both the Jana Sangh (present day Bharatiya Janata Party) and the Communist Party of India-Marxist. Indira Gandhi's contempt for democratic values plummeted from 1975, when she was faced with massive anti-government protests across India, particularly in Gujarat and Bihar.

"From the beginning of 1975, the situation began to deteriorate rapidly. Long established decision-making processes were beginning to be set aside... The earlier practice was to put up the files, papers and correspondence for the PM's orders after a thorough examination."

On 31 October 1984, two of Gandhi's Sikh bodyguards, Satwant Singh and Beant Singh, shot her with their service weapons in the garden of the Prime Minister's residence at 1, Safdarjung Road, New Delhi as she was walking past a wicket gate guarded by Satwant and Beant.

RAJIV GANDHI ERA

Rajiv Gandhi, elder son of Indira Gandhi, remained aloof from politics. It was only following his younger brother's death in 1980, he was pressured by Indian National Congress party politicians and his mother to enter politics. He and his wife were both opposed to the idea, and he even publicly stated that he would not contest for his brother's seat. Nevertheless, he eventually announced his candidacy for the membership of Parliament. His entry was criticized by many in the press, public and by the opposition political parties. He fought and won his first election from Amethi Lok Sabha seat.

After the assassination of her mother, he was immediately sworn in as Prime Minister by Giani Zail Singh, the then President of India.

Anti Sikh Riots

This refers to the statement of Rajiv Gandhi as Prime Minister at a Boat Club rally 19-days after the assassination of Indira Gandhi, which read as "Some riots took place in the country following the murder of Indiraji. We know the people were very angry and for a few days it seemed that India had been shaken. But, when a mighty tree falls, it is only natural that the earth around it does shake a little."

This statement sent a wrong signal to the authorities, who adopted a callous approach of not allowing the truth to come out despite the government setting up probe panels one after the other, including two full fledged judicial commissions, the first headed by retired Chief Justice of India Ranganath Mishra and the second by a former apex court judge G.T. Nanavati. According to the authors of the book titled—"When a Tree Shook Delhi" written by senior advocate H.S. Phoolka and co-author, journalist Manoj Mitta (who have based the details of the book mainly on evidence produced before the nine panels and trial courts, and high courts in the form of sworn affidavits by hundreds of witnesses). Based on eyewitness accounts the book said that instead of targeting the aggressors, the police cracked down on the Sikh victims, who had been defending their properties, when they were attacked by hooligans led by the local Congress leaders.

Bofors Scandal

Rajiv Gandhi's Finance Minister, V.P. Singh, uncovered compromising details about government and political corruption, to the consternation of Congress leaders. Transferred to the Defence Ministry, Singh uncovered what came to be known as the Bofors Scandal, involving tens of millions of dollars - concerned alleged payoffs by the Swedish Bofors arms company through Italian businessman and Gandhi family associate Ottavio Quattrocchi in return for Indian contracts. Upon the uncovering of the scandal, Singh was dismissed from office, and later from Congress membership. Later on Rajiv Gandhi himself was personally implicated in the scandal when the investigation was continued by Narasimhan Ram and Chitra Subramaniam of The Hindu newspaper. This shattered his image as an honest politician; he was posthumously absolved of this allegation in 2004, however.

V.P. Singh's image as an exposer of government corruption made him very popular with the public [citation needed], and opposition parties united under his name to form the Janata Dal coalition. In the 1989 elections, the Congress suffered a major setback. With the support of Indian Communists and the Bharatiya Janata Party, Singh and his Janata Dal formed the government. Rajiv Gandhi became the Leader of the Opposition, while remaining Congress president also. While some believe that Rajiv and Congress leaders influenced the collapse of V.P. Singh's government in October 1990 by promising support to Chandra Shekhar, a high-ranking leader in the Janata Dal, sufficient internal contradictions existed within the ruling coalition, especially over the controversial reservation issue, to cause a fall of the government. Rajiv's Congress offered outside support to Chandra Shekhar for a brief period, who became Prime Minister. They withdrew their support in 1991, however, and fresh elections were announced.

Allegations of Black Money

In November 1991, the Schweizer Illustrierte (Swiss Illustrated) magazine published an article on black money held in secret accounts by Imelda Marcos and 14 other rulers of the Third World countries. Citing McKinsey as a source, the article stated that Rajiv Gandhi held 2.5 billion Swiss Francs in secret Indian accounts in Switzerland. Several leaders of opposition parties in India have raised the issue citing the Schweizer Illustrierte article. In December 1991, Amal Datta raised the issue in the Indian Parliament. The then speaker of the Lok Sabha, Shivrai Patil expunged Rajiv Gandhi's name from the proceedings. In December 2011, Subramanian Swamy wrote a letter to the Director of the Central Bureau of Investigation which cited the article, asking him to take action on black money accounts of the Gandhi family. On December 29, 2011, Ram Jethmalani made an indirect reference to the issue in the Rajya Sabha, calling it a shame that one of India's former Prime Ministers was named by a Swiss magazine. This was met by uproar and a demand for withdrawal of the remark by the ruling Congress party members.

In 1992, two Indian newspapers, the Times of India and The Hindu, published reports alleging that Rajiv Gandhi had received funds from the KGB. The Russian government confirmed this disclosure and defended the payments as necessary for the Soviet ideological interest. In their 1994 book 'The State Within a State', the journalists Yevgenia Albats and Catherine Fitzpatrick quoted a letter signed by Viktor Chebrikov in the 1980s, the then-head of the KGB. The letter says that the KGB maintained contact with Rajiv Gandhi, who expressed his gratitude to the KGB for benefits accruing to his family from commercial dealings of a controlled firm, and a considerable portion of funds obtained from this channel were used to support his party. Aibats later revealed that in December 1985, Chebrikov had asked for authorization from the Central Committee of the Communist Party of the Soviet Union to make payments to family members of Rajiv Gandhi, including Sonia Gandhi and Rahul Gandhi. The payments were authorized by a resolution and endorsed by the USSR Council of Ministers, and had been coming since 1971. In December 2001, Subramaniam Swamy filed a writ petition in the Delhi High Court, acting on which the court ordered CBI to ascertain the truth of the allegations in May 2002. After two years, the CBI told the Court that Russia would not entertain such queries without a registered FIR.

Rajiv Gandhi's last public meeting was at Sriperumbudur on 21 May 1991, in a village approximately 30 miles from Chennai, Tamil Nadu, where he was assassinated while campaigning for the Sriperumbudur Lok Sabha Congress candidate.

Afterwards former treasurer of the party Sitaram Kesari took the reins of the Congress party and oversaw its support to the United Front Government that ruled from 1996-98.

P.V. NARASIMHA RAO ERA

P.V. Narasimha Rao became Prime Minister after the assassination of Rajiv Gandhi. He was the first Prime Minister of India outside the Nehru-Gandhi family to serve in the office for complete five years. He was also the first politician from South India to hold this position. He was also the Prime Minister who was prosecuted on corruption charges.

Narsimha Rao was the first Prime Minister being prosecuted in corruption charges. Cases like Rs.2500 crore -Airbus A-320 deal with France involving kickback (1990), Harshad Mehta security scam (1992), Gold Star Steel and Alloys controversy (1992), JMM bribery case, Hawala scam of Rs. 65 crore and Urea scam (1996) also came up during the period of Narsimha Rao Government.

In July 1993, Rao's government was facing a no-confidence motion, because the opposition felt that it did not have sufficient numbers to prove the majority. It was alleged that Rao, through a representative, offered millions of rupees to members of the Jharkhand Mukti Morcha (JMM), and possibly a breakaway faction of the Janata Dal, to vote for him during the confidence motion. Shailendra Mahato, one of those members who had accepted the bribe, turned approver. In 1996, after Rao's term in office had expired, investigations began in earnest in the case. In 2000, after years of legal proceedings, a special court convicted Rao and his colleague, Buta Singh (who is alleged to have escorted the MPs to the Prime Minister). Rao appealed to a higher court and remained free on bail. The decision was overturned mainly due to the doubt in credibility of Mahato's statements (which were extremely inconsistent) and both Rao and Buta Singh were absolved of the charges in 2002.

Rao, along with fellow minister K.K. Tewary, Chandraswami and K.N. Aggarwal were accused of forging documents showing that Ajeya Singh had opened a bank account in the First Trust Corporation Bank in St. Kitts and deposited $21 million in it, making his father V.P. Singh its beneficiary. The alleged intent was to tarnish V.P. Singh's image. This supposedly happened in 1989. However, only after Rao's term as PM had expired in 1996, he was formally charged by the Central Bureau of Investigation for the crime. Less than a year later the court acquitted him due to lack of evidence linking him with the case.

Lakhubhai Pathak, an Indian businessman living in England alleged that Chandraswami and K.N. Aggarwal alias Mamaji, along with Mr. Rao, cheated him of $100,000. The amount was given for an express promise for allowing supplies of paper pulp in India, and Pathak alleged that he spent an additional $30,000 for entertaining

Chandraswami and his secretary. Rao and Chandraswami were acquitted of the charges in 2003.

After Rao completed his five years tenure as the Prime Minister, in the 1996 general elections Rao's Congress Party was badly defeated and he had to step down from Prime Ministership. He retained the leadership of the Congress party until late 1996 after which he was replaced by Sitaram Kesri. Rao also remained President of the party during his tenure as the Prime Minister. He suffered a heart attack on December 9, 2004 and breathed his last on December 23, 2004.

MANMOHAN SINGH ERA

Dr. Manmohan Singh has been the PM since 2004 till date. His seven year rule has been a period of scandals and scams, corruption and black money. It covers the whole of the next chapter.

CONCLUSION

Our tryst with democracy started with a galaxy of leaders like Mahatma Gandhi, Nehru, Patel, Azad, Shastri and others, and the qualities of honesty, courage and sacrifice that they personified went right down to the village volunteers. It was an age of valor and commitment, not a period of corruption and cowardice as of today with immunity to those who have defrauded the nation of millions. No doubt, power corrupts but never in our worst moments did we ever imagine that within a span 65 years after independence all the merits of our leaders would be lost and a new generation would arise which would make use of the licence-permit Raj to steel from the coffers of the poor. We have reached a stage when there are scams after scams with every passing day. All types of politicians are involved in these scams, even the Prime Minister is accused of corrupt practices. Corruption, black money and rising prices are eating the very vital nerve of our great nation.

Free India's greatest need is that her people should have faith in the bonafide and integuity of their Government. It is no exaggeration to say that congress has lost the confidence of the people. The reason is simple. Congressmen are no longer selfless, there is scramble among them for the prestige and spoils of office. They have lost contact with the people, the contacts are limited to congressmen out of office, and congressmen in the office wiith their narrow interest. The congress ceased a party which was in power for more than 55 years, after independence and as such its idealogy has become flabby and it has ceased to be effective. If India has to be rejuvenated and corruption has to be eradicated, a next party with a new ideology and fresh outlook must come to power through 'pristine purity' of elections organised by an independent agency not sub-servient to executive.

4

UPA Government Neck-deep in Corruption

No doubt, as discussed in the previous chapter, there were scams and scandals during the regimes of Jawahar Lal Nehru, Indira Gandhi, Narasimha Rao and Rajiv Gandhi, however, during the rule of Dr. Manmohan Singh, corruption reached its new heights. In the seven years of his rule Rs.1.76 lakh crore has been siphoned off by his Government in the 2G Spectrum scam and Rs.70,000 crore were cornered in Commonwealth Games scam.

This is the season of scams, and the biggest ever corruption cases in India have been unearthed more recently. So, we decided to dig deep to see which scams were the biggest and most damaging to the country and its citizens alike.

In our daily life, most of us must have been a witness to or a victim of the corruption thriving in some or the other part of the country. It could be in the form of a taxi-driver manipulating the meter to jack-up the reading or a government officer taking bribery to promptly transfer your file to the next department or even yourself offering bribe to a traffic police on breaking a signal.

An average Indian citizen is hard working and diligent, but it is the people in charge of the system *(The Babu's)* or with whom the power lays, that act as a cancer, spreading the venom, slowing down progress and what not! But, somewhere down the line, we ourselves are responsible for allowing and being taken for a ride by these people. Aren't we?

However, it is during a multi-thousand crore scam, that a tax-payer actually realizes the heartburn of being cheated from his valued contribution of funds towards the development and well-being of the nation. But, that's what a scam, be it big or small, means—the act of swindling by some fraudulent scheme or action.

Corruption is endemic and is present in every sector of our society today. There is corruption within the government, the police, the judiciary and the private sector as well. As of now, it has reached its peak. It was during this Government that MPs were offered cash for votes and the Whistle Blowers were sent to jail.

Corruption, black money and rising prices are the gifts of this Government. The free flow of foreign capital in retail trading is now on cards, though it has been put off for sometime because of its opposition by the alliance partners of UPA-II, but the Manmohan Sing's Government is determined to implement it to the detriment of the economy. His Government has shown its helplessness in tackling the issues of graft and price rise. The list of major scams and scandals during his regime given below illustrates this fact.

BOGIE OF SCAMS

UPA Government is the government of scams and scandals. Some of these are given below.

The 2G Spectrum Scam:

It involved officials in the government of India illegally undercharging mobile telephony companies for frequency allocation licenses, which they would use to create 2G subscriptions for cell phones. The shortfall between the money collected and the money which the law mandated to be collected is estimated to be Rs. 176,000 crore (US$33.44 billion) based on 3G auction prices. The issuing of licenses occurred in 2008, but the scam came to public notice when the Indian Income Tax Department was investigating political lobbyist Nira Radia.

The government's investigation and the government's reactions to the findings in the investigation were the subject of debate, as were the nature of the Indian media's reactions. The discussion around the reactions to the 2G spectrum scam became known in the media as the Nira Radia tapes controversy.

Much of the credit of bringing this whole scam into the public light (by pursuing it in the court of law) goes to Subramaniam Swamy who is the chief petitioner for this case in the court of law.

ISRO Spectrum Allocation Scam

The Comptroller and Auditor General (CAG) suspects a scandal in the allocation of S-band spectrum and is reportedly investigating losses worth Rs 2 lakh crore in the scam.

Department of Space and Indian Space Research Organization (ISRO) are under the scanner over the S-band spectrum.

The alleged scam is related to a deal between ISRO's commercial arm Antrix Corp and Devas Multimedia. ISRO is accused of allocating to Devas 70 Mega Hertz of scarce S-band spectrum for a 20-year period.

The CAG was alerted because unlike in earlier contracts, ISRO placed no restrictions on Devas Multimedia for onward leasing of spectrum, which means the company could make huge amounts of money by sub-leasing its privileges.

Commonwealth Games Scam:

Another feather in the cap of Indian scandal list is Commonwealth Games loot. Yes, literally a loot! Even before the long awaited sporting bonanza could see the day of light, the grand event was soaked in the allegations of corruption. It is estimated that out of Rs. 70000 crore spent on the Games, only half the said amount was spent on Indian sportspersons.

The Central Vigilance Commission, involved in probing the

alleged corruption in various Commonwealth Games-related projects, has found discrepancies in tenders—like payment to non-existent parties, willful delays in execution of contracts, over-inflated price and bungling in purchase of equipment through tendering- and misappropriation of funds.

A number of concerns and controversies surfaced before the 2010 Commonwealth Games in New Delhi, India, which received widespread media coverage both in India (the host nation) and internationally.

The Commonwealth Games event was severely criticized by several prominent Indian politicians and social activists because billions of dollars have been spent on the sporting event despite the fact that India has one of the world's largest concentrations of poor people. Additionally, several other problems related to the 2010 Commonwealth Games have been highlighted by Indian investigative agencies and media outlets; these include—serious corruption by officials of the Games' Organizing Committee, delays in the construction of main Games' venues, infrastructural compromise, possibility of a terrorist attack, and exceptionally poor ticket sales before the event.

The Central Bureau of Investigation (CBI) probe has detected irregularities in various areas like merchandising, catering, CWG Village and accreditation. The agency has arrested officials of the Games' Organizing Committee on corruption and delays in the construction of main Games' venues.

Adarsh Society Scam:

In 2010, the Indian media brought to public the alleged violations of rules at various phases of construction in the Adarsh Society. Questions were raised on the manner in which apartments in the building were allocated to bureaucrats, politicians and army personnel who had nothing to do with Kargil War and the way in which clearances were obtained for the construction of the building of the Adarsh Society. The Adarsh society high-rise was constructed in the Colaba locality of Mumbai. which is considered a sensitive coastal area by the Indian Defence forces and houses various Indian Defense establishments. The society is also alleged to have violated the Indian environment ministry rules. Activists like Medha Patkar had been trying to uncover the problems since at least 2004. It had led to resignation of the then Chief Minister, Ashok Chavan.

Several inquiries have been ordered by the army and the Government to probe into the irregularities. Some of the current occupants of the flats in the Adarsh Co-operative Society building have offered to vacate their flats at the earliest, denying allegations that they were allotted flats because they influenced or helped, in some manner, the construction of the society by violating the rules.

Adarsh Housing Society, a cooperative society in Mumbai, was reserved for the war widows and veterans of the Kargil War. However, the flats were allocated to bureaucrats, politicians and army personnel who had nothing to do with the Kargil War.

The 31-floor high-rise is also alleged to have been built in violation of environment rules. The scam led to the resignation of Ashok Chavan as Maharashtra chief minister.

Satyam Scam

Satyam is the biggest fraud in the corporate history to the tune of Rs. 14,000 crore. The company's disgraced former Chairman Ramalinga Raju kept everyone in the dark for a decade by fudging the books of accounts for several years and inflating revenues and profit figures of Satyam. Finally, the company was taken over by the Tech Mahindra which has done wonderfully well to revive the brand Satyam. On 7th January 2009, company Chairman Ramalinga Raju resigned after notifying board members and the Securities and Exchange Board of India (SEBI) that Satyam's accounts had been falsified.

Raju confessed that Satyam's balance sheet of 30 September 2008 contained:

Inflated figures for cash and bank balances of Indian Rupee 5,040 crore (US$1.12 billion) as against Indian Rupee 5,361 crore (US$1.19 billion) reflected in the books, an accrued interest of Indian Rupee 376 crore (US$83.47 million) which was non-existent.

An understated liability of Indian Rupee 1,230 crore (US$273.06 million) on account of funds was arranged by himself.

An understated debtors' position of Indian Rupee 490 crore (US$108.78 million) (as against Indian Rupee D2,651 crore (US$588.52 million) in the books).

Raju claimed in the same letter that neither he nor the Managing Director had benefited financially from the inflated revenues. He claimed that none of the board members had any knowledge of the situation in which the company was placed.

The Cash-for-Vote Scam:

The opposition slammed the UPA government over WikiLeaks cables revelations that the UPA -I paid some MPs to vote in favour of the July 2008 trust vote on the Indo-US nuclear deal.

Telgi Scam

As they say, every scam must have something unique in it to make money out of it in an unscrupulous manner- and Telgi scam had all the suspense and drama that the scandal needed to thrive and be busted.

Abdul Karim Telgi had mastered the art of forgery in printing duplicate stamp papers and sold them to banks and other institutions. The tentacles of the fake stamp and stamp paper case had penetrated 12 states and was estimated at a whooping Rs. 20,000 crore plus. The Telgi clearly had a lot of support from government departments that were responsible for the production and sale of high security stamps.

IPL Scam

Never before has a scam been enjoyed and celebrated by such a massive proportion of Indian people. A lot of the IPL activity has been alleged to be unethical, unlawful and sometimes illegal. Politicians and others are said to be laundering black money via Mauritius and other tax havens which hide investors' identities through shell companies and false names. There are suggestions that matches and bids for team franchises have been fixed, and that there have been bribes, tax evasion, illegal betting, and breaches of foreign investment rules. At the centre of the growth, and the controversy, was Lalit Modi, creator and Chairman of the IPL and former Vice President of the highly politicized Board of Control for Cricket in India (BCCI).

Money-laundering and Mining Scam

On 10 October 2009, he was charged with laundering money. The Income Tax Department uncovered over 4,000 crore in illegal assets owned by Koda. Among others, these assets were reported to include hotels and three companies in Mumbai, property in Kolkata, a hotel in Thailand, and a coal mine in Liberia. This alleged scam is said to be the second-largest scam uncovered in India in 2009 and gets his name included in the list of controversial Indian businessmen like Hasan Ali Khan and Harshad Mehta.

In the probes, it was found that Maoists received a 30% share of the "Koda plunder". This has led to staunch criticism of Koda from sections of society, including the opposition Bharatiya Janata Party. Gujarat Chief Minister Narendra Modi stated Koda was part of a corrupt network of Congress Party who stole money from Jharkhand.

In July 2011, the Member of Parliament, Mr. Madhu Koda was transferred to Delhi's high profile Tihar Jail from Chaibasa Central Jail after being given permission by the Jharkhand Vigilance Court so that he can attend the monsoon session of the Parliament.

Hassan Ali Khan money laundering scam is another one in this row. This scam can be said to be the almost immediate cause of the anti-corruption movement being faced by the country. The revelation about the huge sums of money being stashed away in Swiss banks served as an impetus to rally against the government that had been ignoring it. The magnanimity of the situation came into focus when Indian businessman was arrested on money laundering charges which was to the tune of Rs. 39,120 crores.

INSENSITIVE GOVERNMENT

When Manmohan Singh is asked to reflect upon these scams and scandals he refers them to the compulsions of the 'coalition dharma', a new term coined to come out clean putting the entire onus of corruption on its allies. In the 2G Spectrum Case, the blame has been shifted to A Raja. When asked about food inflation, he directs the querries to Sharad Pawar. When it comes to the scam in purchase of ships he says that Praful Patel will answer. It seems that the Prime Minister has absolved himself of all the responsibilities like the British King:

"Who never said a foolish thing
Nor ever did a wise one."

Then what for is he the Prime Minister? Is he there to dance to Sonia Gandhi's tune?

Manmohan Singh is the weakest Prime Minister, a mouth piece of Sonia Gandhi, who installed him on this post till Rahul is groomed for it. He can't take any decision without consulting Sonia Gandhi and Rahul Gandhi. What can be the greater irony than the fact that the Congress Party's Chief never felt confident about the winability of Manmohan Sigh for a Lok Sabha seat even after his being Prime Minister for the second term. The fact cannot be denied that he has not won even a Municipal election in his life while there are MPs of his party, Pranab Mukherji, the leader of the House in Lok Sabha being among them, who won the Lok Sabha elections several times. As such, he seems to have some sort of complex for which he has little control over his ministers. The ministers who are close to Sonia and Rahul seem to care a fig for him. They seem to consider themselves above the Prime Minister and in Sonia's absence Minmohan Singh finds himself helpless.

Collective responsibility of the Government, one of the basic principles of parliamentary democracy, seems to have lost. The Cabinet Ministers speak against each other. The recent tiff between Pranab Mukherjee, the Finance Minister and P. Chidambaram, the Home Minister on 2G Spectrum issue rocked the Government for several days.

In reality, Manmohan Singh is a puppet, Sonia is the string puller and the Congress leaders are waiting for his pull down and crowning of Rahul Gandhi as the Prime Minister. In this situation would it not be better that he withdraws himself gracefully.

Manmohan Equally Corrupt

Manmohan Singh was considered as Mr. Clean during his UPA-I tenure. When he took over as PM in 2004 people held him in high esteem. People knew him as an honest and competent administrator who would lead the country to great heights. But, during UPA-II he has tarnished his public image presiding over a government mired in some of the biggest scams and scandals in the history of India. People have started disliking him for being weak and too slow to act. He may not be corrupt himself, but he has lost the trust of the public as instead of taking action against the corrupt ministers, he has sheltered and supported them. His hypocrisy has eroded all his moral authority to stop corruption. Given below are the extracts from some of his speeches where he talked about corruption but did nothing to remove it.

HOLLOW PROMISES

Address at the All India Conference of Lokayuktas and Uplokayuktas

September 29, 2004, Dehradun

Mahatma Gandhiji had understood the gathering crisis of corruption and prophesied that the public would need to be in the forefront in exposing corrupt practices and taking to task those who were involved in them. As early as 1928 Mahatma Gandhi wrote in Young India, 'Corruption will be out one day, however much one may try to conceal it; and the public can, as its right and duty, in every case of justifiable suspicion, call its servants to strict account, dismiss them, sue them in a law court or appoint an arbitrator or inspector to scrutinize their conduct, as it likes.'

Convocation Address at Manipur University

November 20, 2004, Manipur

This is important because Governance and development administration should be transparent and participatory. I am acutely aware of the cancer of corruption that is eating into the vitals of development administration all over the country, and not just here. There are no administrative solutions to this problem. The real solution is to empower civil society. You young people can play a vital role in bringing greater transparency into governance and making Governments more accountable not only once in five years, but at all times.

Inaugural Address of Lal Bahadur Shastri Memorial

May 7, 2005, New Delhi

Shastriji not only defended the country against external aggression and internal poverty, he also waged a relentless battle against corruption and in favour of values in our public life. His decision to resign from the position of Union Railway Minister after a rail accident has become a popular tale of public accountability for generations. As the Union Home Minister he was instrumental in appointing one of the first-ever Committees on Prevention of Corruption under the Chairmanship of K. Santhanam. Today, with the benefit of hindsight, the steps taken by Shastriji assume enormous significance in the struggle to eliminate corruption and restore faith in our governance.

Remarks on 90th Birth Anniversary of Shri Bhikhu Ram Jain

August 5, 2005, New Delhi

Shri Bhiku Ramji's role as a representative of the people in the Lok Sabha is inspiring and educative. He worked for the cause of good governance, clean environment and a corruption free administration. I recall that while participating in the discussion on the Finance Bill in 1983, he underlined the role of our cumbersome tax laws in the rising incidence of corruption and believed these were making Indian enterprise uncompetitive. He was in favour of the simplification of the taxation regime and saw this as an important instrument of battling corruption. This influenced my thinking at the time and as Finance Minister I was able to take steps to reform our taxation system. His observation in the early 1980s that more control bred black money and corruption has now come to be accepted as common place.

Prime Minister's Independence Day Address

August 15, 2005, New Delhi

The Central Government, State Governments and Panchayats have to work together so that the expectations of people are fulfilled. If we have to achieve results, there is a need to change the manner in which governments function. There is no space in our government or in our society for corruption and arbitrary action. We are not prepared to tolerate this at any cost. Government servants must work with a sense of public service and they should be held accountable to the people. Governments will have to be made more transparent and accountable. The recently passed Right to Information Act is a landmark step in this direction.

PM's Independence Day Speech

August 15, 2006, New Delhi

We have to pay more attention to the quality of local administration—in our villages and districts, in our towns and cities. We need to rid our municipalities of the cancer of corruption. State governments have a major role to play in this.

We have to work hard to eliminate corruption in the delivery of public services, in fact eliminate it from all walks of life. We will work to put in place a system that rewards honesty, probity and efficiency.

Speech at the Civil Service Day

April 21,2007, New Delhi

Often, policy reform measures do not deliver the desired outcomes because of lack of forward movement in reform of government processes. This is after all, what gives rise to the so-called Inspector Raj. This is what makes the interface of a common citizen with government a cumbersome and daunting affair. This is often the root cause of corruption as well. When I meet individuals or industrialists, it is this aspect of government which is crying out for change.

I sincerely hope we can root out corruption in the civil service and raise the morale of our officers so that they can give their very best to our country. Senior civil servants have a special responsibility to promote a culture of excellence, probity in public conduct and concern for social equity.

Address at the CNBC-TV18 Emerging India Awards, 2007 for Small and Medium Enterprises

June 22, 2007, Mumbai

There are complaints of favouritism and corruption. This is not as it should be. We should free university appointments from unnecessary interventions on the part of governments and must promote autonomy and accountability. I urge states to pay greater attention to this aspect. After all, a dysfunctional education system can only produce dysfunctional future citizens.

Independence Day Speech

August 15, 2007, New Delhi

To make the government, at all levels, more accountable and more transparent, and to fight the cancer of corruption, we had introduced the Right to Information Act. I want every citizen to make full use of this act to ensure that government functions properly and honestly.

Speech on the Occasion of 60th Anniversary of India's Independence

August 15, 2007, New Delhi

For all the benefits of development to reach the poor, it is essential that the delivery systems of the Government, at all levels, are more efficient and purged of corruption. The cancer of corruption must be extinguished if democracy and development have to have a real meaning for our people.

Address at the Conference of Director Generals and Inspector Generals of Police

October 4, 2007, New Delhi

We need greater discipline, lesser politicization and zero corruption. We are committed to supporting your efforts in this direction. However, you need to provide the necessary leadership and direction to the forces under your command.

Speech at the Conference of Chief Ministers & Chief Justices of High Courts

April 19, 2008, New Delhi

Apart from pendency and delayed justice, corruption is another challenge we face both in Government and the judiciary. The Chief Justice of India has written to me suggesting that we create special courts to deal with corruption cases. I agree that there is urgent need to do so. This will instill greater confidence in our justice delivery system, at home and abroad.

Speech on the Occasion of 63rd Anniversary of India's Independence

15 August 2010, New Delhi

Today, we do not need many new programs to achieve our goals. However, we do need to implement the schemes we have already started more effectively, minimizing the chances of corruption and misuse of public money. We want to achieve this in partnership with the State Governments, Panchayati Raj Institutions and civil society groups.

KINGPIN OF CORRUPTION

Manmohan Singh committed to the nation, through his press conferences and addresses at different forums many a times, his intention to overcome corruption, but his actions have never matched his words. Surrounded by corrupt elected representatives of his party he is helpless to take action against them. It is high time for him to give up the greed for Prime Ministership and absolve himself of all the sins of corruption lest he should go down in history as the Kingpin of Corruption.

CONCLUSION

The obvious conclusions from the magnitude and trend in political corruption in India are: One, the growing monopoly of the state in economic affairs has resulted into mal-distribution and increasing inequalities of income in India *vis-a-vis* deteriorating law and order situation. Two, in spite of the increasing claims of policies and programs of the Government to overcome poverty and check exploitation, black money and corruption, the rich, the mafia, the law makers and the executives have become richer and the richest while the poor are starving and committing suicides. What can be greater mockery on the part of the Planning Commission of India when it states on oath before the Supreme Court of the country that a citizen earning Rs. 26/- per day is not poor. It shows how statistics are manipulated in favour of the Government and the people are duped.

The story of Corruption Black Money does not seem to be coming to an end. Every day a new scam seems to be unfolding and the ruling political parties do not seem to yield unless there is a PIL against the corrupt leader and flogging from the High Courts or the Supreme Court to the Governments and Government investigating agencies. So much so that they dare challenge the apex court's jurisdiction for interfering with their failing duties and corrupt practices as if they are above the constitution. In this sort of prevailing situation there have been public cries time and again to have an impartial and independent institution to whom the people can approach and complain about the political and economic excesses and corrupt practices in use of public policies and funds by those in authority for seeking fast redressal at nominal costs.

At the social level, the parallel economy has made people lose faith in society. Its persistent existence is today compelling the *aam-admi* to angrily ask: "What the hell is happening?" Perhaps without it, we would have a far more transparent and technologically efficient economic system. We could have edged ahead of the US and China together in terms of production vis-a-vis consumption. Instead, we now have a generation that is primarily consumption-driven, partly production-driven and wholly caught up in corruption. More importantly, we would not have had to witness the Anna Hazare movement to root out corruption if we didn't have a black economy.

5

Abuse of Political Power

Of late we have seen that there is an over growing tendency in the political parties in power to rule in an autocratic manner overlooking the constitution, the opposition and the civil society, claiming that they are sovereign. They condemn opposition as the voice of the rejected political parties and suppress the peaceful expressions of unrest of the civil society and peaceful civil agitations in a repressive manner by terming them as unconstitutional movements, threats to peace, against the interests of the country and posing law and order problems. All this is against the spirit of democracy and our constitution. The government willfully forgets the preamble of our Constitution that all authority flows from the people of India, the civil society has the right to peaceful protest and that they are deputies in the service of the people and not their masters:

PREAMBLE

WE, THE PEOPLE OF INDIA, having solemnly
resolved to constitute India into a [SOVEREIGN
SOCIALIST SECULAR DEMOCRATIC REPUBLIC] and
to secure to all its citizens:

JUSTICE, social, economic and political;
LIBERTY of thought, expression, belief, faith and worship;
EQUALITY of status and of opportunity;
and to promote among them all
FRATERNITY assuring the dignity of the individual and the [unity and integrity of the Nation];
IN OUR CONSTITUENT ASSEMBLY this twenty sixth day of November, 1949, do HEREBY ADOPT, ENACT AND GIVE TO OURSELVES THIS CONSTITUTION.

The preamble to the constitution of India is the soul of it. In the very beginning it states that India is by the Indians. The people are sovereign; the path is **SECULAR and DEMOCRATIC** governance that has to work for:

JUSTICE, social, economic and political

EQUALITY of status and of opportunity

LIBERTY of thought, expression, belief, faith and worship;

FRATERNITY assuring the dignity of the individual and the [unity and integrity of the Nation]

Thus, defining the responsibilities of the Government it lays down its limits. The actions of the government have to be evaluated with reference to these guiding principles. All the powers and privileges of the institutions under the constitutional framework are subject to the fulfillment of the aspirations of the people expressed in this preamble.

The people have given the Governments sufficient time and a fair chance to play their role, of course with moderate frown at intervals whenever they strayed from the given path. Let us see how much we have moved in these directions so far.

SECULARISM

Though, the use of religion or caste as a vote catching device during elections is a corrupt practice under the Representation of the People

Act 1951, the fact remains that these factors have been playing an important role over the years in deciding the fate of the candidates in elections. A number of petitions containing allegations against the returned candidates for using caste and religion are either dismissed by various courts or pending in absence of substantial evidence.

In 1949 at the instance of Congress rulers the statue of "Ram Lala" was locked in Ayodhya, the Government of the same party put "shilanyas" of the temple in 1996 when it was unlocked by the orders of the court.

Not going too far in time, the recent repeated utterances of Salman Khursid, the Law Minister of India and Beni Prasad, the Union Minister about reservation for Muslims, overlooking of the warnings by the Election Commission, during the recent elections to the U. P. assembly are the examples of blatant shamelessness on the part of those in power challenging a constitutional institution of the country.

Secularism means different things to different people. In the language of Indian politics, the word secularism means the willingness of Hindus to accept the right of the Muslims to maintain their personal community law, use of Urdu and preservation of Islamic institutions but to them, the divisive caste politics in the majority community can go on. For the Congress Party, secularism refers to the willingness of the Government to be the protector of Muslims against hostility and violence on the part of Hindus but they have no qualms in exploiting one caste against another for maximizing their seats. For the BJP secularism means justice for all and appeasement to none. The Communists instead of defining the meaning of this word, accused the BJP as communal and Congress as authoritarian. The Socialists always made special appeal to the backward castes on the ground that in Indian society the interests of castes and classes coincide. Secularism has now become a hat that every party wears and interprets it as per its convenience in the light of suitability of the situation, so it has lost its shape.

DEMOCRACY

B.R. Ambedkar, generally acknowledged to be the father of the Indian Constitution, had warned the Constituent Assembly:

> "I feel, however, good a Constitution may be, it is sure to turn out bad because those who are called to work, happen to be a bad lot...The working of the Constitution does not depend wholly upon the nature of the Constitution. The Constitution can provide only the organs of state such as the Legislature, the Executive and the Judiciary. The factors on which the working of those organs of the state depends are the people and the political parties they will set up as their instruments to carry out their wishes and their politics. Who can say how the people of India and their parties will behave?"

However, insofar as structural changes in Indian politics have led to an adverse self-selection regarding who enters politics, and, thereby the caliber of people likely to enter Parliament, it is not possible to be too optimistic about the capacity of Parliament to rejuvenate itself. More important than changes in the professional background of MPs is the reality that those charged with making laws are sometimes lawbreakers themselves. Recently, India's Supreme Court passed a judgment making it mandatory for candidates contesting parliamentary or assembly polls to disclose their criminal antecedents to the electorate (if any) and information related to their personal finances and education. Parliament tried to evade the judgment by an amendment to the Constitution, which was challenged in the courts and finally struck down in 2003. The judgment attests the degree to which a hobbled legislative has ceded ground not to the executive or external forces, but to the judiciary. Whether the electorate will use the additional information on candidates' backgrounds to better screen their representatives is by no means obvious, but ultimately it is a task that will have to be faced by the Indian voter.

With the passage of time there has been palpable decline in the majesty of Indian Parliament. With much of Parliament's time wasted on rowdiness and disorder and theatrics replacing debate, there are serious concerns of whether it has become "dysfunctional". While "unparliamentarily" behaviour by individual MPs has undoubtedly robbed Parliament of the mystique that often underpins authority, its weakness as an institution of accountability stems from many factors, both within and outside the institution.

Multi Party Democracy

A very large number of candidates contesting for one seat results in vote wastage and party or parties hardly representing less than one fourth of the electorate constitute government claiming to be undisputed true representatives of the people. It needs evolution of a two party system so that the true majority of the electorate gets represented. Going a step further the best solution is to move towards a National Government so that it becomes a truly participative democracy and delivers political justice. In 2009 General Elections 364 political parties contested and the turnout of voters was 56.97% and the UPA got 37.22% of the polled votes that comes to about 16% of the whole electorate.

Loss of Faith and Credibility in Government

In addition to "systemic" problems, like erosion of collective responsibility, excessive centralization and widespread political corruption, the faith of the ordinary citizen in the working of their elected government has been further shaken by two landmark events. In December 2009, there was a sudden announcement in favour of a separate state of Telangana, followed by an equally abrupt decision to postpone it and the spectacle of some MPs being forcibly carried out of the Rajya Sabha so as the landmark legislation on women's reservation could be approved the same day. And then, the pause—and announcement that this Bill will be introduced in the Lok Sabha later after consultation with all parties! So was the case with FDI in retail trading in India and more recently decision about NCTC.

Suggestion to Strengthen Democracy

An unintended consequence of some recent amendments to the Constitution (*i.e.,* the 52nd Amendment of 1985 and the 91st Amendment of 2003), combined with the power of parties to issue whips, has been to make individual members of Parliament fully subordinate to their leaders. The power of party leaders *vis-a-vis* elected members has been further compounded by an amendment in 2003 in the Representation of the People's Act which removed the domicile requirement for election to the so-called Council of States

(Rajya Sabha). An immediate priority is to revoke all amendments, which are designed to "disempowering" elected members.

Cutting across political parties—in power and in Opposition—nearly 25 per cent of elected members in the Lok Sabha have criminal antecedents. An important reason for the attractiveness of politics as a career of choice by persons with criminal records is the enormous judicial delay in deciding such cases, and the power of political leaders to further delay the investigation and prosecution.

This incentive may be completely reversed by a relatively simple measure—by providing that elected candidates with pending criminal cases cannot take the "oath of office" until their cases have been heard by courts, and that such cases would have priority over other pending cases. Just consider the impact of this "reverse incentive" in order to avoid immediate hearing of cases, the incentive would be to avoid getting elected to Parliament or state legislatures!

A related measure to make politics less remunerative is to reduce the power of ministries to "allocate" public resources, such as mineral rights, spectrum, gas etc. If an autonomous Election Commission, appointed by the government, can organize free and fair elections in the largest democracy in the world, similar agencies can be established to allocate public resources as per policies approved by the Cabinet.

Finally, the prevailing practice of passing several Bills at the end of the day at the discretion of the executive branch, without discussion or actual voting, has to be simply abolished—except in an emergency—to enable Parliament to perform its assigned role under the Constitution.

If the above measures are taken, or at least considered by Parliament, the working of Indian democracy by the people would become less oligarchic and more accountable.

JUSTICE AND EQUALITY

When it comes to justice it includes social, economic and political justice to provide a level playing ground for all irrespective of class, cast or creed considerations.

Social Justice

"First work of this assembly is to make India independent by a new constitution through which starving people will get complete meal and cloths, and each Indian will get best option that he can progress himself." **V.R. Krishna Iyear.**

"In this sense social justice holds the aims of equal opportunity to every citizen in the matter of social & economical activities and to prevent inequalities." **P.B. Ganendragadkar**

There is a very wide planning of justice according to necessity in the constitution. It expects distribution of social benefits according to necessity by which more needy persons can get benefits. It is expected of the state that the state shall in particular, direct its policy towards securing that children are given opportunities and facilities to develop in a healthy manner and in conditions of freedom and dignity and that childhood and youth are protected against exploitation and against moral and material abandonment. Under Article 41, it is expected the state that the State shall, within the limits of its economic capacity and development, make effective provision for securing the right to work, to education and to public assistance in case of unemployment, old age, sickness and disablement, and in other cases of underserved want. It is provided under Article 42 that the state shall make provision for securing just and humane conditions of work and for maternity relief. In Article 43 it is expected that the State shall endeavor to secure, by suitable legislation or economic organization or in any other way, to all workers agricultural, industrial or otherwise, work, a living wage, conditions of work ensuring a decent standard of life and full enjoyment of leisure and social and cultural opportunities and, in particular, the state shall endeavor to promote cottage industries on an individual or co-operative basis in rural areas. In PUDR vs. Union of India, the Supreme Court has held that minimum wages must be given and not to pay minimum wages is the violation of human dignity and it is also known as exploitation.

The following human development indices over the years since 1980 reveal that compared to the rate of increase in the index during 2000-2005 in the following years the rate has slowed down reflecting growing negligence of the Government towards social justice.

Human Development Index*

Year	*India*	*World*
1980	0.320	0.455
1990	0.389	0.526
2000	0.440	0.570
2005	0.482	0.598
2006	0.491	0.604
2007	0.500	0.611
2008	0.506	0.615
2009	0.512	0.619
2010	0.519	0.624

Source : UNDP Human Development Report, 2011.

*Human Development Index (HDI) is a comparative measure of life expectancy, literacy, education and standards of living for countries worldwide. It is a standard means of measuring well-being, especially child welfare.

According to the newly revised official definition of the poverty line, 37 per cent of India's population (or about 410 million people) falls below the poverty line, making the country home of one-third of the world's poor. Disparities in income and human development are on the rise. The rich seems to have grown richer. The new revised official poverty line seems to have cleverly divided the poor into two categories, less poor and more poor and shifting the less poor driving out of the category of people below the poverty line for window dressing by our Planning Commission.

Economic justice

India saw an annual growth rate of GDP (Gross Domestic Product) of only 3.6% during the 3 decades, post-independence. It's a growth of only 1.4% in terms of per capita. The economy of the country only moved towards higher growth trajectory during 1980s, when it saw a growth rate of 5.4%. The growth rate of GDP soared up to 7.3% by 2007-08, whereas the per capita GDP saw a growth of 5.7%. Due to sufficient foreign exchange reserves, moderate inflation, stable exchange rates and adequate food stocks, the country achieved a sustainable growth rate.

States	*GSDP*		*Per Capita GSDP*	
	1980-81/ 1992-93	*1993-94/ 2005-06*	*1980-81/ 1992-93*	*1993-94/ 2005-06*
Andhra Pradesh	5.72	6.53	3.50	5.51
Assam	3.98	3.54	1.75	2.14
Bihar	3.41	4.73	1.23	5.26
Gujarat	6.77	7.10	4.74	5.30
Haryana	5.75	6.98	3.24	4.81
Karnataka	5.57	6.88	3.59	5.50
Kerala	3.82	6.28	2.44	5.51
Madhya Pradesh	4.49	4.91	2.07	6.00
Maharashtra	6.32	6.17	3.97	4.42
Orissa	3.67	5.53	1.80	4.31
Punjab	5.21	4.53	3.23	2.93
Rajasthan	7.37	5.44	4.74	3.29
Tamil Nadu	5.46	6.12	4.03	5.16
Uttar Pradesh	4.47	4.19	2.17	2.59
West Bengal	4.57	6.61	2.35	5.23

Source : CSO.

However, the gross state domestic product growth rates largely varied between states in India. The states like Assam, Uttar Pradesh, Madhya Pradesh and Bihar saw a growth rate of less than 5% in pre and post reform period. On the other hand, states like Andhra Pradesh, Tamil Nadu, Gujarat, Karnataka, Haryana saw a growth rate of less than 5% during 1980-93, which improved considerably during 1993-2006.

The second in our semi-annual series of India Updates points out that India's economic growth seems to be back to the pre-crisis trend, but inflation is worrying. The RBI is likely to continue its policy of cautious rate hikes in an uncertain environment. The signals are not clear whether, core inflation is caused by more general demand pressures, which would best be addressed with more aggressive policy tightening, or by second round effects of earlier food and commodity price shocks, for which the current monetary policy stance is likely to be adequate. The December 2010 Update also discusses several medium-term issues: the link between the real exchange rate and growth, a long-term look at education, demographics and growth, the challenges facing the introduction of the GST, and the mid-term evaluation of the Eleventh Development Plan.

Political Justice

Political justice implies that all citizens should have equal political rights, equal voice in the government. Conferral of one-man-one-vote' right is not by itself political freedom. The little man of India must be able to exercise his voting right, well equipped with knowledge of whom to vote and then with full freedom to vote for his choice. The doors of the court are open to all but that by itself is not justice so long as the weakest of the weak is not empowered enough to have access to justice. The core of the commitment of the Constitution to the social revolution through Rule of Law lies in the effectuation of the Fundamental Rights and Directive Principles as supplementary and complimentary to each other. Political democracy has to be stable. Socio-economic democracy has to become a way of life. On the economic plane, we shall have to get rid of the contradictions, failing which, generation of immense wealth would not be able to eliminate exact poverty.

The term 'equality' means the absence of special privileges to any section of the society, and provision of adequate opportunities for all individuals without any discrimination. The Preamble secures at all citizens of India equality of status and opportunity. This provision embraces three dimensions of equality- civic, political and economic.

The following provisions of the chapter on Fundamental Rights ensure civic equality:

- Equality before the Law (Article 14).
- Prohibition of discrimination on grounds of religion, race, caste, sex, place of birth (Article 15).
- Equality of opportunity in matters of public employment (Article 16).
- Abolition of untouchability (Article 17).
- Abolition of titles (Article 18).

There are two provisions in the Constitution that seek to achieve political equality.

- No person is to be declared ineligible for inclusion in electoral rolls on grounds of religion, race, caste or sex (Article 325).
- Elections to the Lok Sabha and the state assemblies to be on the basis of adult suffrage (Article 326).

It has been seen that in spite of the efforts of Election Commission to ensure free and fair election, there are certain shortcomings of our electoral system. But several examples have been seen in the past elections where voters have not been registered because their illiteracy, poverty and lack of political awareness have been hurdles in this regard. Ballot riggings and criminalisation of politics at increasing rate have also come in the way of political justice in India. The most important development against social justice has been the delimitation of legislative and parliamentary constituencies according to the convenience of the parties in power. Some of its notable weaknesses are discussed below:

Money Power

The role of unaccounted money in elections has become a serious problem. The political parties collect funds from companies and business houses, and then use this money to influence the voter to vote in their favour. The business contributions are mostly in cash and are not unaccounted. Many other corrupt practices are also adopted during election such as bribing, rigging or voters intimidation, impersonation and providing transport and conveyance of voters to and fro the polling stations. The reports of liquor being distributed in poor areas are frequent during election.

Muscle Power

Earlier the criminals used to support the candidates by intimidating the voter at a gunpoint to vote according to their direction. Now they themselves have come out openly by contesting the elections leading to criminalization of politics. As a result violence during elections has also increased.

Misuse of Government Machinery

All the political parties do not have equal opportunity in respect of access to resources. The party in power is always in advantageous position than the opposition parties. There is widespread allegation that the party in power accomplishes misuse of government machinery. All these features lead to violence, booth capturing, rigging bogus voting, forcible removal of ballot papers, ballot boxes burning of vehicles, etc. which result into loss of public faith in elections.

LIBERTY

The Preamble also mentions about liberty of thought and expression. These freedoms have been guaranteed in the Constitution through the Fundamental Rights. Though freedom from want has not been guaranteed in the Fundamental Rights, certain directives to the State have been mentioned in the Directive Principles.

Talking about the liberty of thought and expression, the individual and public voices against the unsound and wrongful policies of the Government are not only suppressed but repressive measures are adopted attributing them to law and order maintaining machinery as if they are beyond them. Those in power consider them above law and interpret constitutional provision according to their suitability taking advantage of public ignorance of law and individuals' ability to protest against misuse of authority by those in Government.

The above discussion shows that drunk with power those in Government exploit democratic institution for their personal ends wilfully neglectful of their constitutional responsibilities challenging that they have the verdict and if the public wants something different they should wait for another five years. The public demand for justice and just democratic institutions are crushed down labelling them as undemocratic, unconstitutional and attempts of destabilizing the Government with foreign hands in them. Prime Minister's speech on India's on 65th Independence Day from the ramparts of the Red Fort implicating Anna's Jan Lokpal Movement in this manner and his Government's handling of the movement later on is the blatant recent example of how undemocratically the elected Governments try to throttle the public voice. Indira Gandhi did it earlier, to retain power after her election was set aside by the Supreme Court, by declaring internal emergency in the country resorting to excesses on the public overlooking the fundamental rights of the people.

The naked show of this despotic democracy was also seen during agitation against black money on the Ramlila Grounds . On Feb. 23, 2012, the Supreme Court bench of justice BS Chauhan and justice Swatanter Kumar said in its judgment that the midnight crackdown on the supporters of Baba Ramdev on June 5, 2011 was a "reflection of the might of the state which struck at the foundation of democracy." The bench also said the police had indulged in "unjustifiable and brutal acts" on the gathering by using teargas and lathi-charge to chase people out. Declaring that Ramdev's threat to go on strike could not be termed as unconstitutional, the court questioned the police's decision to invoke section 144 of the Criminal Procedure Code on the night of June 4 without any "emergency threat". If even then the Congress says that they are bound by the constitution, there can be no greater mockery of the constitution than this.

FRATERNITY

Fraternity refers to promotion of brotherhood, between all Indian's irrespective of their caste/creed. In the background of India's multi-lingual, multi-cultural and multi- religious society and keeping in view the partition of the country, the framers of the Constitution were very much concerned about the unity and integrity of our newly independent country. There was a need for harmonious co-existence among various religions, linguistic, cultural and economic groups. Phrases like 'dignity of individuals', 'fraternity among people' and 'unity and integrity of the nation' in the Preamble highlight its need. But the Indian polity seems to be utterly irresponsive to it.

Divisive Politics

The way the opportunistic combination of castes, religious and regional groups are emerging simply for the sake of grabbing political power raises a big question: whether our political leaders are adhering to the basic features of Indian constitution or taking the nation further to a chaotic condition? Mushrooming of caste associations has now become the bane of Indian politics, but our political rulers instead of taking a lesson from the history continue to play communal/caste politics. The unity shown by our people during wars and more recently in Kargil operations are proof enough that the Indians are basically patriotic. In peacetime our political leaders unfortunately start playing divisive politics for their personal gains.

Use of Religion, Cast and Class in Elections

Providing for reservation of certain number of seats for scheduled castes and scheduled tribes in parliament, state assemblies, in government jobs and its gradual extension after every ten years were viewed by a section of population as an attempt to create a permanent division in the society on caste lines. Similarly, the politics of majority versus minority played by the political rulers was another attempt to divide the country on the basis of religion. Unfortunately, the situation gradually deteriorated from bad to worse and reached its nadir when a former Prime Minister created a caste-war situation in the country through implementation of Mandal Commission report. Our political leaders who swear in the name of Indian constitution have forgotten its spirit and basic features and are making continued efforts to capture political power by dividing the country on the basis of caste, religion, language, sect and region.

Instead of doing away with this system, demand from divergent groups for reservation for religious minorities and OBCs (other backward classes) in parliament, state legislative assemblies and jobs is gaining ground to get political mileage during elections? Religion and Caste have become a way of political life in India. Come elections, the use of communal and caste politics gets intensified.

CONCLUSION

The political parties in power have been misusing their authority and have been violating the spirit of the constitution for narrow political gains. The main reason for this has been the absence of an institution to check them. Hence, there is a strong case for an effective Lokpal.

6

Misuse of Agencies Dealing with Corruption

The Government feels that already an independent institutional set up exists to tackle the problem of corruption in India. At the central Government level, there is Central Vigilance Commission, Departmental Vigilance and CBI. CVC and Departmental Vigilance deal with vigilance (disciplinary proceedings) aspect of a corruption case and CBI deals with criminal aspect of that case. Central Vigilance Commission is the apex body for all vigilance cases in Government of India. Let us have a look at what they are and evaluate their independence, impartiality and potential to face the challenge.

LAWS DEALING WITH CORRUPTION: KEY FEATURES

Public servants in India can be penalized for corruption under the Indian Penal Code, 1860 and the Prevention of Corruption Act, 1988. The Benami Transactions (Prohibition) Act, 1988 prohibits benami transactions. The Prevention of Money Laundering Act, 2002 penalizes public servants for the offence of money laundering. India is also a signatory (not ratified) to the UN Convention against Corruption since 2005. The Convention covers a wide range of acts of corruption and also proposes certain preventive policies.

Indian Penal Code, 1860:

The IPC defines "public servant" as a government employee, officers in the military, navy or air force; police, judges, officers of Court of Justice, and any local authority established by a central or state Act.

Section 169 pertains to a public servant unlawfully buying or bidding for property. The public servant shall be punished with imprisonment of upto two years or with fine or both. If the property is purchased, it shall be confiscated.

Section 409 pertains to criminal breach of trust by a public servant. The public servant shall be punished with life imprisonment or with imprisonment of upto 10 years and a fine.

The Prevention of Corruption Act, 1988:

In addition to the categories included in the 1PC, the definition of "public servant" includes office bearers of cooperative societies receiving financial aid from the government, employees of universities, Public Service Commission and banks.

If a public servant takes gratification other than his legal remuneration in respect of an official act or to influence public servants is liable to minimum punishment of six months and maximum punishment of five years and fine. The Act also penalizes a public servant for taking gratification to influence the public by illegal means and for exercising his personal influence with a public servant.

If a public servant accepts a valuable thing without paying for it or paying inadequately from a person with whom he is involved in a business transaction in his official capacity, he shall be penalized with minimum punishment of six months and maximum punishment of five years and fine.

It is necessary to obtain prior sanction from the central or state government in order to prosecute a public servant.

The Benami Transactions (Prohibition) Act, 1988:

The Act prohibits any benami transaction (purchase of property in false name of another person who does not pay for the property) except when a person purchases property in his wife's or unmarried daughter's name.

Any person who enters into a benami transaction shall be punishable with imprisonment of upto three years and/or a fine.

All properties that are held to be benami can be acquired by a prescribed authority and no money shall be paid for such acquisition.

The Prevention of Money Laundering Act, 2002:

The Act states that an offence of money laundering has been committed if a person is a party to any process connected with the proceeds of crime and projects such proceeds as untainted property. "Proceeds of crime" means any property obtained by a person as a result of criminal activity related to certain offences listed in the schedule to the Act. A person can be charged with the offence of money laundering only if he has been charged with committing a scheduled offence.

The penalty for committing the offence of money laundering is rigorous imprisonment for three to seven years and a fine of upto Rs 5 lakh. If a person is convicted of an offence under the Narcotics Drugs and Psychotropic Substances Act, 1985 the term of imprisonment can extend upto 10 years.

The Adjudicating Authority, appointed by the central government, shall decide whether any of the property attached or seized is involved in money laundering. An Appellate Tribunal shall hear appeals against the orders of the Adjudicating Authority and any other authority under the Act.

Every banking company, financial institution and intermediary shall maintain a record of all transactions of a specified nature and value, and verify and maintain records of all its customers, and furnish such information to the specified authorities.

PROCESS TO INVESTIGATE AND PROSECUTE THE CORRUPT:

The three main authorities involved in inquiring, investigating and prosecuting corruption cases are the Central Vigilance

Commission (CVC), the Central Bureau of Investigation (CB1) and the state Anti-Corruption Bureau (ACB). Cases related to money laundering by public servants are investigated and prosecuted by the Directorate of Enforcement and the Financial Intelligence Unit, which are under the Ministry of Finance.

The CBI and state ACBs investigate cases related to corruption under the Prevention of Corruption Act, 1988 and the Indian Penal Code, 1860. The CBI's jurisdiction is the central government and Union Territories while the state ACBs investigate cases within the states. States can refer cases to the CBI.

The CVC is a statutory body that supervises corruption cases in government departments.

The CBI is under its supervision. The CVC can refer cases either to the Central Vigilance Officer (CVO) in each department or to the CBI. The CVC or the CVO recommends the action to be taken against a public servant but the decision to take any disciplinary action against a civil servant rests on the department authority.

Prosecution can be initiated by an investigating agency only after it has the prior sanction of the central or state government. Government appointed prosecutors undertake the prosecution proceeding in the courts.

All cases under the Prevention of Corruption Act, 1988 are tried by Special Judges who are appointed by the central or state government.

CENTRAL VIGILANCE COMMISSION

The Central Vigilance Commission was set up by the Government in February, 1964 on the recommendations of the Committee on Prevention of Corruption, headed by Shri K. Santhanam, to advise and guide Central Government agencies in the field of vigilance. It is conceived to be the apex vigilance institution, free of control from any executive authority, monitoring all vigilance activity under the Central Government and advising various authorities in Central Government organizations in planning, executing, reviewing and reforming their vigilance work.

Consequent upon promulgation of an Ordinance by the President, the Central Vigilance Commission has been made a multi member Commission with "statutory status" with effect from 25th August, 1998.

The CVC Bill was passed by both the houses of Parliament in 2003 and the President gave its assent on September 11, 2003. Thus the Central Vigilance Commission Act 2003 (No. 45 Of 2003) came into effect from that date.

The Commission shall consist of:

A Central Vigilance Commissioner - Chairperson;

Not more than two Vigilance Commissioners - Members;

Vide GOI Resolution on "Public Interest Disclosure and Protection of Informer" dated April 2004, the Government of India has authorized the Central Vigilance Commission as the "Designated Agency" to receive written complaints for disclosure on any allegation of corruption or misuse of office and recommend appropriate action.

Organization:

The Central Vigilance Commission has its own Secretariat, Chief Technical Examiners' Wing (CTE) and a wing of Commissioners for Departmental Inquiries (CDI).

• Secretariat

The Secretariat consists of a Secretary of the rank of Additional Secretary to the GOI, one officer of the rank of Joint Secretary to the GOI, ten officers of the rank of Director/Deputy Secretary, four Under Secretaries and office staff.

• Chief Technical Examiners' Wing (CTE)

The Chief Technical Examiner's Organization constitutes the technical wing of the Central Vigilance Commission (India) and is manned by two Engineers of the rank of Chief Engineers(designated as Chief Technical Examiners) with supporting engineering staff. The main functions assigned to this organization are :

Technical audit of construction works of Governmental organizations from a vigilance angle;

Investigation of specific cases of complaints relating to construction works;

Extension of assistance to CBI in their investigations involving technical matters and for evaluation of properties in Delhi; and

Tendering of advice/assistance to the Commission and Chief Vigilance Officers in vigilance cases involving technical matters. Commissioners for Departmental Inquiries (CDIs)

There are fifteen posts of Commissioners for Departmental Inquiries (CDI) in the Commission, 14 in the rank of Deputy Secretaries/Directors and one in the rank of Joint Secretary to Government of India. The CDIs function as Inquiry Officers to conduct Oral inquiries in departmental proceeding initiated against public servants.

Powers and Functions:

to exercise superintendence over the functioning of the Delhi Special Police Establishment (DSPE) with respect to investigation under the Prevention of Corruption Act, 1988; or offence under CRPC for certain categories of public servants and to give directions to the DSPE for purpose of discharging this responsibility;

• to review the progress of investigations conducted by the DSPE into offences alleged to have been committed under the PC Act;

• to undertake an inquiry or cause an inquiry or investigation to be made into any transaction in which a public servant working in any organization, to which the executive control of the Government of India extends, is suspected or alleged to have acted for an improper purpose or in a corrupt manner; to tender independent and impartial advice to the disciplinary and other authorities in disciplinary cases, involving vigilance angle at different stages i.e. investigation, inquiry, appeal, review etc.; to exercise a general check and supervision over vigilance and anti-corruption work in Ministries or Departments of the Govt. of India and other organizations to which the executive power of the Union extends; and

• to chair the Committee for selection of Director (CBI), Director (Enforcement Directorate) and officers of the level of SP and above in DSPE. to undertake or cause an inquiry into complaints received under the Public Interest Disclosure and Protection of Informer and recommend appropriate action.

Jurisdiction:

Commission's Jurisdiction under CVC Act :

- Members of All India Service serving in connection with the affairs of the Union and Group A officers of the Central Government.
- Officers of the rank of Scale V and above in the Public Sector Banks.
- Officers in Grade D and above in Reserve Bank of India, NABARD and SIDBI.
- Chief Executives and Executives on the Board and other officers of E-8 and above in Schedule 'A' and 'B' Public Sector Undertakings.
- Chief Executives and Executives on the Board and other officers of E-7 and above in Schedule 'C' and 'D' Public Sector Undertakings.
- Managers and above in General Insurance Companies.
- Senior Divisional Managers and above in Life Insurance Corporations.
- Officers drawing salary of Rs.8700/- p.m. and above on Central Government D.A. pattern, as on the date of the notification and as may be revised from time to time in Societies and other Local Authorities.

THE CHIEF VIGILANCE OFFICERS (CVO)

The Chief Vigilance Officers are extended hands of the CVC. The Chief Vigilance Officers are considerably higher level officers who are appointed in each and every Department/Organization to assist the Head of the Department/Organization in all vigilance matters.

Selection and Appointment

The Chief Vigilance Officers constitute an important link between the organizations concerned and the Central Vigilance Commission (as also the CBI). The following procedures have been laid down/ evolved in the matter of appointment of CVOs:

(a) Prior approval of the Commission for appointment of an officer as CVO;

(b) As far as possible, the Chief Vigilance Officers should be from outside the Organization in which he is to be appointed. The initial tenure of full-time CVO in PSUs is for three years extendable by two years in the same organization with the approval of the Commission or up to a further period of three years on transfer to another PSU on completion of initial tenure of three years in the previous PSU;

(c) In cases where the scale of operation of a particular organization does not justify creation of a full-time post, an officer within the organization sufficiently senior in rank to be able to report directly to the Chief Executive on vigilance matters may be considered for such appointments;

(d) The officer to be given additional charge of the post of CVO should not be one whose normal duties involve dealing with matters sensitive from vigilance point of view (like recruitment, purchase, etc.);

(e) Once an officer has worked as CVO in an organization, he should not go back as CVO to the same organization again;

(f) An officer who is appointed from outside as CVO in Central Public Undertaking shall not be permanently absorbed in the same organization on expiry or in continuation of his tenure as CVO in that organization; and

(g) The "Vigilance" and "Security" function in an organization should be separated as both the activities are equally demanding and the discharge of "security" functions by a Chief Vigilance Officer only leads to dilution of supervision on vigilance matters. However, an exception has been made in respect of the hotel industry.

Role and functions of Chief Vigilance Officers:

Even though detection and punishment of corruption and other malpractices are certainly important, what is more important is taking preventive measures instead of hunting for the guilty in the post corruption stage. Therefore, the role and functions of CVOs has been broadly divided in to two parts, which are:

(a) Preventive and

(b) Punitive

• Preventive functions:

The CVOs undertake various measures, which include:

(a) To examine in detail the existing Rules and procedures of the Organization with a view to eliminate or minimize the scope for corruption or malpractices;

(b) To identify the sensitive/corruption prone spots in the Organization and keep an eye on personnel posted in such areas;

(c) To plan and enforce surprise inspections and regular inspections to detect the system failures and existence of corruption or malpractices;

(d) To maintain proper surveillance on officers of doubtful integrity; and

(e) To ensure prompt observance of Conduct Rules relating to integrity of the Officers like

(i) The Annual Property Returns;

(ii) Gifts accepted by the officials;

(iii) Benami transactions;

(iv) Regarding relatives employed in private firms or doing private business etc.

• Punitive Functions:

(i) To ensure speedy processing of vigilance cases at all stages. In regard to cases requiring consultation with the Central Vigilance

Commission, a decision as to whether the case had a vigilance angle shall in every case be taken by the CVO who, when in doubt, may refer the matter to his administrative head, i.e. Secretary in the case of Ministries/Departments and Chief Executive in the case of public sector organizations;

(ii) To ensure that charge-sheet, statement of imputations, lists of witness and documents etc. are carefully prepared and copies of ail the documents relied upon and the statements of witnesses cited on behalf of the disciplinary authority are supplied wherever possible to the accused officer along with the charge-sheet;

(iii) To ensure that all documents required to be forwarded to the Inquiring Officer are carefully sorted out and sent promptly;

(iv) To ensure that there is no delay in the^appointment of the Inquiring Officer, and that no dilatory tactics are adopted by the accused officer or the Presenting Officer;

(v) To ensure that the processing of the Inquiry Officer's Reports for final orders of the Disciplinary Authority is done properly and quickly;

(vi) To scrutinize final orders passed by the Disciplinary Authorities subordinate to the Ministry/Department, with a view to see whether a case for review is made out or not;

(vii) To see that proper assistance is given to the CBI, in the investigation of cases entrusted to them or started by them on their own source of information;

(viii) To take proper and adequate action with regard to writ petitions filed by accused officers;

(ix) To ensure that the Central Vigilance Commission is consulted at all stages where it is to be consulted and that as far as possible, the time limits prescribed in the Vigilance Manual for various stages are adhered to;

(x) To ensure prompt submission of returns to the Commission;

(xi) To review from time to time the existing arrangements for vigilance work in the Ministry/Department for vigilance work

subordinate officers to see if they are adequate to ensure expeditious and effective disposal of vigilance work;

(xii) To ensure that the competent disciplinary authorities do not adopt a dilatory or law attitude in processing vigilance cases, thus knowingly otherwise helping the subject public servants, particularly in cases of officers due to retire;

(xiii) To ensure that cases against the public servants on the verge of retirement do not lapse due to time-limit for reasons such as misplacement of files etc. and that the orders passed in the cases of retiring officers are implemented in time; and

(xiv) To ensure that the period from the date of serving a charge-sheet in a disciplinary case to the submission of the report of the Enquiry Officer, should, ordinarily, not exceed six months.

CENTRAL BUREAU OF INVESTIGATION

The Central Bureau of Investigation traces its origin to the Special Police Establishment (SPE) which was set up in 1941 by the Government of India. The functions of the SPE then were to investigate cases of bribery and corruption in transactions with the War & Supply Deptt. of India during World War II. Superintendence of the SPE was vested with the War Department.

Even after the end of the War, the need for a Central Government agency to investigate cases of bribery and corruption by Central Government employees was felt. The Delhi Special Police Establishment Act was, therefore, brought into force in 1946. This Act transferred the superintendence of the SPE to the Home Department and its functions were enlarged to cover all departments of the Govt. of India. The jurisdiction of the SPE extended to all the Union Territories and could be extended also to the States with the consent of the State Government concerned.

The DSPE acquired its popular current name, Central Bureau of Investigation (CBI), through a Home Ministry resolution dated 1.4.1963. Initially the offences that were notified by the Central Government related only to corruption by Central Govt. servants. In due course, with the setting up of a large number of public sector undertakings, the employees of these undertakings were also brought under CBI purview. Similarly, with the nationalization of the banks in 1969, the Public Sector Banks and their employees also came within the ambit of the CBI.

Emergence as a National Investigative Agency

From 1965 onwards, the CBI has also been entrusted with the investigation of Economic Offences and important conventional crimes such as murders, kidnapping, terrorist crimes, etc., on a selective basis.

The SPE initially had two Wings. They were the General Offences Wing (GOW) and Economic Offences Wing (EOW). The GOW dealt with cases of bribery and corruption involving the employees of Central Government and Public Sector Undertakings. The EOW dealt with cases of violation of various economic/fiscal laws. Under this set-up, the GOW had at least one Branch in each State and the EOW in the four metropolitan cities, *i.e.,* Delhi, Madras (Chennai), Bombay (Mumbai) and Calcutta (Kolkata). These EOW Branches dealt with offences reported from the Regions, *i.e.,* each Branch had jurisdiction over several States.

Widening Role

As the CBI, over the years, established a reputation for impartiality and competence, demands were made on it to take up investigation of more cases of conventional crime such as murder, kidnapping, terrorist crime, etc. Apart from this, even the Supreme court and the various High Courts of the country also started entrusting such cases for investigation to the CBI on petitions filed by aggrieved parties. Taking into account the fact that several cases falling under this category were being taken up for investigation by the CBI, it was found expedient to entrust such cases to the Branches having local jurisdiction.

It was therefore decided in 1987 to constitute two investigation divisions in the CBI, namely, Anti-Corruption Division and Special Crimes Division, the latter dealing with cases of conventional crime, besides economic offences.

Mission

To uphold the Constitution of India and law of the land through in-depth investigation and successful prosecution of offences; to provide leadership and direction to police forces and to act as the nodal agency for enhancing inter-state and international cooperation in law enforcement.

Vision

Based on its motto, mission and the need to develop professionalism, transparency, adaptability to change and use of science and technology in its working, the CBI will focus on

1. Combating corruption in public life, curb economic and violent crimes through meticulous investigation and prosecution.

2. Evolve effective systems and procedures for successful investigation and prosecution of cases in various law courts.

3. Help fight cyber and high technology crime.

4. Create a healthy work environment that encourages team-building, free communication and mutual trust.

5. Support state police organizations and law enforcement agencies in national and international cooperation particularly relating to enquiries and investigation of cases.

6. Play a lead role in the war against national and transnational organized crime.

7. Uphold Human Rights, protect the environment, arts, antiques and heritage of our civilization.

8. Develop a scientific temper, humanism and the spirit of inquiry and reform.

9. Strive for excellence and professionalism in all spheres of functioning so that the organization rises to high levels of endeavor and achievement.

The CBI is a central subject under the Constitution of India, meaning that it reports to the Indian Government and not to the individual states.

Normally, cases assigned to the CBI are sensitive and of national importance. It is a usual practice for the respective state police departments, to initially register any case coming under its jurisdiction, and if necessary, through mediation by the central government, the cases may be transferred to the CBI. The CBI handles many high profile cases, and is never far from controversy.

Because of its intensely political overtones, it has been exposed by its former bigwigs like Joginder Singh and BR Lall who were Director and Joint Director respectively, to be engaging in nepotism , mal-prosecution and outright corruption. In his book, Who Owns CBI, BR Lall, an honest and upright officer details the modus operandi of manipulating and derailing investigation. This organization has become synonymous with corruption as information obtained under the RTI Act has revealed. Even the Top Bosses are known for stooping to illegal fund diversions. RTI activist Krishnanand Tripathi has alleged harassment from CBI in order to save itself from exposure through RTI. CBI has now been exempted from RTI act.

However, in recent years, the CBI has been seen as refusing to abide by the laws of the government. On September 24, 2011, it has advised the Supreme Court, to violate its legal jurisdiction, and pursue cases past the point of which it has legal right. It has now become an organization that is violating the laws-of the land, rather than upholding it. In view of this violation of Constitution, the CBI is being seen as a rogue organization, which has lost its authority to be an effective branch of the government.

WEAKNESSES OF THE EXISTING SYSTEM

Central Vigilance Commission

• It does not have adequate resources commensurate with the large number of complaints that it receives. CVC is a very small set up with a staff strength less than 200. It is supposed to check corruption in more than 1500 central government departments and ministries, some of them being as big as Central Excise, Railways, Income Tax etc. Therefore, it has to depend on the vigilance wings of respective departments and forwards most of the complaints for inquiry and report to them. While it monitors the progress of these complaints, there is delay and the complainants are often disturbed by this. It directly enquires into a few complaints on its own, especially when it suspects motivated delays or where senior officials could be implicated. But given the constraints of manpower, such number is really small.

• CVC is merely an advisory body. Central Government Departments seek CVC's advice on various corruption cases. However, they are free to accept or reject CVC's advice. Even in those cases, which are directly enquired into by the CVC, it can only advise government. CVC mentions these cases of non-acceptance in its monthly reports and the Annual Report to Parliament. But these are not much in focus in Parliamentary debates or by the media.

• Experience shows that CVC's advice to initiate prosecution is rarely accepted and whenever CVC advised major penalty, it was reduced to minor penalty. Therefore, CVC can hardly be treated as an effective deterrent against corruption.

• CVC cannot direct CBI to initiate enquiries against any officer of the level of Joint Secretary and above on its own. The CBI has to seek the permission of that department, which obviously would not be granted if the senior officers of that department are involved and they could delay the case or see to it that permission would not be granted.

• CVC does not have powers to register criminal case. It deals only with vigilance or disciplinary matters.

• It does not have powers over politicians. If there is an involvement of a politician in any case, CVC could at best bring it to the notice of the Government. There are several cases of serious corruption in which officials and political executive are involved together.

• It does not have any direct powers over departmental vigilance wings. Often it is seen that CVC forwards a complaint to a department and then keeps sending reminders to them to enquire and send report. Many a times, the departments just do not comply. CVC does not have any really effective powers over them to seek compliance of its orders.

• CVC does not have administrative control over officials in vigilance wings of various central government departments to which it forwards corruption complaints. Though the government does consult CVC before appointing the Chief Vigilance Officers of various departments, however, the final decision lies with the government. Also, the officials below CVO are appointed/transferred by that department only. Only in exceptional cases, if the CVO chooses to bring it to the notice of CVC, CVC could bring pressure on the Department to revoke orders but again such recommendations are not binding.

• Appointments to CVC are directly under the control of ruling political party, though the leader of the Opposition is a member of the Committee to select CVC and VCs. But the Committee only considers names put up before it and that is decided by the Government. The appointments are opaque.

• CVC Act gives supervisory powers to CVC over CBI. However, these supervisory powers have remained ineffective. CVC does not have the power to call for any file from CBI or to direct them to do any case in a particular manner. Besides, CBI is, under administrative control of DOPT rather than CVC.

Therefore, though CVC is relatively independent in its functioning, it neither has resources nor powers to enquire and take action on complaints of corruption in a manner that meets the expectations of people or act as an effective deterrence against corruption.

Departmental Vigilance Wings

Each Department has a vigilance wing, which is manned by officials from the same department barring a few which have an outsider as Chief Vigilance Officer. However, all the officers under him belong to the same department.

• Since the officers in the vigilance wing of a department are from the same department and they can be posted to any position in that department anytime, it is practically impossible for them to be independent and objective while inquiring into complaints against their colleagues and seniors. If a complaint is received against a senior officer, it is impossible to enquire into that complaint because an officer who is in vigilance today might get posted under that senior officer some time in future.

•In some departments, especially in the Ministries, some officials double up as vigilance officials. It means that an existing official is given additional duty of vigilance also. So, if some citizen complaints against that officer, the complaint is expected to be enquired into by the same officer. Even if someone complaints against that officer to the CVC or to the Head of that Department or to any other authority, the complaint is forwarded by all these agencies and it finally lands up in his own lap to enquire against himself. Even if he rescues himself from such inquiries, still they have to be handled by those who otherwise report to him. There are indeed examples of such, absurdity.

There have been instances of the officials posted in vigilance wing by that department having had a very corrupt past. While in vigilance, they try to scuttle all cases against themselves. They also turn vigilance wing into a hub of corruption, where cases are closed for consideration.

• Departmental vigilance does not investigate into criminal aspect of any case. It does not have the powers to register an FIR.

• They also do not have any powers against politicians.

• Since the vigilance wing is directly under the control of the Head of that Department, it is practically impossible for them to enquire against senior officials of that department.

Therefore, the vigilance wing of any department is seen to soft pedal on genuine complaints or used to enquire against "inconvenient" officers.

Central Bureau of Investigation (CBI)

CBI has powers of a police station to investigate and register FIR. It can investigate any case related to a Central Government department on its own or any case referred to it by any state government or any court. But its functioning so far has revealed that it has inherent weaknesses:

- CBI is overburdened and does not accept cases even where amount of defalcation is alleged to be around Rs. 1 crore.
- CBI is directly under the administrative control of Central Government.
- So, if a complaint pertains to any minister or politician who is part of a ruling coalition or a bureaucrat who is close to them, CBI's credibility has suffered and there is increasing public perception that it cannot do a fair investigation and that it is influenced to scuttle these cases.
- Again, because CBI is directly under the control of Central Government, CBI is perceived to have been often used to settle scores against inconvenient politicians.

Therefore, if a citizen wants to make a complaint about corruption by a politician or an official in the Central Government, there isn't a single anti-corruption agency which is effective and independent of the government, whose wrongdoings are sought to be investigated. CBI has powers but it is not independent. CVC is independent but it does not have sufficient powers or resources.

SUPREME COURT ON THESE INSTITUTIONS:

Thus while throwing out the prosecution case in the famous Jain Hawala scandal, the Supreme Court in December 1997 laid down a string of measures to extricate the investigating agencies (CBI & ED) from the clutches of Government to ensure free and fair investigation of matters involving the ruling establishment. The chief directives of SC were:-

1. Single Directive (an executive order to CBI directing it to seek Government permission before investigating officials above a certain level) was invalidated.

2. CVC to be accorded statutory status.

3. CVC to be entrusted with the superintendence of CBI instead of the Government.

4. Appointment of CVC to be done by a 3 member panel including the leader of opposition besides the PM and the HM, forcing Govt to take on board the voice of the opposition.

5. The appointment was to be done from a panel of three *outstanding civil servants and others with impeccable integrity.*

Other directives of the Supreme Court pertained to the appointment and functioning of CBI & ED. The Government was expected to expeditiously bring in legislation to implement these directives.

SUPREME COURT JUDGMENT-VINEET NARAIN CASE THE COURT OBSERVED:

Independent Review Committee

The IRC is a body constituted by the Central Government itself as a result of its perception that the constitution and functioning of the CBI, CVC and Directorate of Enforcement require a close scrutiny in the background of the recent unsatisfactory functioning of these agencies with a view to improve their functioning. The view taken by the IRC is a reaffirmation of this belief shared by everyone. The preface to the report indicates the reason for the constitution of the IRC and says:

"In the past several years, there has been progressive increase in allegations of corruption involving public servants. Understandably, cases of this nature have attracted heightened media and public attention. A general impression appears to have gained ground that the Central investigating agencies concerned are subject to extraneous pressures and have been indulging in dilatory tactics in not bringing the guilty to book. The decisions of higher courts to directly monitor investigation in certain cases have added to the aforesaid belief."

DIRECTIONS OF COURT:

CENTRAL BUREAU OF INVESTIGATION (CBI) AND CENTRAL VIGILANCE COMMISSION (CVC):

1. The Central Vigilance Commission (CVC) shall be given statutory status.

2. Selection for the post of Central Vigilance Commissioner shall be made by a Committee comprising the Prime Minister, Home Minister and the Leader of the Opposition from a panel of outstanding

civil servants and others with impeccable integrity, to be furnished by the Cabinet Secretary. The appointment shall be made by the President on the basis of the recommendations made by the Committee. This shall be done immediately.

3. The CVC shall be responsible for the efficient functioning of the CBI. While Government shall remain answerable for the CBI's functioning, to introduce visible objectivity in the mechanism to be established for over viewing the CBI's working, the CVC shall be entrusted with the responsibility of superintendence over the CBI's functioning. The CBI shall report to the CVC about cases taken up by it for investigation; progress of investigation; cases in which charge-sheets are filed and their progress. The CVC shall review the progress of all cases moved by the CBI for sanction of prosecution of public servants which are pending with the competent authorities, specially those in which sanction has been delayed or refused.

4. The Central Government shall take all measures necessary to ensure that the CBI functions effectively and efficiently and is viewed as a non-partisan agency.

5. The CVC shall have a separate section in its Annual Report on the CBI's functioning after the supervisory function is transferred to it.

6. Recommendations for appointment of the Director, CBI shall be made by a Committee headed by the Central Vigilance Commissioner with the Home Secretary and Secretary (Personnel) as members. The views of the incumbent Director shall be considered by the Committee for making the best choice. The Committee shall draw up a panel of IPS officers on the basis of their seniority, integrity, experience in investigation and anti-corruption work. The final selection shall be made by the Appointments Committee of the Cabinet (ACC) from the panel recommended by the Selection Committee. If none among the panel is found suitable, the reasons thereof shall be recorded and the Committee asked to draw up a fresh panel.

7. The Director, CBI shall have a minimum tenure of two years, regardless of the date of his superannuation. This would ensure that an officer suitable in all respects is not ignored merely because he

has less than two years to superannuate from the date of his appointment.

8. The transfer of an incumbent Director, CBI in an extraordinary situation, including the need for him to take up a more important assignment, should have the approval of the Selection Committee.

9. The Director, CBI shall have full freedom for allocation of work within the agency as also for constituting teams for investigations. Any change made by the Director, CBI in the Head of an investigative team should be for cogent reasons and for improvement in investigation, the reasons being recorded.

10. Selection/extension of tenure of officers up to the level of Joint Director (JD) shall be decided by a Board comprising the Central Vigilance Commissioner, Home Secretary and Secretary (Personnel) with the Director, CBI providing the necessary inputs. The extension of tenure or premature repatriation of officers up to the level of Joint Director shall be with final approval of this Board. Only cases pertaining to the appointment or extension of tenure of officers of the rank of Joint Director or above shall bee referred to the Appointments Committee of the Cabinet (ACC) for decision.

11. Proposals for improvement of infrastructure, methods of investigation, etc. should be decided urgently. In order to strengthen CBI's in-house expertise, professionals from the Revenue, Banking and Security sectors should be inducted into the CBI.

12. The CBI Manual based on statutory provisions of the Cr PC provides essential guidelines for the CBI's functioning. It is imperative that the CBI adheres scrupulously to the provisions in the Manual in relation to its investigative functions, like raids, seizure and arrests. Any deviation from the established procedure should be viewed seriously and severe disciplinary action taken against the officials concerned.

13. The Director, CBI shall be responsible for ensuring the filing of charge-sheets in courts within the stipulated time-limits, and the matter should be kept under constant review by the Director, CBI.

14. A document on CBI's functioning should be published within three months to provide the general public with a feedback on

investigations and information for redress of genuine grievances in a manner which does not compromise with the operational requirements of the CBI.

15. Time-limit of three months for grant of sanction for prosecution must be strictly adhered to. However, additional time of one month may be allowed where consultation is required with the Attorney General (AG) or any other law officer in the AG's office.

16. The Director, CBI should conduct regular appraisal of personnel to prevent corruption and/ or inefficiency in the agency.

Enforcement Directorate

1. A Selection Committee headed by the Central Vigilance Commissioner and including the Home Secretary, Secretary (Personnel) and Revenue Secretary, shall prepare a panel for appointment of the Director, Enforcement Directorate. The appointment to the post of Director shall be made by the Appointments Committee of the Cabinet (ACC) from the panel recommended by the Selection Committee.

2. The Director, Enforcement Directorate like the Director, CBI shall have a minimum tenure of two years. In his case also, premature transfer for any extraordinary reason should be approved by the aforesaid Selection Committee headed by the Central Vigilance Commissioner.

3. In view of the importance of the post of Director, Enforcement Directorate, it shall be upgraded to that of an Additional Secretary/ Special Secretary to the Government.

4. Officers of the Enforcement Directorate handling sensitive assignments shall be provided adequate security to enable them to discharge their functions fearlessly.

5. Extension of tenure up to the level of Joint Director in the Enforcement Directorate should be decided by the said Committee headed by the Central Vigilance Commissioner.

6. There shall be no premature media publicity by the CBI/ Enforcement Directorate.

7. Adjudication/commencement of prosecution shall be made by the Enforcement Directorate within a period of one year.

8. The Director, Enforcement Directorate shall monitor and ensure speedy completion of investigations/adjudications and launching of prosecutions. Revenue Secretary must review their progress regularly.

9. For speedy conduct of investigations abroad, the procedure to approve filing of applications for Letters Rogatory shall be streamlined and, if necessary, Revenue Secretary authorized to grant the approval.

10. A comprehensive circular shall be published by the Directorate to inform the public about the procedures/systems of its functioning for the sake of transparency.

11. In-house legal advice mechanism shall be strengthened by appointment of competent legal advisers in the CBI/ Directorate of Enforcement.

12. The Annual Report of the Department,of Revenue shall contain a detailed account on the working of the Enforcement Directorate.

Nodal Agency

1. A Nodal Agency headed by the Home Secretary with Member (Investigation), Central Board of Direct Taxes, Director General, Revenue Intelligence, Director, Enforcement and Director CBI as members, shall be constituted for coordinated action in cases having politico-bureaucrat-criminal nexus.

2. The Nodal Agency shall meet at least once every month.

3. Working and efficacy of the Nodal Agency should be watched for about one year so as 'to improve it upon the basis of the experience gained within this period.

Prosecution Agency

1. A panel of competent lawyers of experience and impeccable reputation shall be prepared with the advice of the Attorney General.

Their services shall be utilized as prosecuting counsel in cases of significance. Even during the course of investigation of an offence, the advice of a lawyer chosen from the panel should be taken by the CBI/ Enforcement Directorate.

2. Every prosecution which results in the discharge or acquittal of the accused must be reviewed by a lawyer on the panel and, on the basis of the opinion given, responsibility should be fixed for dereliction of duty, if any, of the officer concerned. In such cases, strict action should be taken against the officer found guilty of dereliction of duty.

3. The preparation of the panel of lawyers with thee approval of the Attorney General shall be completed within three months.

4. Steps shall be taken immediately for the constitution of an able and impartial agency comprising persons of unimpeachable integrity to perform functions akin to those of the Director of Prosecutions in U.K. On the constitution of such a body, the task of supervising prosecutions launched by the CBI/Enforcement Directorate shall be entrusted to it.

5. Till the constitution of the aforesaid body, Special Counsel shall be appointed for the conduct of important trials on the recommendation of the Attorney General or any other law officer designated by him.

The appointment of P.J. Thomas was seen as the final nail in the coffin to which the CVC has been relegated. The Government of the day contended that the appointment of the CVC can be made by a majority decision virtually nullifying the presence of the leader of opposition in the selection panel. While the SC directive envisaged a panel of 3 names, the government insisted on one name despite strong objections from opposition. The biggest irony is that while CVC was envisaged by SC as the top sanctioning authority for prosecution against corrupt officials, Thomas himself, it turned out, was a beneficiary of the Government inaction over request for prosecution sanction in an old Palmolive Oil import scam in Kerala.

CONCLUSION

The present Government has been misusing the agencies dealing with corruption for its political gains. It is because these agencies are directly under its conttrol. CBI, one of these agencies, is generally used as an instrument to cow down corrupt leaders of opposition parties to seek their support. Hence, these agencies must be independent of the Government control.

7

The Public Wrath

Autocratic governance through democratic means has crept through in India for cultural and social reasons. The rulers were held in reverence as representatives of God to deliver justice to the people with the idealistic governance of 'Ramrajya' had always been at their heart in which the voice of the meanest was heard even if it meant the greatest sacrifice on the part of the ruler. This outlook towards the rulers has changed at a very slow pace over time. This is why the Indian people have shown great tolerance even against the foreign rulers until there had been an outrageous use of authority by them, we may call it their orthodoxy or give it any other name. The poverty and illiteracy of the masses might have been the other reasons for which they had been indifferent to the behaviour of the ruling class. But whenever the rulers tried to encroach upon the limits of morality and social justice they have come out in the open and fought against injustice united with all their might. The Mughals and the British saw it and the present day popular Governments should be aware of it.

FIRST PHASE

The first phase of Indian politics was dominated by the euphoria of independence from the foreign rule and Nehru's personality bathed in Gandhiji's halo. On 15 January 1941 Gandhiji said,

"Some say Pandit Nehru and I were estranged. It will require much more than difference of opinion to estrange us. We had differences from the time we became co-workers and yet I have said for some years and say so now that not Rajaji but Jawaharlal will be my successor."

But Gandhiji felt betrayed after the meeting of All India Congress Committee in November 1947 when inspite of his repeated reminders the Congress Party was not dissolved. Gandhiji could foresee the degeneration of the Congress into a corrupt and timid organization that would "scramble for loves and fishes ....and discord and personal rivalries among the members of the Congress High Command." But Gandhji's soulful moan can be heard when he said, "I can carry no one with me in this." This reveals the selflessness of Gandhi and the lust for power and pelf in the Congress Party.

But the Indian public tolerated all Nehru's freaks because it had regard for him to a fault for the sacrifices that he and his party colleagues made towards independence of the country. Otherwise also Pt. Nehru and his colleagues were held in great esteem for their integrity. Therefore, there was not much outburst of anger against his regime. An objective assessment today, however, reveals that for Nehru's personality cult, his fancy for westernized outlook vis-a-vis Gandhian outlook and his defense perceptions the nation had to pay a heavy price and for a few of them we are still paying.

(a) Intolerance for opposition and leadership.

(b) Communal politics in the name of secularism.

(c) Lack of zero tolerance for corrupt politicians and administration.

(d) Urban based economic planning giving rise to inequalities.

(e) Kashmir problem and insufficient defense concerns.

(f) Only lip service to Gandhi to the utter neglect of his philosophy in implementation.

From them sprouted many of the social, political and economic ills like terrorism, corruption, parochial politics, price rise, and ever growing conflict between the rich and the poor that have achieved alarming dimensions now.

SECOND PHASE

Following the death of Shri Lal Bahadur Shastri (1964-1966), Indira Gandhi was elected as Prime Minister by the Congress party. She led the party to a fourth successive general election victory, though with a greatly reduced majority. In 1969 her nominee for President of India was successfully elected but it precipitated a split within the Congress between the parliamentary and organizational wings. The split was followed by a radical left turn which included the nationalization of banks and insurance companies.

In 1971 Indira Gandhi went into a national election on a slogan of "eradicate poverty". Her appeal projected her as a national leader and undermined organizational opposition to her within the party. The successful execution of the Indo-Pak War (1971) under Gandhi's guidance led to the creation of Bangladesh. Her popularity was at an all time high and was followed by Congress victories in the states.

After the 1973 global increase in oil prices, the opposition parties led a countrywide agitation against inflation and corruption. 1974 ushered in a year of high inflation, unemployment and lack of supplies and essential commodities. Jayaprakash was asked to lead a peaceful agitation by the Navanirman Andolan of Gujarat. On April 8, 1974, at the age of 72, he led a silent procession at Patna. The procession was lathi charged. On June 5, 1974, JP addressed a mammoth crowd at Gandhi Maidan in Patna. He declared, "This is a revolution, friends! We are not here merely to see the Vidhan Sabha dissolved. That is only one milestone on our journey. But we have a long way to go... After 27 years of freedom, people of this country are wracked by hunger, rising prices, corruption... oppressed by every kind of injustice... it is a Total Revolution we want, nothing less!"

Raj Narain, who had been defeated in parliamentary election by Indira Gandhi, lodged cases of election fraud and use of state machinery for election purposes against Mrs. Indira Gandhi in the Allahabad High Court. On 12 June 1975, Justice Jagmohanlal Sinha of the Allahabad High Court found the Prime Minister guilty on the charge of misuse of government machinery for her election campaign. The court declared her election null and void and unseated her from her seat in the Lok Sabha. The court also banned her from contesting any election for an additional six years.

However, strikes in labour and trade unions, student unions and government unions swept across the country. Protests led by J.P.Narayan, Raj Narain,Satyendra Narayan Sinha and Morarji Desai flooded the streets of Delhi close to the Parliament building and the Prime Minister's residence. The persistent efforts of Raj Narain, was praised worldwide as it took over four years for Justice Jagmohan Lal Sinha to finally pass judgment against Indira Gandhi. The ruling later became the primary reason for the imposition of emergency by Indira Gandhi.

Jayaprakash Narayan attracted a gathering of 1,00,000 people at the Ramlila Grounds and thunderously recited *Rashtrakavi* Ramdhari Singh 'Dinkar's wonderfully evocative poetry: *Singhasan Khaali Kara Ke Janata Aaati Hai* He called for Indira to resign, and advocated a program of social transformation which he termed *Sampoorna kraanti* [Total Revolution].

JP had called for the PM's resignation and had asked the military and the police to disregard unconstitutional and immoral orders; JP, opposition leaders, and dissenting members of her own party (the 'Young Turks') were arrested on that day.

The response of the government was to declare a state of emergency. On 25 June 1975, the government declared that there was a threat of internal disturbances and therefore, it invoked Article 352 of the Constitution. Under the provision of this article the government could declare a state of emergency on grounds of external threat or a threat of internal disturbances. The government decided that a grave crisis had arisen which made the proclamation of a state of emergency necessary. Technically speaking this was within the powers of the government, for our Constitution provides for some special powers to the government once an emergency is declared.

Once an emergency is proclaimed, the federal distribution of powers remains practically suspended and all the powers are concentrated in the hands of the union government. Secondly, the government also gets the power to curtail or restrict any or all of the Fundamental Rights of the people under the emergency clause. From the wording of the provisions of the Constitution, it is clear that an Emergency is seen as an extra-ordinary condition in which normal democratic politics cannot function. Therefore, special powers are granted to the government.

JP was kept as *detenu* at Chandigarh even after he had asked for a month's parole for mobilising relief in areas of Bihar gravely affected by flood. His health suddenly deteriorated on October 24, and he was released on November 12; diagnosis at Jaslok Hospital, Bombay, revealed kidney failure; he would be on dialysis for the rest of his life.

Within a few months, President's Rule was imposed on the two opposition party ruled states of Gujarat and Tamil Nadu thereby bringing the entire country under direct Central rule or by governments led by the ruling Congress party. Police were granted powers to impose curfews and indefinitely detain citizens and all publications were subjected to substantial censorship by the Ministry of Information and Broadcasting. Inder Kumar Gujral, a future prime minister himself, resigned as Minister for Information and Broadcasting to protest Sanjay Gandhi's interference in his work. Finally, impending legislative assembly elections were indefinitely postponed, with all opposition-controlled state governments being removed by virtue of the constitutional provision allowing for a dismissal of a state government on recommendation of the state's governor. Indira Gandhi used the emergency provisions to grant herself extraordinary powers.

"Unlike her father Jawaharlal Nehru, who preferred to deal with strong chief ministers in control of their legislative parties and state party organizations, Mrs. Gandhi set out to remove every Congress chief minister who had an independent base and to replace each of them with ministers personally loyal to her...Even so, stability could not be maintained in the states..."

It is alleged that she further moved President Ahmed to issue ordinances that did not need to be debated in the Parliament, allowing her to rule by decree.

Simultaneously, Indira Gandhi's government undertook a campaign to stamp out dissent including the arrest and detention of thousands of political activists; Sanjay was instrumental in initiating the clearing of slums around Delhi's Jama Masjid under the supervision of Jag Mohan, later Lt. Governor of Delhi, which allegedly left thousands of people homeless and hundreds killed, and led to communal embitterment in those parts of the nation's capital; and the family planning program which forcibly imposed vasectomy on thousands of fathers and was often poorly administered.

The white paper prepared predominantly on the basis of government records and the report submitted by a former secretary to the information and broadcasting ministry, Mr. K.K. Dass sums up: Of the 253 journalists taken into custody 110 were arrested under the MISA, 60 under the DIR and 83 for "other reasons."

The white paper relates to the misuse of censorship provisions, harassment of journalists, allegations about certification of films, manipulation of news agencies and other mass media and other incidental matters.

Listing several cases of complaints, it says the pre-censorship covered, among other things, court proceedings, Views critical of Maruti and Mr. Sanjay Gandhi came in for unfavorable notice by the authorities.

Publishers were often subjected to punitive action such as detention under the MISA, seizure of presses, cancellation of declaration, withdrawal of accreditation facilities, stoppage of government advertisements and demands for security deposits.

In support of this contention the white paper has cited judgments by high courts, notably those of Bombay and Gujarat Some of the complaints received by the Dass committee speak of lack of courage shown by newspaper establishments and the manner in which they vied with one another to applaud the government.

Illustrative of Mrs.Gandhi's approach to media is a remark she made at a conference of AIR station directors, ridiculing questions being raised about the credibility of broadcasts. "Quite honestly I don't understand what it means. Who has credibility? The newspapers who had day in and day out printed falsehood?" The white paper explains that this kind of utter unconcern for credibility marked the attitude of the government throughout the emergency. "No wonder by the time the emergency ended public faith in reliability of the media had been completely shattered. Even news items referring to absence of press freedom in far off countries like Portugal had to be discouraged."

Major fallouts of Emergency:

Mulling of the constitution for personal and party gains.

Under the provisions of Emergency, the various Fundamental Rights of citizens stood suspended, including the right of citizens to move the Court for restoring their Fundamental Rights.

Detention of people by police without charge or notification of families.

Abuse and torture of detainees and political prisoners.

Use of public and private media institutions, like the national television network Doordarshan, for propaganda.

Forced sterilization of men and women under the family planning initiative. Indira's son, Sanjay Gandhi, was blamed for this forcible treatment of people.

Destruction of the slum and low-income housing in the Turkmen Gate and Jama Masjid area of old Delhi.

Large scale and illegal enactment of laws (including modifications to the Constitution) which shifted the country towards socialism.

The Emergency years were the biggest challenge to India's commitment to democracy, which proved vulnerable to the manipulation of powerful leaders and large parliamentary majorities

Indira Gandhi was from royalty school of thought. She had the mentality of a dictator. All the actions she had taken in her tenure suggested this. Bangladesh war, emergency, destroying Golden temple, massacre of Sikhs, all these actions are in line with British Raj. The British Raj was continued by Nehru-Indira regime till 1984.

After Indira revoked the emergency on January 18, 1977 and announced elections, it was under JP's guidance that the Janata Party (a vehicle for the broad spectrum of the anti-Indira Gandhi opposition)

was formed. The Janata Party was voted into power, and became the first non-Congress party to form a government at the Centre.

THIRD PHASE

Following his younger brother's death in 1980, Rajiv was pressured by Indian National Congress party politicians and his mother to enter politics. He and his wife were both opposed to the idea, and he even publicly stated that he would not contest for his brother's seat. Nevertheless, he eventually announced his candidacy for Parliament. His entry was criticized by many in the press, public and opposition political parties. He fought his first election from Amethi Lok Sabha seat. In this by-election, he defeated Lokdal leader Sharad Yadav by more than 200,000 votes.

Elected to Sanjay's Lok Sabha constituency of Amethi in Uttar Pradesh state in February 1981, Rajiv Gandhi became an important political advisor to his mother. It was widely perceived that Indira Gandhi was grooming Rajiv for the prime minister's job, and he soon became the president of the Youth Congress—the Congress party's youth wing.

Rajiv Gandhi was in West Bengal when his mother was assassinated on 31 October 1984 by her bodyguards. Top Congress leaders, as well as President Zail Singh pressed Rajiv to become India's Prime Minister, within hours of his mother's assassination by two of her Sikh bodyguards. Commenting on the anti-Sikh riots in the national capital Delhi, Rajiv Gandhi said, "When a giant tree falls, the earth below shakes"; a statement for which he was widely criticised. Many Congress politicians were accused of orchestrating the violence. Soon after assuming office, Rajiv asked President Zail Singh to dissolve Parliament and hold fresh elections, as the Lok Sabha completed its five year term. Rajiv Gandhi also officially became the President of the Congress party. The Congress party won a landslide victory—with the largest majority in history of Indian Parliament—giving Gandhi absolute control of government. He also benefited from his youth and a general perception of being *Mr. Clean,* or free of a background in corrupt politics. Rajiv thus revived hopes and enthusiasm amongst the Indian public for the Congress.

Anti-Sikh riots

This refers to the statement of Rajiv Gandhi as Prime Minister at a Boat Club rally 19-days after the assassination of Indira Gandhi, which read as "Some riots took place in the country following the murder of Indiraji. We know the people were very angry and for a few days it seemed that India had been shaken. But, when a mighty tree falls, it is only natural that the earth around it does shake a little."

This statement sent a wrong signal to the authorities, who adopted a callous approach of not allowing the truth to come out despite the government setting up probe panels one after the other, including two full fledged judicial commissions, the first headed by retired Chief Justice of India Ranganath Mishra and the second by a former apex court judge G.T. Nanavati. According to the authors of the book titled - "When a Tree Shook Delhi" written by senior advocate H.S. Phoolka and co-author, journalist Manoj Mitta (who have based the details of the book mainly on evidence produced before the nine panels and trial courts and high courts in the form of sworn affidavits by hundreds of witnesses). Based on eyewitness accounts the book said that instead of targeting the aggressors the police cracked down on the Sikh victims, who had been defending their properties when they were attacked by hooligans led by local Congress leaders.

Bofors scandal

V.P. Singh, Indira Gandhi's finance minister, uncovered compromising details about government and political corruption to the consternation of Congress leaders. Transferred to the Defence ministry, Singh uncovered what became known as the Bofors scandal, involving tens of millions of dollars - concerned alleged payoffs by the Swedish Bofors arms company through Italian businessman and Gandhi family associate Ottavio Quattrocchi, in return for Indian contracts.'Upon the uncovering of the scandal, Singh was dismissed from office, and later from Congress membership. Rajiv Gandhi himself was later personally implicated in the scandal when the investigation was continued by Narasimhan Rao and Chitra Subramaniam of *The Hindu* newspaper. This shattered his image as an honest politician; he was posthumously cleared over this allegation in 2004, however.

V.P. Singh's image as an exposer of government corruption made him very popular with the public, and opposition parties united under his name to form the Janata Dal coalition. In the 1989 elections, the Congress suffered a major setback. With the support of Indian communists and the Bharatiya Janata Party, Singh and his Janata Dal formed a government. Rajiv Gandhi became the Leader of the Opposition, while remaining Congress president. While some believe that Rajiv and Congress leaders influenced the collapse of V.P. Singh's government in October 1990 by promising support to Chandra Shekhar, a high-ranking leader in the Janata Dal, sufficient internal contradictions existed, within the ruling coalition, especially over the controversial reservation issue, to cause a fall of government. Rajiv's Congress offered outside support briefly to Chandra Sekhar, who became Prime Minister. They withdrew their support in 1991, however, and fresh elections were announced.

Sri Lanka policy

Then Sri Lankan Prime Minister Ranasinghe Premadasa opposed the Indo-Sri Lanka Peace Accord, but accepted it due to pressure from then President Junius Richard Jayewardene. In January 1989 Premadasa was elected President and on a platform that promised that the Indian Peace Keeping Force (IPKF) leave within three months. In the 1989 elections, both the Sri Lanka Freedom Party and United National Party wanted the IPKF to withdraw, and they got 95 per cent of the vote.

The police action was unpopular in India as well, especially in Tamil Nadu, as India was fighting the Tamil separatists. Rajiv refused to withdraw the IPKF, believing that the only way to end the civil war was to politically force Premadasa and militarily force the LTTE to accept the accord. In December 1989, V.P. Singh was elected Prime Minister and completed the pullout. The IPKF operation killed over 1,100 Indian soldiers, 5,000 Tamil civilians and cost over 10,000 crores.

Shah Bano Case

In 1985, the Supreme Court of India ruled in favour of Muslim divorcee Shah Bano, declaring that her husband should give her alimony. Muslim fundamentalists in India treated it as an encroachment in Muslim Personal Law and protested against it. Gandhi agreed to their demands. In 1986, the Congress (I) party, which had an absolute majority in Parliament at the time, passed an act that nullified the Supreme Court's judgement in the Shah Bano case. This was viewed by many in India, including the Bharatiya Janata Party as appeasement of Muslims. Some Congress members believed the same and they influenced Rajiv, to either revoke the act or to pacify Hindu sentiments too. The opening up of the gates of the Ram Janmabhoomi—Babri Masjid gates for worship of the Ram Lala idols at Ayodhya was an event which would go on to haunt India for several years.

Allegations of Black Money

Opposition parties in India, including Janata Party, claim that Rajiv Gandhi has black money in Swiss Bank accounts to the tune of billions of dollars. This was first raised by the Swiss magazine, Schweitzer Illustrated in 1991.

Rajiv Gandhi's last public meeting was at Sriperumbudur on 21 May 1991, in a village approximately 30 miles from Chennai, Tamil Nadu, where he was assassinated while campaigning for the Sriperumbudur Lok Sabha Congress candidate. The assassination was carried out by the Liberation Tigers of Tamil Eelam.

FOURTH PHASE

After Rajiv Gandhi's assassination in 1991, Narsimah Rao came back into power. As the Congress had won the largest number of seats in the 1991 elections, he got the opportunity to head the minority government as Prime Minister. He was the first person outside the Nehru-Gandhi family to serve as Prime Minister for five continuous years, the first to hail from South India and also the first from the state of Andhra Pradesh. Since Rao had not contested the general elections, he then participated in a by-election in Nandyal to join the parliament. N.T. Rama Rao (then leader of the Chief Opposition party of Telugu Desam) did not want to put a contestant against Rao, because he was the First Prime Minister of India from Andhra Pradesh, and NTR did not want to create an obstacle on his path. By that, Rao won from Nandyal with a victory margin of a record 5 lakh (5,00,000) votes and his win was recorded in the Guinness Book of World Records. His cabinet included Sharad Pawar, himself a strong contender for the Prime Minister's post, as defense minister. He also broke convention by appointing a non-political economist and future prime minister, Manmohan Singh as his finance minister.

In July 1993, Rao's government was facing a no-confidence motion, because the opposition felt that it did not have sufficient numbers to prove a majority. It was alleged that Rao, through a representative, offered millions of rupees to members of the Jharkhand Mukti Morcha (JMM), and possibly a breakaway faction of the Janata Dal, to vote for him during the confidence motion. Shailendra Mahato, one of those members who had accepted the bribe, turned approver. In 1996, after Rao's term in office had expired, investigations began in earnest in the case. In 2000, after years of legal proceedings, a special court convicted Rao and his colleague, Buta Singh (who is alleged to have escorted the MPs to the Prime Minister). Rao appealed to a higher court and remained free on bail. The decision was overturned mainly due to the doubt in credibility of Mahato's statements (which were extremely inconsistent) and both Rao and Buta Singh were cleared of the charges in 2002.

Rao, along with fellow minister K.K. Tewary, Chandraswami and K.N. Aggarwal were accused of forging documents showing that Ajeya Singh had opened a bank account in the First Trust Corporation Bank in St. Kitts and deposited $21 million in it, making his father V.P. Singh its beneficiary. The alleged intent was to tarnish V.P. Singh's image. This supposedly happened in 1989. However only after Rao's term as PM had expired in 1996, was he formally charged by the Central Bureau of Investigation for the crime. Less than a year later the court acquitted him due to lack of evidence linking him with the case.

Lakhubhai Pathak, an Indian businessman living in England alleged that Chandraswami and K.N. Aggarwal alias Mamaji, along with Mr. Rao, cheated him out of $100,000. The amount was given for an express promise for allowing supplies of paper pulp in India, and Pathak alleged that he spent an additional $30,000 entertaining Chandraswami and his secretary. Rao and Chandraswami were acquitted of the charges in 2003.

FIFTH PHASE

Dr. Manmohan singh is the Prime Minister of India from 2004 till date. His era has been a saga of the volcanic eruptions against corruption and black money. During the discussion for the vote of confidence, BJP MP's produced cash in the parliament, as viewed on Lok Sabha TV, alleging a bribe by the Samajwadi Party to vote for the government. The BJP claimed to have documentary evidence in a "cash for vote" scam and submitted a report before the parliamentary committee probing the matter. The BJP also wrote a 17-page letter to the Parliamentary committee headed by Congress member V. Kishore Chandradeo in this regard. Arun Jaitley said Samajwadi MP Reoti Raman Singh had offered his party's MPs the cash on the night of July 21. He also alleged that SP leader Amar Singh was behind the entire episode. Jaitley said: "The investigating agencies did not do their job. So we inquired into the matter and gathered documentary evidence in the case." He alleged the 'cash for vote' scam reflected the subversion of the Indian Parliament, as well as a section of the media.

The winter session of parliament in October 2008 came under intense criticism from the Left parties and the BJP to demand a full fledged winter session instead of what was seen as the UPA to having "scuttled the voice of Parliament" by bringing down the sittings to a record low of 30 days in the year. The tensions between the UPA and the opposition parties became evident at an all party meeting convened by Lok Sabha speaker Somnath Chatterjee when the leader of opposition, LK Advani questioned the status, timing and schedule of the current session of parliament.

In early November 2008, months before a new general election, RJD chief Laloo Prasad Yadav, along with other MP's from Bihar, threatened to resign en masse from the central government as well as with their MLA's in Bihar and Jharkhand if the central government did not take steps to arrest Raj Thackeray under the NSA for the recent actions against north Indian students in Maharashtra, as well as to initiate a CBI inquiry in the killing of a Bihari in Mumbai. The opposition BJP termed this "another spell of rhetoric" on the issue of attacks on North Indians in Mumbai.

ANTI CORRUPTION MOVEMENT

The 2011 Indian anti-corruption movement is a series of ongoing demonstrations and protests across India intended to establish strong legislation and enforcement against endemic corruption. The movement has gained momentum since April 5, 2011, when anti-corruption activist Anna Hazare began his now-famous hunger strike at Jantar Mantar in New Delhi.

The chief aim of the movement is to alleviate corruption in the Indian government through a piece of legislation called the Jan Lokpal Bill. Another important aim, led by protests under Swami Ramdev, is the repatriation of black money from Swiss and other foreign banks.

The movement is primarily one of Gandhian non-violent civil resistance, featuring demonstrations, marches and acts of civil disobedience, hunger strikes and the use of social media. The protests are unusual as they have no political affiliation; most protesters have been hostile to attempts by political parties to use them to strengthen their own personal political agendas.

Issues regarding corruption in India have become increasingly prominent in recent years. The country was subject to socialist-inspired economic policies dating from independence in 1947 until the 1980s. Over-regulation, protectionism, and government ownership of industry led to slow economic growth, high unemployment, and wide-spread poverty. This system of bureaucratic control by government is called the License Raj and lies at the core of endemic corruption.

The Vohra Report of 1993, submitted by the former Indian Union Home Secretary N.N. Vohra, studied the issue of the criminalization of politics. The report contained several observations made by official agencies on the criminal network which was virtually running a parallel government. It also discussed criminal gangs who enjoyed the patronage of politicians and the protection of government functionaries. It revealed that political leaders had become leaders of street gangs and rogue elements in the military. Over the years, criminals had been elected to local bodies, State Assemblies, and the Parliament.

The Right to Information Act of 2005 helped civilians work effectively towards tackling corruption. It allows Indian citizens to request information, for a fixed fee of Rs. 10, from a "public authority" (a body of Government or "instrumentality of State"). In turn, this public authority is required to reply to the request within thirty days. Activists have used this to uncover corruption cases against various politicians and bureaucrats - one consequence being that some of those activists have been attacked and even killed.

PRE-LAUNCH OF THE MOVEMENT

Although Anna Hazare and Swami Ramdev now stand in the public limelight, the movement was pre-launched by several anti-corruption campaigns occurring from late October 2010 through late March 2011, The following table summarizes the first Indian anti-corruption campaigns that built the foundation under the global movement:

Oct 29, 2010

An anti-corruption press conference organized by NGO India Against Corruption was held at the Press Club of India to highlight the fact that the government-appointed Shunglu Committee had inadequate powers to investigate the Commonwealth Games scam.

November 1, 2010

By order of Defence Minister of India A.K. Antony, the Indian Army establishes a court of inquiry into the Adarsh Housing Society Scam.

November 14, 2010

After India Against Corruption registers a complaint regarding corruption in the Commonwealth Games scam, nearly 10,000 people assembled at the Parliament Street Police Station.

November 24, 2010

The Central Bureau of Investigation's arrests of several senior bankers under allegations of receiving bribes to issue corporate loans in the 2010 housing loan scam.

December 10, 2010

The Central Government of India and the Directorate General of Income Tax (Investigation) file a delayed joint affidavit to the Supreme Court of India declaring the Nov. 2007 wiretapping of corporate lobbyist Nira Radia in the Radia tapes controversy.

December 22, 2010

A 20,000-person anti-corruption protest in response to the 2G spectrum scam held at New Delhi's Ramlila ground.

January 17, 2011

The Supreme Court of India criticizes the administration for not publicly disclosing Indian nationals named on Rudolf Elmer's "black money" list revealed to Julian Assange's Wikileaks.

January 18, 2011

The public release of an anti-corruption open letter from Azim Premji, Keshub Mahindra, and other leading Indian industrialists demanding reform of "the widespread governance deficit in almost every sphere,of national activity, covering government, business and institutions."

January 29, 2011

Former Chief Minister Chandra Babu Naidu announces launch of his "war on corruption" through his NTR Memorial Trust and Jana Chaitanya Vedika.

January 30, 2011

Thousands of people marched against corruption in more than 52 cities in India and abroad. Copies of the CVC Act, the CBI Act and the Government's Lokpal Bill were torn up by the thousands, sending a strong message that the people lack faith in the ineffective anti-corruption measures.

February-March, 2011

The Central Bureau of Investigation's arrests of co-conspirators implicated in the 2G spectrum scam.

February 10, 2011

The Supreme Court of India orders all trial courts in the country to expedite handling of corruption cases; also, all High Courts of India ordered to seek quarterly reports from lower trial courts on the progress of corruption cases.

February 21, 2011

In a public address to the Parliament of India, the President of India Pratibha Patil stated that measures to ratify the United Nations Convention Against Corruption and other legislative and administrative measures necessary to improve transparency will be taken.

March 1, 2011

The SEC action against Indian School of Business Chairman Rajat Gupta in the Galleon insider trading scandal; Gupta had also violated McKinsey & Co.'s firm policy by corruptly backdealing through his own consulting firm, MindSpirit LLC.

March 3, 2011

The forced resignation of Chief Vigilance Commissioner P.J. Thomas on charges of corruption by the Supreme Court of India.

March 12, 2011

The worldwide 50-city Dandi March II organized by People for Lok Satta and India Against Corruption.

March 13, 2011

The "Drive around Delhi" protest organized by India Against Corruption.

March 17, 2011

The Wikileaks' Cash-for-votes scandal involving the delayed leak of a diplomatic cable describing an Indian legislative aide showing a US embassy official "chests of cash" used to bribe Indian lawmakers over a vote on an Indo-U.S. nuclear deal back in July 2008.

March 30, 2011

Famous cricketer Kapil Dev's letter to Prime Minister Manmohan Singh, complaining of the inadequacy of Commonwealth Games corruption investigations and petitioning for the Jan Lokpal Bill.

DETAILED TIMELINE

4 April 2011

Anna Hazare announced that he would commence his "fast unto death" and that this would last until a comprehensive measure to tackle corruption was introduced. He claimed that the government had excluded "civil society" from the panel set up to draft the Jan Lokpal Bill, and implied that at least one of the persons who was to be on the drafting committee - Sharad Pawar - might be unsuitable for that role because of his large landholdings. Kiran Bedi and Swami Agnivesh voiced their support for Hazare. Later a video exposed Agnivesh talking to Kapil Sibal and saying that Anna is behaving like a mad man. The more concessions are given, the more these people are trying to climb over the head and that no more concession be given and the movement need to be stopped.

5 April 2011

Protesters have come out in support of Anna Hazare

Hazare initiated his fast at Jantar Mantar in Delhi. Elsewhere, people attended a protest at Freedom Park, Bangalore.

Campaigners for India Against Corruption (IAC) estimated that a petition circulated in the city of Pune which demanded that the government enact a bill had attracted between 5000 and 6000 signatures between 3 April and 5 April. Hazare has been involved with IAC, a group established by various prominent activists with the primary purpose of achieving the legal enactment and subsequent enforcement of a strong version of the Jan Lokpal bill.

7 April 2011

Protests have continued as the Government fails to offer better terms to the activists

Two rounds of talks failed. There was agreement regarding constituting a panel to examine the Bill but the government would not accede to demands that it should be a formally constituted panel or that Hazare should lead it. As a consequence of this, Hazare continued his fast.

Narendra Modi, the chief Minister of Gujarat lashes out at Manmohan Singh for resisting the passage of the Jan Lokpal Bill.

Sonia Gandhi, the president of the Indian National Congress party and the head of the National Advisory Council appealed to Hazare to end his indefinite fast.

Hazare and the protesters tried to keep the protests non-political. No politicians were welcome at the site of the fast. Former Haryana Chief Minister Om Prakash Chautala, former Madhya Pradesh Chief Minister Uma Bharti and journalist Barkha Dutt were forced by civilians to leave, after the protesters objected to their presence, which they believed was harming the integrity of their movement.

8 April 2011

Protesters in Pune

Protests spread to numerous other places, including Mumbai, Kolkata, Thiruvananthapuram, Hyderabad, Jaipur, Chennai, Patna, Bhopal, Ahmedabad, Ranchi, Pune, and the University of Jammu.

The government continued to squabble with the activists stating that the bill drafting committee will be headed by a government appointed minister and not a civil society member as the protesters demanded to avoid allowing the government to make the bill less powerful.

The Prime Minister, Manmohan Singh, met with the President of India to outline to her how the government was going ahead with the demands of the population.

15 supporters of Hazare on fast were hospitalized.

Bollywood came out in support of the protests, with actors, musicians and directors speaking in support of the movement and Hazare. Director Farah Khan, actor Anupam Kher, music director

Vishal Dadlani, poet-filmmaker Pritish Nandy and actor Tom Alter all visited Jantar Mantar; others stated their support for the movement via social networking websites or the media. Oscar winning Indian composer A.R. Rahman also declared his support for the anti-graft movement.

Renowned Indian/Qatari artist Late M.F. Hussain showed his support by drawing a cartoon of Hazare.

Indian students at Cambridge University, the former alma mater of the Indian Prime Minister also expressed their support for the movement.

Many prominent people from government agencies as well as from various corporate houses came out in support of the movement. Some of them were -Delhi Metro chief E. Sreedharan (also called the Metro Man of India), Punj Lloyd chairman Atul Punj, Maruti Suzuki chairman R.C. Bhargava, Hero group's Sunii Munjal, Tata Steel vice-chairman B. Muthuraman, Bajaj Auto Chairman Rahul Bajaj, Godrej Group head Adi Godrej, Biocon Chairman and Managing Director Kiran Mazumdar-Shaw and Kotak. Mahindra Bank vice-chairman & managing director Uday Kotak. They all declared their support for Hazare and the movement.

ASSOCHAM President Dilip Modi and FICCI Director General Rajiv Kumar, too came out in support of the movement.

The Government of India accepted the compromise formula that there be a politician chairman and an activist non-politician Co-Chairman. It was reported that Pranab Mukherjee will be the Chairman of the draft committee while Shanti Bhushan will be the co-chairman. Bhushan was one of the original drafters of the Lokpal Bill along with Hazare, Justice N. Santosh Hegde, advocate Prashant Bhushan, and RTI activist Arvind Kejriwal.

9 April 2011

After accepting all the demands of Hazare, the Government of India issued a Official Gazette saying that the draft of the lokpal would be made and presented in the coming monsoon session of Lok Sabha.

Victory celebrations took place at locations throughout the country and even Hazare's village.

Bollywood lauded the outcome, repeating their support for the movement. Protesters and leaders of the movement alike stated that the path to attaining complete passage of the bill is still a difficult one, and the movement may see harsher days ahead.

Many commentators have called the movement the 'wake-up' call for India.

Within a day of the beginning of the agitation, more than 30,000 people had pledged their support to the Lokpal Bill. Organisers of the India Against Corruption said 30,000 people from Maharashtra expressed their support on their website. The website has 20,000 members in Mumbai alone. Within a few days the Facebook page for India Against Corruption had more than 2,20,000 likes.

16 April 2011

The first meeting regarding a draft of the Lokpal Bill was held on 16 April, The government agreed to audio-record all meetings of the Lokpal Bill panel and to hold public consultations before a final draft is prepared. Hazare demanded that the proceedings be televised live but the government refused.

4 June 2011

Swami Ramdev begins his indefinite hunger strike at Ramlila Maidan in Delhi to bring back the black money stashed in tax havens abroad.

65,000 followers gathered at Ramlila Maidan.

In a press conference in the evening Kapil Sibbal made public a letter from Ramdev's camp to call off the hunger strike. Ramdev took it as a betrayal and hardened his position.

5 June 2011

At midnight, police raided the grounds when most protesters were sleeping and Ramdev was busy at a meeting with his core group.

A large police force lobbed tear gas shells, burned the place and lathicharge the crowd at 1 am (IST) to evict them.

Police had arranged buses to drop supporters at railway stations and bus stands in advance; had ammunition ready and were in battle-gear wearing vests and helmets and kept some ambulances on standby.

Delhi Police arrested Ramdev, who was disguised in a salwar kameez with a group of female protesters heading peacefully towards the New Delhi Railway Station.

Ramdev was held in a government'guesthouse for a few hours and then sent to Dehradun in a BSF aircraft.

Ramdev was sent to his Patanjali Yogpeeth ashram in Haridwar where he delivered a press conference.

53 people were injured and were treated at the Lok Nayak Jai Prakash (LNJP) hospital, AIIMS Trauma Center and Ram Manohar Lohia Hospital.

One of Baba Ramdev's supporters was injured in the incident and her condition was still critical as of 17th August 2011.

Protesters huddled near the Metro station, bus depots and railway stations. Many walked down to Gurdwara Bangla Sahib and other nearby ashrams. According to New Delhi railway station authorities, supporters continued to leave in batches through the course of the day. While several supporters spent the day at a park near Ramlila Maidan, others took shelter at an Arya Samaj facility in Paharganj.

Ramdev was prohibited from entering Delhi for 15 days.

6 June 2011

Prime Minister Manmohan Singh justified the action against Baba Ramdev as an operation that had to be conducted, and that there was no alternative. However Manmohan Singh did not elaborate as to why force was used on a peaceful gathering and why the swoop was done at 1 AM in the morning.

9 June 2011

Hazare described his fight against corruption as the "Second Freedom Struggle" and set an ultimatum of 15 August 2011, as the last date to pass a strong Jan Lokpal Bill, threatening to otherwise intensify his anti-corruption agitation and start another fast from 16 August.

16 June 2011

The Government and the civil society split wide open due to differences in jointly drafting the bill. Government representatives said that if a consensus on the common bill was not reached, two drafts would be sent to the Cabinet, one drafted by the Government and the other drafted by the civil society. Team Anna also claimed that only 15 points, out of a total 71 recommended, were agreed upon and included in the joint draft. Hazare declared that if the government version of the bill was passed in the Parliament, he would start his hunger strike from August 16, 2011.

22 June 2011

In a veiled warning to Anna Hazare for his proposed fast, Congress leader Digvijay Singh on Wednesday indicated that the Gandhian might be meted out the same treatment, depending upon the prevailing situation at that time, as yoga guru Ramdev was given at Ramlila ground.

14 August 2011

In a scathing attack on Anna Hazare, Congress spokesperson, Manish Tewari, and an MP from Ludhiana constituency, described Anna Hazare as being "involved in corruption from top to bottom", "neck deep in corruption", and also mentioning that the social activist needed to be "shown his place".

15 August 2011

Anna Hazare announced at a press conference that he and his supporters were determined to go ahead with the fast on 16 August 2011 as planned. He also urged people to court arrest to push for a stronger Lokpal bill.

Section 144 was imposed a night before the planned protest date, at JP Park, Rajghat and Dilli Gate, which prohibited assembly of five or more persons.

16 August 2011

Anna Hazare was detained by Delhi Police in the early morning before he could start his hunger strike at JP park, Delhi. Delhi Police had asked Anna not to leave his home, which he declined, and Anna was detained at his residence in Mayur Vihar. Arvind Kejriwal, Kiran Bedi, Manish Sisodia and more than 1,200 supporters were also taken into preventive custody by the Police.

Anna Hazare was sent to seven days judicial custody to Tihar jail after refusing to sign a personal bond to be released on bail.

Shehla Masood, an RTI activist and a strong supporter of Anna Hazare's anti-corruption movement, was shot dead around 11.30am IST. An unidentified assailant shot her in front of her house in Koh-e-Fiza, Bhopal.

Kiran Bedi and Shanti Bhushan, detained by Delhi Police on the morning ahead of Anna Hazare's fast-unto-death, were released in the evening at around 6:30pm IST.

The current telecom minister Kapil Sibai was greeted with black flags and booed by a group of students at a seminar on the Jan Lokpal bill.

With the Government of India, preparing to release Anna Hazare late in the night, however Anna refused to come out of Tihar jail until the government agreed to an unconditional permission to hold protests at JP Park.

Demonstrations were held all over India protesting Anna Hazare's arrest. In Chennai, Mahatma Gandhi's secretary, V Kalyanam led the protestors. He said —"India will get a sure gold medal if corruption is entered as an item in the Olympic Games. We may not be a force in football or athletics or hockey. But India is the undisputed global leader in corruption." Referring to Anna Hazare's arrest in New Delhi, Kalyanam said it was easier to fight foreign tyranny than the tyranny of our own people. He ridiculed the contention of Union ministers like Kapil Sibal and Chidambaram that Parliament was supreme and civil society had no voice.

17 August 2011

After almost a day, Anna still refused to leave jail and spent the night in a room in Tihar jail, despite the government decision to free him.

Delhi Police made concessions for Anna Hazare to fast, stepping up from seven days to 14 days and finally 21 days at Ramlila Maidan.

Congress made a statement that they suspected a foreign hand in the protests and asked the government to probe if the US was behind Anna's agitation.

18 August 2011

Anna Hazare agreed to leave jail after Delhi Police granted him permission to fast for 15-days against corruption at Ramlila Maidan. However, he would spend another night in Jail till the venue is ready.

Arvind Kejriwal left Tihar jail being there for two days. Kejriwal called this move as just the beginning of their fight against corruption, and also confirmed that Anna Hazare would leave the jail once the grounds at Ramlila Maidan are ready for the fast.

19 August 2011

Anna Hazare left Tihar Jail at 15 minutes to noon IST after 3 days, to a spontaneous roar of welcome from the huge crowd assembled near the Jail. Just past the gates, he raised his hand in the air and shouted "Bharat mata ki Jai (Victory to Mother India)'[1]. He also addressed the public stating: "Whether I am there or not, this fight will continue." which too received a huge roar of applause. Anna waved the national flag towards the crowd, who responded by waving hundreds of smaller flags and chanted "Anna zindabad (long live Anna)".

Paying obeisance to Mahatma Gandhi at Rajghat and Amar Jawan Jyoti at the India Gate, Anna Hazare reached Delhi's Ramlila Maidan to launch a 15-day mass protest against corruption.

Anna Hazare finally launched his protest at Ramlila Maidan as he declared that he will not quit the venue till the Jan Lokpal Bill is passed.

Varun Gandhi, Bharatiya Janata Party MP announced that he will introduce Anna Hazare's Jan Lokpal Bill in the Lok Sabha as a private member's bill, saying that Jan Lokpal Bill is better than anything the nation has seen before and would like to make a small contribution in his own way.

21 August 2011

Anna Hazare's camp on Sunday called their supporters to confront individual Members of Parliament and Union Ministers at their residence and also warned the UPA government that its days would be numbered if it failed to pass the Bill by August 30.

Over 1,00,000 supporters had thronged Ramliia Maidan on Sunday, to show their support against corruption.

Around 50,000 supporters marched in the streets on Mumbai to support Anna Hazare's call for an effective anti-corruption legislation. The marchers started from the Bandra railway station and walked all the way to Juhu, reportedly in one of the biggest protests in Mumbai.

22 August 2011

On behalf of Anna Hazare, Sri Sri Ravishankar on Monday met NDA leaders at L.K. Advani's residence to discuss the Lokpal issue and garner opposition support.

Anna Hazare, on his 7th day of fast said he would not negotiate with any other mediator, including P. Chidambaram or Kapil Sibal. He also said he would only negotiate with Congress MP Rahul Gandhi, the Prime Minister's Office (PMO) or Maharashtra Chief minister Prithviraj Chavan regarding the Jan Lokpal Bill.

23 August 2011

South Indian superstar Rajinikanth pledged his support for Anna Hazare's movement for the Jan Lokpal bill stating that he was happy that an able and dedicated leader like Anna Hazare is leading the fight against corruption. He also congratulated all Indians for lending their support to the 'bloodless revolution'.

Prime Minister Manmohan Singh on Tuesday appealed Anna Hazare to end his fast. He wrote a letter to Anna stating that he will ask Lok Sabha Speaker Meira Kumar if Anna's Jan Lokpal Bill can be sent to the Standing Committee. Prime Minister also said that the government was concerned about Anna's health.

24 August 2011

Bharatiya Janata Party MP Varun Gandhi visited Ramliia Maidan on Wednesday morning. He stated his visit was as a common man and had nothing to do with his party as he supported the cause of Anna Hazare.

An all-party meeting was chaired by Prime Minister Manmohan Singh at his official residence in New Delhi represented by finance minister Pranab Mukheriee. However the meeting ended with Mukherjee appealing Anna Hazare to end his fast, prompting the civil society to declare that they were "back to square one".

25 August 2011

Prime Minister Manmohan Singh on Thursday offered a new formula saying that the Government was ready to debate all versions of the Lokpal Bill in circulation at Parliament. He also said that the bills prepared by Aruna Roy's NCPRT and Jaiprakash Narain will also be debated by the Parliament alongwith the Jan Lokpal Bill.

Union Minister Vilasrao Deshmukh met Anna Hazare at his protest camp at Ramlila Maidan. Deshmukh reportedly conveyed a message from the Prime Minister to urge Anna to end his fast and also asked him to consider the Prime Minister offer to debate all versions of Lokpal Bill in Parliament.

Anna Hazare had asked Prime Minister Manmohan Singh to start the parliamentary discussion the next morning itself. Hazare had also put forward his three demands to the Prime Minister - Citizen's Charter, Lokayuktas in all states with Lokpal powers and inclusion of lowest to highest bureaucracy.

Popular South Indian actor Vijay met Anna Hazare at Ramlila Maidan and also fasted through out the day to express his support towards anti-corruption. Saluting Hazare's "will-power", Vijay said its praiseworthy the way the movement got public support that too without any political background.

26 August 2011

Government asked Anna Hazare to guarantee of ending his fast once the discussion (debate) opens in Parliament.

Veteran Bollywood actor Om Puri visited Ramlila Maidan and met Anna Hazare on his 11th day of fast, expressing his support to anti-corruption movement.

27 August 2011

Bollywood actor Aamir Khan met Anna Hazare at Ramlila Maidan. Supporting the anti-corruption campaign, Khan urged Anna to end his fast stating his leadership is required for the campaign as passing the bill will be a long process.

Finance minister Pranab Mukherjee on Saturday initiated his debate in the Parliament on the Lokpal Bill issue. Initiating the speech, Mukherjee again requested Anna to end his fast.

Bharatiya Janata Party MP Sushma Swaraj, during the debate in Lok Sabha, expressed her party's support for Anna Hazare, and said the BJP largely agrees with the three pre-conditions (Citizen's Charter, Lokayuktas in all states with Lokpal powers and inclusion of lowest to highest bureaucracy) laid down by Anna to end his hunger strike and is willing to vote in favour it.

Supporting Anna Hazare anti-corruption movement, singer Sonu Nigam performed at Ramlila Maidan on Saturday. Sonu took blessings of Anna, who was on his 12th day of his indefinite fast.

Government agreed to voice vote on Lokpal debate in Parliament.

Both the houses have passed the resolution agreeing upon all the three conditions set by Anna in Jan Lokpal Bill. "We have won only half the battle," said Hazare standing before wildly cheering crowds and flanked by his key aides and Union minister Vilasrao Deshmukh, former Maharashtra chief minister who has been an interlocutor. "I congratulate every MP on what has happened today." Anna Hazare said. Anna Hazare also declared of breaking fast on Sunday morning at 10 am.

28 August 2011

Anna Hazare ended his 12-day fast after 288 hours on Sunday morning at around 10 am IST (UTC+05:30) before thousands of cheering supporters at Ramlila Maidan. Hazare was driven straight to Medanta Medicity run by eminent cardiologist Dr. Naresh Trehan who was attending to him along with his team during his entire period of fast.

Thousands of supporters gathered at India Gate following anti-corruption crusader's call to celebrate their victory.

CONCLUSION

Anna Hazare's agitation is the latest expression of the impotent public wrath against corruption and black money. It has awakened the masses which will ultimately help in rooting out the cancer of corruption and black money that is eating the very vital nerve of economy and polity of our nation. Now, the masses have become so enlightened and agitated that this impotent public wrath will become so potent that none will be able to suppress it. This public wrath will over throw all corrupt political leaders and free India from corruption and black money.

8

Sad Story of Lokpal Bills

The Indian 'Lokpal is synonymous to the institution of Ombudsman' existing in the Scandinavian countries. The institution of'Ombudsman' first came into being in Sweden in 1713 when a 'Chancellor of Justice' was appointed by the King to act as invigilator to look into the functioning of war-time government. Thereafter, a new beginning was made in 1809, when it was laid down that the Ombudsman would be made thereafter by the legislature. Thereafter, this institution remained confined only to Scandinavian countries such as Finland and Denmark. The first Commonwealth country where the institution of Ombudsman was accepted was New Zealand where this office came into being in 1962. A modified version of the Ombudsman, that is, the Office of the Parliamentary Commissioner was established in the United Kingdom in 1967. Since then, the institution office of the ombudsman had spread to several countries from the sixties.

The ombudsmen can investigate a complaint by themselves or through any public or private agency. After investigation, in Sweden and Finland, the Ombudsman has the power to prosecute erring public servants; whereas in Denmark, he can only order prosecution.

However, the power of prosecution is very rarely used. The strength of the ombudsman lies in the publicity attached to the office, and the negative view that attaches itself to all that the office it scrutinizes. In Sweden and Finland, ombudsmen can also supervise the courts. In other countries,, their authority is only over the non-judicial public servants. In almost all the cases they deal with complaints relating to both corruption and mal-administration.

NEED OF LOKPAL

After independence, increasing magnitude of developmental and welfare responsibilities of the government has boosted the proliferation of the administrative machinery. Consequently, over the years numerous cases of corruption, maladministration and misuse of authority and resources have started coming to light. Since such practices couldn't be curbed by the existing measures, under the Indian Penal Code 1860 and the Prevention of Corruption Act, 1988. (The Code of Criminal Procedure and the Prevention of Corruption Act requires the investigating/prosecuting agency to get prior sanction of the central or state government before it can initiate the prosecution process in a court). Therefore, the need for an agency independent of the executive, legislative and judiciary, to look into citizens' grievances and cases of corruption have been widely felt and the central government have at several times considered the introduction of a 'Lok Pal Bill' to put it in place as a mechanism to tackle corruption.

There have been animated discussions in Parliament on various facets of the problems of corruption at the time of consideration of the Prevention of Corruption Bill, the Criminal Law Amendment Bill and the Commissions of Inquiry Bill. In 1959, Shri C.D. Deshmukh had suggested for the establishment of, "a high-level impartial standing judicial tribunal to investigate and report on complaints pertaining to corruption."

On 3 April 1963, during a debate on the Demands for Grants of the Ministry of Law, Dr. L.M. Singhvi stressed the need for setting up of a Parliamentary Commissioner—an Ombudsman like institution and suggested an amendment of the Constitution to set up such an office and define its function and possibly even the procedure which it had to follow. The same year Shri P.B. Gajendrakar, the then Chief

Justice of India, pleaded for the establishment of an independent authority for the redress of public grievances. In September 1963, the Administrative Reforms Committee of Rajasthan under the Chairmanship of Shri H.C. Mathur, recommended the appointment of an Ombudsman to look into the complaints against high State officials and Ministers. In December 1963, while accepting the recommendation of the Santhanam Committee for the setting up of the Central Vigilance Commission, the Government promised to examine further the question of evolving machinery for dealing with the grievances of citizens against the administration. Dr. L.M. Singhvi moved a resolution in the Lok Sabha on 3 April 1964, reiterating his demand for setting up an officer of Parliament known as People's Procurator. The resolution was discussed in detail by all sections of the House but was withdrawn on the assurance of the Government that it would look into the matter. In pursuance of this assurance, the Government constituted a Special Consultative Group of Members of Parliament on administrative reforms, in early 1965, which favoured a high powered inquiry commission on administrative reforms. Accordingly, an Administrative Reforms Commission (ARC) was appointed in January 1966, for making recommendations on the reorganisation of the administrative system of the country.

The ARC was required to consider, among other things, problems of existing arrangement and need for a special institution for the redress of citizens' grievances keeping in mind the need for ensuring the highest standards of efficiency and integrity in public services, and also for making public administration responsive to the people. More specifically, the commission was expected to examine:

1. The adequacy of the existing arrangements for the redress of grievances; and

2. The need for introduction of any new machinery or special institution for redress of grievances.

The ARC appointed on 25 June 1966, a study group to go into these problems. On the basis of recommendations of this group, the ARC made an interim report on 20 October 1966, in which it took note of the often expressed public out-cry against the prevalence of corruption, the existence of widespread inefficiency and the unresponsiveness of administration to popular needs. It felt that the answer to this lay in the provision of a machinery which would examine public complaints and shift the genuine from the false or the untenable so that failures and achievements of the administration could be publicly viewed in the correct perspective. Such an institution was regarded necessary even from the point of view of affording protection to the services. The Commission, therefore, recommended that there should be a statutory machinery to enquire into complaints alleging corruption or injustice arising out of maladministration. In other words, the ARC while preparing its report had three ends in view:

1. Evolution of a suitable grievance procedure for the individuals to invoke in complaints of maladministration,

2. Creation of a mechanism which would reduce corruption in the administrative services; and

3. Setting up a mechanism which would take cognizance of complaints of favouritism and nepotism against Central and State Ministers.

The Administrative Reforms Commission (ARC) also appended to its report a draft Bill on the subject with a view to enable the Government to take a prompt and speedy action to set up the institution of Lokpal and Lokayukta.

LEGISLATIVE HISTORY OF LOKPAL IN INDIA

In the annals of Indian Parliament, no bill had a more checkered history than the Lokpal Bill. In 1966 the then Rashtrapati Dr. Radhakrishanan had sct up an Administrative Reforms Commission headed by Morarji Bhai Desai. It was this commission that recommended enacting a law for the establishment of a Lokpal.

The first Bill of this genre was introduced in the fourth Lok Sabha in 1966. Today's is the fifteenth Lok Sabha, more than 45 years have elapsed but the Bill is still lingering on in the air. Different governments came into power over the years but the Congress Party -whether in power or opposition has always let down this Bill on one pretext or the other as it could be the biggest hurdle for the entry of the corrupt politicians in the party.

THE LOKPAL AND LOKAYUKTAS BILL, 1966

The first major attempt on the legislative plans for providing an Ombudsman like institution in India was made with the introduction of "the Lokpal and Lokayukta Bill" in the Lok Sabha, on 9 May 1968. The Bill was referred to a Joint Committee of the Houses of Parliament which presented its report to the Lok Sabha on 26 March 1969.

The Bill, as reported by the Joint Committee, was passed by the Lok Sabha after being discussed elaborately. The Bill, as passed by the Lok Sabha, was sent to the Rajya Sabha on 22 August 1969. But, while it was pending in the Rajya Sabha, the fourth Lok Sabha was dissolved on 27 December 1970. The Bill consequently lapsed.

The Bill sought to give effect to the recommendations of the ARC in so far as they related to matters within the purview of the Union Government, In its scope, it differed from the draft Bill proposed by the ARC in two major respects. It did not extend to public servants in the States. Secondly, it did not confine itself to Ministers and Secretaries alone. In other words, the Bill sought to provide a statutory machinery to enquire into complaints based on actions of the all Union public servants, including Ministers.

THE LOKPAL AND LOKAYUKTAS BILL, 1971

Since the earlier Bill had lapsed, the Bill as passed by the Lok Sabha in 1969 was reintroduced in the Lok Sabha on 11 August 1971. This Bill also lapsed due to dissolution of the fifth Lok Sabha.

THE LOKPAL BILL, 1977

After the Janata Party came to power in 1977, the matter was re-examined having regard to the recommendations of the ARC, the provisions of the 1971 Bill and other laws on the subject enacted in various States from time to time and the experience of the functioning of such institutions in the States where they had been set up. In the light of this re-examination, it was proposed to alter the scheme of the Lokpal as incorporated in the 1971 Bill in material respects for making the institutions of Lokpal an effective instrument to combat the problems posed by corruption.

Accordingly, a fresh Bill called the "Lokpal Bill, 1977" was introduced in the Lok Sabha on 28 July 1977. This Bill was referred to a Joint Committee of the Houses of Parliament which submitted its report on 20 July 1978. While the Bill was under consideration of the Lok Sabha, the sixth Lok Sabha got dissolved. Consequently this Bill also lapsed.

Under the scheme proposed by the Lokpal Bill, 1977, the jurisdiction of the Lokpal was to cover any complaints of misconduct against the Prime Minister, Members of Parliament and Chief Ministers of States. Allegations against civil servants were excluded from the purview of the Lokpal. Grivances due to mal-administration etc., as distinct from allegations of misconduct, were also excluded from its jurisdiction.

THE LOKPAL BILL, 1985

Yet another Lokpal Bill was introduced in the Lok Sabha on 26 August 1985. The 1985 Bill empowered the Lokpal to inquire into complaints against a "public functionary" (as defined in the Bill) alleging that he has committed an offence punishable under Chapter IX of the Indian Penal Code or under the Prevention of Corruption Act, 1947. The expression "public functionary" covered Ministers, Ministers of State, Deputy Ministers and Parliamentary Secretaries of the Union. The Bill was referred to a Joint Committee which recommended withdrawal of the Bill as several of its embers felt that the Bill in its then existing form would not, if enacted, serve the purpose for which it was intended . The Government argued that the Bill did not make any provision for the redress of grievances arising out of any act or omission of the Government or a public functionary or an employee of the Government which did not involve any element of corruption. It was common experience that many grievances of citizens arose because of inefficiency, tardiness, delay, red-tape, outmoded rules and procedures which did not involve any corrupt motive. It was, therefore, necessary, the Government emphasized, to evolve a system or machinery to redress the grievances of citizens, otherwise the Lokpal would not serve the objectives which were envisaged by the ARC. The Government offered to re-examine the entire issue relating to the establishment of Lokpal, its powers and jurisdiction.

The withdrawal of the Bill was opposed vehemently by the Members belonging to the opposition not only on the floor of the Lok Sabha when the report of the Joint Committee was tabled but a strong note of dissent was also appended to the Report. Nine Members of the Committee belonging to opposition parties described the Bill as the most anemic in content and the most restricted in scope. They, however, fett that the withdrawal of the Bill at that stage would render the three years' labor of the Committee as extravagant and futile. They held that the need for the institutions of Lokpal was overdue which should not be shelved on any pretext whatsoever and the amendments suggested by them, if incorporated, would provide the Bill with necessary teeth. They felt that the Committee was fully competent or enlarge the definition of "complaint' so as to cover complaints about abuse of power, gross misconduct, maladministration causing harassment to citizens, etc. Two other reasons advanced by the Government for not proceeding with the Bill, *i.e.,* passing of the Prevention of Corruption act, 3988, and setting up a Directorate of Public Grievances were also found by them to be unconvincing. They contended that any subordinate department cannot be a substitute for the Lokpal.

The members belonging to the opposition further demanded that the office of the Prime Minister should also be brought under the purview of the Lokpal as was done by the Lokpal Bill, 1977. They cited, in this regard example of several States where the Chief Ministers have been put under the jurisdiction of their respective Lokayuktas. The Bill was, however, withdrawn by the leave of the House.

THE LOKPAL BILL, 1989

The Lokpal Bill, 1989 was introduced in the Lok Sabha on 29 December 1989 for constituting the institution of Lokpal to combat the problem of corruption at higher levels. Like the previous two Lokpal Bills, the Lokpal Bill, 1989 did not cover public servant under its ambit. Instead the Bill sought to deal with the problem of corruption at higher political levels.

The Bill sought to equip Lokpal with necessary powers and immunities to create greater assurance of justice and fair play in the mind of all. It proposed that the jurisdiction of Lokpal should cover the complaints of corruption within the meaning of the Prevention of Corruption Act, 1988, against the Council of Ministers including the Prime Minister. It also provided that in case of complaints against a Minister, the competent authority should be the Prime Minister to decide about the action to be taken on the recommendation of the Lokpal, and in the case of the Prime Minister, it should be the House of the People.

The Lokpal Bill, 1989, lapsed with the dissolution of the ninth Lok Sabha.

THE LOKPAL BILL, 1996

After coming to power at the Centre, the United Front Government introduced a fresh Lokpal Bill on 13 September 1996, with a view to providing for the institution of Lokpal to inquire into allegations of corruption against public functionaries and for matters connected therewith. The Bill sought to provide the citizen a convenient and effective forum for determination of complaints and thereby save him from pursuing his remedy through the process of Courts, which is usually expensive or dilatory. The Bill sought to ensure that the Lokpal was able to act independently and discharge his functions without fear or favor.

The Bill too was referred to the Standing Committee on Home Affairs for examination and report. The Standing Committee presented its Report to the Parliament on 9.5.1997 making wide ranging amendments to the various provisions of this Bill. Before the Government could finalize its stand on the various recommendations of the Standing Committee, the Eleventh Lok Sabha was dissolved and consequently the Bill also lapsed,

THE LOKPAL BILL, 1998

The NDA government under Atal Bihari Vajpayee introduced a new 'Lokpal Bill' (on 03.08.1998) and it was also referred to the Department related Parliamentary Standing Committee on Home Affairs for examination and report. The Standing Committee presented its report to the Parliament on 25.02.1999. However, before the

Government could take a view on the various recommendations made by the Parliamentary Standing Committee, the Twelfth Lok Sabha was dissolved on 26.4.1999 and consequently the Bill also lapsed.

THE LOKPAL BILL, 2001

The Lokpal Bill, 2003 (introduced on 14.08.2001) was the eighth attempt by the Government to establish the institution of Lokpal at the federal level during the last six decades. The 2001 Lok Pal Bill, provided' for the establishment of the institution of Lokpal to inquire into allegations of corruption against public functionaries, including the Prime Minister and it proposed to appoint the Lokpal and two members by the President on the recommendation of a committee headed by the Vice-president and comprising the Prime Minister, the Lok Sabha Speaker, the Home Minister, Leader of the House other than the House in which the Prime Minister is a member and Leaders of the Opposition in the Lok Sabha and the Rajya Sabha. The 2001 Bill provided for a fixed tenure of three years for the Chairperson and the members. The Lokpal would inquire into complaints alleging that a public functionary has committed an offence punishable under the Prevention of Corruption Act, 1988. The "public functionary" will cover the Prime Minister, the Ministers, the Ministers of State, the Deputy Ministers and the Members of Parliament. Other constitutional functionaries such as Judges of the Supreme Court, the Election Commissioners have been kept out of the purview of the bill. With a view to ensuring that the Lokpal is able to act independently and discharge its functions without fear or favour, the bill provided that the Chairperson or a Member of the Lokpal shall not be removed from office, except by an order made by the President on the ground of proved misbehaviour or incapacity after an inquiry by a committee consisting of the Chief Justice of India and two other Judges of the Supreme Court next to the Chief Justice in seniority.

SUMMARY OF THE BILLS

It would be seen that the Lok Pal Bill was introduced for the first time in 1968 but it lapsed with the dissolution of the Lok Sabha. Thereafter, it was introduced seven more times in Parliament, the last time in 2001. However, the Bill lapsed each time except in 1985 when it was withdrawn. Out of Eight Bills, Six Bills were referred to the Committees of Parliament - three to Joint Select Committee and three to the Standing Committee on Home Affairs. Though the attempts at the Union/Central level to institute Lokpal were unsuccessful for one reason or other, some State Governments have set up Lokayuktas/Upa-Lokayuktas for redressal of public grievances against administrative acts of that Government in pursuance of the recommendations of ARC. The States like Orissa, Maharashtra, Rajasthan and Bihar were the leading States in setting up the institution of Lokayuktas. At the state level, so far 18 states have created the institution of the Lokayukta through the Lokayukta Acts.

Throughout its arduous journey, the concept of Lokpal has undergone many a change both in its form and content. So much so, the original concept of Lokpal as suggested by the Administrative Reforms Commission (ARC) appears to have undergone a metamorphosis. Even the first Bill which was brought with a view to giving effect to the recommendations of the ARC was different in its scope from the draft Bill proposed by the Commission. The first two Bills (1968 and 1971) had recommended two separate institutions, "Lokpal" and "Lokayukta". Former was meant to look into complaints against Ministers and Secretaries while the latter was to deal with those against all lower level public servants. The Bill brought in 1971, except for some modifications of formal nature, was an exact replica of the 1968 Bill. Both the Bills were named as the Lokpal and Lokayuktas Bill.

The scheme of the Lokpal under the 1977 Bill prepared by the Janata Government was materially different in many important respects from the earlier Bills. Unlike the 1968 and 1971 Bills, the Lokpal Bill, 1977, did not talk about the Lokayukta; it provided instead for the appointment of 'Special Lokpal(s)' for the expeditious disposal of cases. Secondly, it included the Prime Minister also in its ambit whereas the other Bills did not include him. Thirdly, while the earlier Bills covered both "allegations of misconduct" and "grievances", the 1977 Bill excluded the latter from its jurisdiction. It defined the word "misconduct" in wider terms. Fourthly, unlike the earlier Bills, the 1977 Bill embraced Ministers and Members of Parliament but excluded bureaucracy from its purview. Finally, while earlier Bills provided for consulting the Leader of the Opposition in the appointment of Lokpal, the 1977 Bill was silent about it.

In 1985, the Government introduced another Bill which was, again, different in certain respects from the earlier Bills. First, the Prime Minister and members of Parliament were excluded from the purview of this Bill. Secondly, the all-inclusive nature of the definition of "corruption" given in the 1977 Bill, was done away with the scope of complaints was restricted to the relevant provisions of the Prevention of Corruption Act and the Indian Penal Code and thirdly, prosecution on allegations held unproved or false by the Lokpal was barred.

The fifth Bill, introduced on 29 December 1989 in the Lok Sabha, aimed at curbing corruption at the higher political levels, as claimed in its Statement of Objects and Reasons. This Bill made many departures from those brought forward previously in terrain important respects. First, the Prime Minister once again was brought within the purview of the Lokpal. Secondly, the competent authority to whom the Lokpal was to forward his report in the 1989 Bill in relation to Prime Minister was the House of the People and about a public functionary, other than the Prime Minister, was the Prime Minister. In contrast, the Lokpal Bill, 1985, provided that the competent authority to whom the report would be sent by the Lokpal was the Prime Minister. The 1985 Bill empowered the President to appoint as Lokpal " a person who is or has been or is qualified to be a Judge of the Supreme Court", while the 1989 Bill said that the President would appoint persons who are or have been Judges of the Supreme Court as the Chairman and members of the Lokpal. Besides, unlike all the previous Bills, the 1989 Bill proposed to set up a three-Member Lokpal with a Chairman and two Members. Like the Lokpal Bill 1989, the Lokpal Bill 1996 also proposed to set up a three-member Lokpal. However, the Lokpal was to be appointed by the President on the recommendation of the Committee consisting of seven members *viz.,* the Prime Minister who will be the chairman of the committee, Speaker of the Lok Sabha, Minister-in-charge of the Ministry of Home Affairs, Minister-in-charge of the Ministry of Personnel, Public Grievances and Pensions, Leader of the Opposition in the Rajya Sabha and the Lok Sabha and the Deputy Chairman of the Rajya Sabha.

Upon perusal of all eight Government Bills, one finds that there is perceptible shift in the central focus of the legislation from the issue of redressal of public grievances to corruption at high places. This radical departure can be observed from the Lokpal Bill, 1977 and Bills introduced thereafter have no provision for redressal of citizens' grievances and thereby stripped off Lokpal its intrinsic concept. In the first two Bills (Lokpal and Lokayuktas Bill, 1968 and Lokpal and Lokayuktas Bill, 1971) clause 2 contained definition of the terms 'grievance' and 'mal-administrations' which were conspicuously missing in the proposed legislations introduced from 1977 onwards. Rest of the Bills in their clause 2 had inter-alias the definition of the terms 'complaint' or 'corruption' instead of'grievance' or 'mal-administration'. Therefore, it is evident that over the years Parliament's concern appears to have been growing more with matters relating to corruption than with the citizens' grievances. While in the first two Bills (1968 and 1971) the emphasis was on 'complaints' and 'grievances' of mal-administration against public servants, in the latter Bills of 1977, 1985, 1989, 1996, 1998 and 2001 the emphasis had shifted to 'allegations of corruption' against' public functionaries'.

In 2002, the report of the National Commission to Review the Working of the Constitution (headed by Justice M.N. Venkatachiliah) urged that the Constitution should provide for the appointment of the Lok Pal and Lokayuktas in the states but suggested that the Prime Minister should be kept out of the purview of the authority. In 2004, the UPA government's National Common Minimum Programme promised that the Lok Pal Bill would be enacted. The Second Administrative Commission (chaired by Shri Veerappa Moily), formed in 2005, also recommended that the office of the Lok Pal be established without delay.

In January 2011, the government formed a Group of Ministers, chaired by Shri Pranab Mukherjee to suggest measures to tackle corruption, including examination of the proposal of a Lok Pal Bill.

9

Jan Lokpal Bill and Government Bills

Forty-three years and at least eight versions of the Lokpal bill have come but the Parliament still hasn't reached consensus on who and what, exactly, it should cover. All that everyone can agree on is that Lokpal should be responsible for investigating into complaints of corruption against public officials.

The Lokpal bill, first introduced in the Lok Sabha in 1968, failed to be legislated into law as it lapsed after the fourth Lok Sabha session was dissolved. At the time, it had neither members of Parliament nor the prime minister under its purview. The Lokpal bill was later introduced in 1971, 1977, 1985, 1989, 1996, 1998, 2001, 2008 and finally in 2010.

LOKPAL BILL 2010

The Government Lokpal Bill 2010 was proposed to be passed as an ordinance by the Central government.

UPA government has been under constant attack due to exposure of one scam after the other on the issue of corruption. In order to salvage its image, the government proposed to set up an institution of Lokpal to check corruption at high places.

Main Features of the Bill

1. Lokpal will not have any power to either initiate action suo moto in any case or even receive complaints of corruption from general public. The general public will make complaints to the speaker of Lok Sabha or chairperson of Rajya Sabha. Only those complaints forwarded by Speaker of Lok Sabha/Chairperson of Rajya Sabha to Lokpal would be investigated by Lokpal.

2. Lokpal will be an advisory body. Lokpal, after enquiry in any case, will forward its report to the competent authority. The competent authority will have final powers to decide whether to take action on Lokpal's report or not. In the case of cabinet ministers, the competent authority is Prime Minister. In the case of PM and MPs the competent authority is Lok Sabha or Rajya Sabha, as the case may be.

3. Lokpal will have no police powers. Therefore, Lokpal will not have the power to register an FIR. Therefore, all the enquiries conducted by Lokpal will tantamount to "preliminary enquiries".

4. There will be a strong punishment for "frivolous" complaints. If any complaint is found to be false and frivolous, Lokpal will have the power to send the complainant to jail through summary trial but if the complaint were found to be true, the Lokpal will not have the power to send the corrupt politicians to jail!

5. Lokpal will have jurisdiction only on MPs, ministers and PM. It will not have jurisdiction over officers.

6. Lokpal will consist of three members, all of them being retired judges.

7. The selection committee will consist of Vice President, PM, Leaders of both Houses and the leaders of opposition in both houses Law and Home Ministers.

8. Lokpal will not have powers to investigate any case against PM, which deals with foreign affairs, security and defense. This means that corruption in defence deals will be out of any scrutiny whatsoever. It will become impossible to investigate into any Bofors in future. Therefore, the draft Lokpal ordinance is eyewash, a sham. It is sad that despite so much of embarrassment caused to UPA due to so many

scams,UPA is still making a fool of the people in the form of this draft ordinance.

Criticism of the Bill

However the remedy seems to be worse than the disease. Rather than strengthening anti corruption systems, this bill if passed, will end up weakening whatever exists in the name of anti corruption today. The principal objections to government's proposal are as follows:

1. This not only severely restricts the functioning of Lokpal, it also provides a tool in the hands of the ruling party to have only those cases referred to Lokpal which pertain to political opponents (since speaker is always from the ruling party). It will also provide a tool in the hands of the ruling party to protect its own politicians.

2. In the coalition era when the government of the day depends upon the support of its political partners, it will be impossible for the PM to act against any of his cabinet ministers on the basis of Lokpal's report. For instance, if there were such a Lokpal today and if Lokpal made a recommendation to the PM to prosecute A. Raja, obviously the PM will not have the political courage to initiate prosecution against A. Raja. Likewise, if Lokpal made a report against the PM or any MP of the ruling party, will the house ever pass a resolution to prosecute the PM or the ruling party MP? Obviously, they will never do that.

3. The bill is legally unsound. Even if the report of Lokpal is accepted, who will file the charge sheet in the court? Who will initiate prosecution? Who will appoint the prosecution lawyer? The entire bill is silent on that.

9. The bill does not say what will be the role of CBI after this bill. Can CBI and Lokpal investigate the same case or CBI will lose its powers to investigate politicians? If the latter is true, then this bill is meant to completely insulate politicians from any investigations whatsoever which are possible today through CBI.

10. The bill appears to be meant to browbeat, threaten and discourage those fighting against corruption.

11. The officers and politicians do not indulge incorruption

separately. In any case of corruption, there is always an involvement of both of them. So according to government's proposal, every case would need to be investigated by both CVC and Lokpal. So now, in each case, CVC will look into the role of bureaucrats while Lokpal will look into the role of politicians. Obviously the case records will be with one agency and the way government functions it will not share its records with the other agency. It is also possible that in the same case the two agencies arrive at completely opposite conclusions. Therefore it appears to be a sure way of killing any case.

12. There is no reason why the choice should be restricted to judiciary. By creating so many post retirement posts for judges, the government will make the retiring judges vulnerable to government influences just before retirement as is already happening in the case of retiring bureaucrats. The retiring judges, in the hope of getting post retirement employment would do the bidding of the government in their last few years.

13. As regards the selection committee, barring Vice President, all of them are politicians whose corruption Lokpal is supposed to investigate. So there is a direct conflict of interest. Also selection committee is heavily loaded in favour of the ruling party. Effectively ruling party will make the final selections. And obviously ruling party will never appoint strong and effective Lokpal.

The first version of the Lokpal Bill drafted by the Government of India in 2010 was considered ineffective by anti-corruption activists from the civil society. These activists, under the banner of India Against Corruption, came together to draft a citizen's version of the Lokpal Bill later called the Jan Lokpal.

JAN LOKPAL BILL

Justice Santosh Hegde, Lokayukta of Karnataka, and Prashant Bhushan, Supreme Court lawyer in consultation with other Members of Civil Society, have drafted an alternative 'Lokpal Bill' with the aim of replacing the existing, mutually exclusive anti-corruption agencies with a single, autonomous apex body empowered to investigate and prosecute politicians, bureaucrats and judges. The bill proposes institution of the office of Lokpal at the federal level and Lok Akyukta at state level. Jan Lokpal Bill is designed to create an effective anti-corruption and grievance redressal systems at centre and to assure that effective deterrent is created against corruption and to provide effective protection to whistleblowers. This has been done after the government of India has failed to pass the Lokpal Bill for 42 years reflecting the systemic corruption as the members of the legislature don't want their powers to be curbed and their actions made accountable.

The draft bill also aims to bring whistleblower protection, currently in the form of a separate bill, within the ambit of the Lokpal. This 'Jan Lok Pal Bill' proposes a single, autonomous Lokpal combining within it the powers and mandate of the CBI and the CVC and with jurisdiction over politicians, bureaucrats and judges. Besides being able to independently initiate investigation and prosecution without prior permission from any other agency, the body will act as an appellate authority in respect of public grievances linked to bribery. The whistleblowers, currently under the supervision of the CVC, will also come under the protective purview of the Lokpal. The members and the chairperson of the Lokpal, 11 in all, will be selected by a transparent and participatory process and any complaint of wrongdoing against a member will be required by law to be investigated and acted upon within a month through a transparent process. In the event that the charges are upheld, the.loss to the exchequer by the officer's wrongdoing will be recovered.

The Jan Lokpal Bill is supposed to be the answer to India's massive endemic corruption which strikes daily in the form of a new scam or scandal. The government has proven to be woefully inadequate in taking on the corrupt politicians, bureaucrats and businessmen. This corrupt nexus has been repeatedly exposed and its structure exposed through the Nira Radia Tapes. The Indian administration has shamefully failed to take action only promising to do something without doing anything worthwhile. The Indian Judiciary has also castigated the government numerous times for its abject failure in the 2G Telecom Scam, Black Money Scandal etc. However the government instead of strengthening anti-corruption measures has only put obstacles in the way. Its no wonder when the committee meant to look after the Bill comprises of ministers tainted with a number of scams themselves. Anna Hazare has held a fast unto death to put pressure on the government to pass the draft bill but the Minister appear unconcerned. Here is a short summary and guide to the main points of the Jan Lokpal Bill which IMHO deserves the support of the whole Indian civil society.

Main Features of the Bill

1. There shall be an institution known as Lokpal which shall consist of one Chairperson and ten members along with its officers and employees. The Lokpal shall be headed by its Chairperson. The Government will appoint the members of the Lokpal though Chairperson and members of Lokpal shall not be serving or former member of either the Parliament or the Legislature of any State and shall not hold any office or trust of profit

2. There shall be a separate fund by the name of "Lokpal fund" in which penalties/fines imposed by the Lokpal shall be deposited and in which 10% of the loss of Public Money detected/prevented on account of investigations by Lokpal shall also be deposited by the Government.

The administrative expenses of the office of the Lokpal including all salaries, allowances and pensions payable to or in respect of persons serving in that office, shall be charged on the Consolidated Fund of India.

3. A selection committee consisting of the following shall be set up which will have representatives from the government, judiciary and civil society. The members shall have unimpeachable integrity with 4 members from the legal background.

4. These will be the powers of the Lokpal:

(a) Initiate prosecution against public servants as well as those private entities.

(b) Order cancellation or modification of a-license or lease or permission or contract.

(c) Blacklist the concerned firm or company or contractor.

(d) Take necessary action to provide protection to a whistleblower

(e) Suo moto initiate appropriate action under this Act.

(f) Power to Issue Search Warrants.

(g) For the purpose of any such investigation (including the preliminary inquiry) the Lokpal shall have all the powers of a civil court.

(h) Lokpal to be a deemed police officer.

(i) Lokpal may decide to impose a fine on the officials responsible for the non-compliance of its orders.

(j) Assess Number of Special Judges for Corruption in an Area.

(k) Power to issue Letter of Rogatory.

The functioning of the Lokpal will be as follows:

5. Lokpal shall function in benches of three or more members. Chairperson shall be responsible for overall administration and supervision of the institution of Lokpal.

6. For offences mentioned in Chapter 111 of Prevention of Corruption Act, punishment shall not be less than five years which may extend upto life imprisonment.

Provided that if the accused is any officer of the rank of Joint Secretary in the state or above or a Minister, the punishment shall not be less than ten years.

Criticisms of the Bill

1. The bill has been criticised as being naive in its approach to combating corruption. According to Pratap Bhanu Mehta, President of the Center for Policy Research Delhi, the bill "is premised on an institutional imagination that is at best naive; at worst subversive of representative democracy". The very concept of a Lokpal has received criticism from HRD minister Kapil Sibal in that it will lack accountability, be oppressive and undemocratic.

2. The critics feel that the exact judicial powers of Lokpal are rather unclear in comparison with its investigative powers. The bill requires "...members of Lokpal and the officers in investigation wing of Lokpal shall be deemed to be police officers". Although some supporters have denied any judicial powers of Lokpal, the government

and some critics have recognised Lokpal to have quasi-judicial powers.

3. The bill also states that "Lokpal shall have, and exercise the same jurisdiction powers and authority in respect of contempt of itself as a High court has and may exercise, and, for this purpose, the provisions of the Contempt of Courts Act, 1971 (Central Act 70 of 1971) shall have the effect subject to the modification that the references therein to the High Court shall be construed as including a reference to the Lokpal." Review of proceedings and decisions by Lokpal is prevented in the bill by the statement "...no proceedings or decision of the Lokpal shall be liable to be challenged, reviewed, quashed or called in question in any court of ordinary Civil Jurisdiction." As a result, how the trials will be conducted is unclear in the bill, although the bill outlines requiring judges for special courts, presumably to conduct trial that should be completed within one year. The critics hence express concern that, without judicial review, Lokpal could potentially become an extra-constitutional body with investigative and judicial powers whose decisions cannot be reviewed in regular courts.

4. The matter of whether the Indian Prime Minister and higher judiciary should or should not be prosecutable by the Lokpal remains as one of the major issues of dispute. Anna's own nominee for co-chairing the joint panel Justice Verma, the former Chief Justice of the Supreme Court, has expressed his constitutional objections for including the Prime Minister and higher judiciary under Lokpal According to him, "this would foul with the basic structure of the constitution".

5. Magsaysay Award winner Aruna Roy who has said "Vesting jurisdiction over the length and breadth of the government machinery in one institution will concentrate too much power in the institution, while the volume of work will make it difficult to carry out its tasks". She and her colleagues at the National Campaign for People's Right to Information (NCPRI) have proposed an alternative mechanism consisting of five institutions.

6. Noted author and social activist Arundhati Roy was highly critical of Lokpal, stating "you could say that the Maoists and the Jan

Lokpal Bill have one thing in common—they both seek the overthrow of the Indian State", and While his means may be Gandhian, Anna Hazare's demands are certainly not. Contrary to Gandhiji's ideas about the decentralisation of power, the Jan Lokpal Bill is a draconian, anti-corruption law, in which a panel of carefully chosen people will administer a giant bureaucracy.

FIGHT FOR EFFECTIVE LOKPAL

Public awareness drives and protest marches were carried out to campaign for the bill. However, public support for the Jan Lokpal Bill draft started gathering steam after Anna Hazare, a noted Gandhian announced that he would hold an indefinite fast from 5 April 2011 for the passing of the Jan Lokpal Bill.

To dissuade Hazare from going on an indefinite hunger strike, the Prime Minister's Office directed the ministries of personnel and law to examine how the views of society activists can be included in the Lokpal Bill. On 5 April, the National Advisory Council rejected the Lokpal bill drafted by the government. Union Human Resource Development Minister Kapil Sibal then met social activists Swami Agnivesh and Arvind Kejriwal on 7 April to find ways to bridge differences over the bill. However, no consensus could be reached on 7 April owing to several differences of opinion between the social activists and the Government.

On 7 April 2011 Anna Hazare called for a *Jail Bharo Andolan* from 13 April to protest against Government's rejection of their demands. Anna Hazare also claimed that his group has received six crore (60 million) text messages of support and that he had further backing from a large number of Internet activists. The outpouring of support was largely free of political overtones; political parties were specifically discouraged from participating in the movement. The fast ended on 9 April, after 98 hours, when the Government accepted most demands due to public pressure.

Joint Drafting Committee

The drafting committee was officially formed on 8 April 2011. It consisted of the following ten members, including five from the government and five drawn from the civil society.

Member	Qualifications and status
Pranab Mukheriee	Finance Minister. *Co-Chairman*
Shanti Bhushan	Former Minister of Law and Justice, *Co-Chairman*
P. Chidambaram	Minister of Home Affairs
Veerappa Moily	Minister of Corporate Affairs
Kapil Sibal	Minister for human resource & devlopement
Salman Khursid	Minister of Law
Anna Hazare	Social Activist
Prashant Bhushan	Lawyer
N. Santosh Hegde	Former Lokayukta (Karnataka) and Supreme Court Justice
Arvind Kejriwal	RTI Activist.

The Government's handling of the formation of the draft committee, involving the civil society in preparation of the draft Lokpal bill, was criticised by various political parties including BJP, BJD, TDP, AIADMK, CPI-M, RJD, JD(U) and Samajwadi Party.

Anna Hazare set at 15 August deadline for the passing of the Lokpal Bill in the Parliament, failing which he would start atiunger strike from 16 August. The fast also led to the Government of India agreeing to setting up a Joint Drafting Committee, which would complete its work by 30 June.

The committee failed to agree on the terms of a compromise bill and the government promised to introduce both the bills in Parliament but it actually introduced its own version in the parliament in August 2011.

GOVERNMENT LOKPAL BILL 2011

The Lokpal Bill, 2011, was introduced in the Lok Sabha on August 4, 2011 by Shri V. Narayanaswamy, Union Minister of State, Personnel, Public Grievances & Pensions. The Bill was referred to the Standing Committee on Personnel, Public Grievances, Law and Justice. The report of the Committee was expected within three months. But it was submitted to the Rajya Sabha on......

Main Features of the Bill

• The Bill provides for establishment of the Lokpal for inquiring into complaints of corruption against certain public servants.

• The members of the Lokpal shall be appointed by the President on the basis of the recommendations of the Selection Committee.

• The Selection Committee shall comprise of the Prime Minister, Speaker of the Lok Sabha, Leaders of the Opposition in both houses, a Union Cabinet Minister nominated by the Prime Minister, one sitting judge of the Supreme Court, and one sitting Chief Justice of the High Courts both nominated by the Chief Justice of India, an eminent jurist nominated by the central government and a person of eminence in public life with knowledge of public administration, policy making, anti-corruption policy, vigilance and finance.

• The Lokpal shall consist of one chairperson and up to eight other members. The Chairperson shall be a present or former judge of the Supreme Court. Fifty per cent of the other members shall be judicial members (judges of the Supreme Court and Chief Justices of the High Court). A non-judicial member is required to have 25 years experience in anti-corruption policy, public administration, vigilance and finance.

• A Lokpal can enquire into offences under the Prevention of Corruption Act, 1988 committed by;

(a) the PM once he has demitted the office,

(b) current and former Union Ministers,

(c) current and former MPs,

(d) group A officers and above,

(e) persons of equivalent ranks in public sector undertakings and other government bodies,

(f) officers of organizations having an annual income above a specified amount receiving funds from the government or the public.

• The Lokpal shall be constituted of two wings: the Investigation Wing and the Prosecution Wing.

• The central government is required to constitute Special Courts to hear cases referred to it by the Lokpal under this Bill. The Lokpal shall recommend the number of such courts.

• A complaint against the specified officials may be made to the Lokpal for actions committed within seven years of the date of complaint. The Lokpal can ask the Investigation Wing to conduct preliminary investigation of any offence alleged to be committed under the PCA. The Lokpal shall provide the accused with copies of the complaint and secure him a hearing. In case *aprima facie* case is made out it may then conduct a public inquiry.

• If the inquiry concludes that an offence was committed, the Lokpal may recommend disciplinary action to the competent authority. It can also file a case before the Special Court through its Prosecution Wing. The competent authority shall within 30 days of receipt of the recommendation initiate disciplinary proceedings and inform the Lokpal of the action proposed or taken.

• The Bill removes the requirement of sanction for initiating investigation and prosecution.

• The preliminary investigation or inquiry has to be completed within a maximum period of three months. The following inquiry by the Lokpal is to be completed within a maximum period of one year. The trial before the Special Court is to be completed within a maximum timeframe of two years.

• The penalty for filing false and frivolous complaints is imprisonment for a minimum of two years to a maximum of five years and a fine of Rs. 25,000 upto Rs. 2 lakh.

• The Lokpal may be removed by an order of the President on the basis of the report of the Supreme Court on a reference by the President. A reference to the Supreme Court may be made by *(a)* the President, *(b)* the President on the basis of a petition signed by 100 Members of the Parliament and *(c)* the President if he is satisfied on the basis of a petition by a citizen.

THE BILL INTRODUCED IN LOK SABHA

The much-debated Lokpal Bill was introduced in the Lok Sabha on

August 4, 2011 amid objections from the BJP and its NDA partners over exclusion of the Prime Minister from the purview of the proposed legislation.

Just before introduction of the Bill, Speaker Meira Kumar gave permission to Leader of the Opposition Sushma Swaraj to express her views as a special case under Rule 72. Swaraj said when the Prime Minister does not enjoy immunity from prosecution under the criminal law and Prevention of Corruption Act, why is he being kept out of the ambit of the Lokpal.

She maintained that as per the Constitution, everybody was equal and there is no immunity from IPC, CrPC or the Prevention of Corruption Act.

"It is for the first time that under Clause 2 of the Lokpal Bill, all Union ministers are included except the Prime Minister. I don't understand why. How can anybody occupying any position be a holy cow? Why is the Prime Minister being kept out of its purview?" Swaraj posed.

She stated that then Prime Minister Atal Bihari Vajpayee had put the debate to rest during the NDA rule by saying that if he is not under its purview it will have no meaning. She was referring to the Lokpal Bill proposed by the NDA government which was ultimately not introduced in the Parliament.

"As chairperson of the then Standing Committee on Home, Pranab Mukherjee had accepted that the Prime Minister should be within the purview of the Lokpal. The Prime Minister (Manmohan Singh) has himself said he wants to be within its ambit. Why is the Cabinet not paying heed to his views?" she asked.

Swaraj said the BJP had several objections to the proposed Bill but would, for the moment, confine herself to only the exclusion of the PM. "We will object to introduction of the Lokpal Bill," she said.

Minister of State in PMO V. Narayanasamy, who introduced the Bill, said the Prime Minister had offered to be within the purview of the Lokpal but the Cabinet did not agree. "Ultimately this bill will go to the Standing Committee. Your objection cannot be sustained," he told the Opposition benches.

Mukherjee told the House that Swaraj's contention that he gave his nod to the NDA's Lokpal Bill is true.

"On February 16, 2002 as Chairperson of the Standing Committee on Home, I had placed that Bill on the table of the House. NDA had two full years after that. Why did they not bring the Bill," Mukherjee said.

When Narayanasamy introduced the Bill, the BJP and NDA members objected to it.

Earlier, in his reply to the motion on price rise, Mukherjee said the government has taken views of the civil society but "there was no question of diluting the authority of Parliament in making the legislation." He said that in the case of Lokpal Bill, normal legislative process will be followed.

AFTERMATH

The presentation of the Bill gave birth to a strong reaction against this it from Team Anna, other political parties and public in general.

Team Anna Burns Copies of Bill

Meanwhile, Anna Hazare and his team members burnt copies of the "anti-poor, anti-Dalit" law with the Gandhian asserting that he would go ahead with his fast beginning August 16 till a strong law is brought in.

Hazare and his supporters burnt copies of the Bill in Maharashtra's Ralegaon Siddhi while his supporters Arvind Kejriwal, Prashant Bhushan and Kiran Bedi led the protest in Uttar Pradesh's Kaushambi area in Ghaziabad.

Amidst sloganeering against the government, Hazare said it was the last chance to eradicate corruption from the country and that the protest should be organised all over to ensure that a strong Lokpal Bill is brought in.

"This is a bad and weak Bill which is introduced in Parliament. We need a new and strong Bill. I trusted them when they said they will bring a strong law and ended my fast in April. They cheated me,' he said.

He claimed the government would have fallen if he had continued his fast then for another three days. The government does not fear fast or protests but they fear the voice of people, he said, adding that people should acquire this power to overthrow governments.

Alleging that it was an insult to Parliament and people, Kejriwal described the Bill as "anti-poor and anti- Dalit[11] which does not help the poor in fighting corruption. Countering suggestions that the Bill can be further debated in the Standing Committee, Kejriwal said the panel cannot alter or change the provisions as it can only give suggestions.

"Parliament has been given a fait accompli. This is insult of the people and the Parliament," he added.

Bhushan and Bed! said what they were demanding was an independent agency which could probe corruption.

Government's Reaction Against Burning of the Bill

Slamming Team Anna for burning copies of the Lokpal Bill, government on Wednesday, August 17, 2011 said actions of the civil society members was an insult to Parliament and posed a danger to deniocracy.

"Today, this Bill is a property of Parliament and to burn this Bill publicly is an insult to Parliament. If our democracy continues to function in this fashion, then I feel it poses a danger to democracy," HRD Minister Kapil Sibal said.

He said if Anna Hazare and his colleagues wanted to put across their views on the Bill, they should approach the Parliamentary Standing Committee.

"The Bill is Parliament's property, there are Parliamentary procedures. If Mr. Hazare wants to put his point of view he is entitled to do so by moving to the Standing Committee and saying that the provisions of my Bill be taken into account," Sibal said.

Asked whether any action would be taken against Hazare and his colleagues for burning copies of the Lokpal Bill, he said this issue would be decided by someone else.

"Whether to take action or not will be decided by someone else. We have said this is against democracy and against the Constitution and it is an insult to Parliament," he said.

Law Minister Salman Khurshid asked team Anna to come clean on whether they have faith in Parliamentary democracy.

"You should ask them (Team Anna) about this as the Lokpal Bill is now the property of Parliament. They claim that they have full faith in Parliament," he said.

"Those who express faith in Parliament are themselves burning the copy of the Bill. You should ask them what kind of belief is this," he said.

Government Charges BJP With Double-speak

Government on Thursday, August 18, 2011 dubbed as "political opportunism and double speak" the BJP's objection to exclusion of the office of Prime Minister from the ambit of Lokpal, pointing out that the Lokayukta Act in states ruled by the party did not cover the chief ministers.

"The statement of the Leader of the Opposition in the Lok Sabha is a classic example of political opportunism. If the BJP is so concerned about Lokpal, the states they are in power would have had a Lokpal," Telecom Minister Kapil Sibal said.

Home Minister P Chidambaram said Leader of the Opposition Sushma Swaraj made the statement objecting to provisions of the Lokpal Bill to make a political point.

On Swaraj's argument that Pranab Mukherjee, as chairman of the Parliamentary Standing Committee, had included Prime Minister in the ambit of the Lokpal, Chidambaram said the NDA, which was in power for two years after the report was submitted, should have got the Bill passed in Parliament.

"Mukherjee had submitted the report of the Standing Committee on February 16, 2002. The NDA had two years and two months to get the Bill passed in Parliament. They did not," he said.

Sibal questioned why there was no Lokayukta in Gujarat from

2003 to 2011. He said the then Gujarat Chief Minister Keshubhai Patel had appointed a Lokayukta in the state in 1998 and the term of the ombudsman ended in 2003.

"From 2003 to 2011, there has been no Lokayukta in Gujarat. If the Leader of the Opposition is so concerned that the people's grievances be addressed, the BJP should have asked the Chief Minister to appoint a Lokayukta," Sibal said.

No Compromise on Basic Structure of the Constitutions

Amid protests over tabling of the government version of the Lokpal Bill in Parliament, Congress on Thursday said there could be no compromise on the basic structure of the Constitution and wondered why Anna and his friends do not understand a fact even a school child can!

"There is a Constitutional structure in the country and this structure has not fallen from above but has been put in place by people of the country through their elected representatives," Congress spokesperson Manish Tewari said.

"In India's democratic structure, everybody can give an advice but it is only people's representatives, who can introduce a bill in Parliament and enact a law. This basic fact is understood by even *a* school child. Either Anna and his friends do not understand or do not want to understand. The question is why they do not want to understand it," he said.

When told that team Anna has burnt copies of the Lokpal Bill of the government, Tewari said the country has seen people and parties burning even the Indian Constitution and then finally agreeing to work within its framework.

"Akali leader Prakash Singh Badal had burnt Indian Constitution in Rakabaganj. Now he is Punjab's Chief Minister.

"Similar unfortunate incidents had also happened in Assam. Even those, who burnt the Constitution of India realized the futility of such exercises and finally reconciled to work within the parameters of the same. Why the Anna team is refusing to recognize this reality," Tewari asked.

SUPPORT FOR JAN LOKPAL BILL

Surveys

India Against Corruption conducted a survey on the draft Lokpal Bill presented by the Indian Government in parliament. It showed that 85% of the particpiants were opposed to the government's bill. The team especially cited the results from the Chandni Chowk constituency, the constituency of Telecom Minister Kapil Sibal, who is a vehement voice for the government's version of the bill.

According to a nationwide survey conducted by CNN-IBN & CNBC-TV18 and published in early August, only a shade over a third of respondents have heard of Lokpal. 34% of all respondents said they have heard of the ombudsman and only 24% knew what it actually Prashant Bhushan, one of Anna Hazare's associates and a drafter of the Jan Lokpal Bill, has demanded a nation-wide referendum on the Jan Lokpal Bill to gauge the mood of the nation.

Legislator support

Post the massive support to Anna Hazare's movement, several of the MPs across party lines have come out in support to the Jan Lokpal Bill. Most notable names are Congress MPs from Maharashtra Priya Dutt and Datta Meghe. Datta Meghe also demanded that his party spokesperson Manish Tiwari should apologise to Anna Hazare for his uncharitable comments.

This support started coming as over 150 MPs and Ministers from different states were forced to remain confined to their houses as Anna supporters protested outside their houses. Protests were also seen outside the residence of Sheila Dixit CM of Delhi, Kapil Sibal, Pranab Mukheriee amongst others.

BJP MP Varun Gandhi is introducing Jan Lokpal Bill as a private member's bill in the parliament.

Social media

As per the reports, Anna Hazare's fast was successful in mobilising the support of thousands in the virtual world of social media. On Independence Day, Anna had over 5,00,000 mentions through status updates and comments across top social networking sites, including

Facebook and Twitter in the country. Two days later, the number had shot up to 9 million. On YouTube, over 40,000 people watched the video shot by Kiran Bed! inside Tihar Jail in which Anna has addressed his supporters. Facebook has 542 fan pages by Anna's name.

Online surveys

• According to the survey conducted by STAR News and Nielsen, 87% of the 8,900 respondents of the survey supported the Jan Lokpal Bill. The survey—conducted in 28 cities across the country, including all four metres—mainly deals with three important points: public's knowledge about the Lokpal Bill; awareness about Anna's campaign; and the perceived problems with the Jan Lokpal Bill.

• Over a million people joined the Times of India online anti-graft campaign, in one of the biggest ever voting exercises in the virtual world. The news analysis points that citizens want to make their voices heard and have found the platform offered by the campaign' a viable one to do so.

Parliamentary Support and PM's Assurance

On 27 August 2011, a special and all exclusive session of Parliament was conducted and a resolution was unanimously passed after deliberations in both the houses of Indian Parliament by sense of the house.

The resolution, in principle, agreed on the following subjects and forwarded the Bill to related standing committee for structure and finalise a report.

1. A citizen charter on the bill
2. An appropriate mechanism to subject lower bureaucracy to lokpal
3. The establishment of Lokayuktas (ombudsmen at state level) in states

Anna Hazare, civil rights activists along with protestors at site of the fast welcomed this development on being informed, terming it as a battle "half won" while ending the protest.

CONCLUSION

The Jan Lokpal is a stringent law against corruption that envisages hard punishment for corruption doers while protecting whistle-blowers. This Bill will be opposed tooth and nail by the executive and the legislature as it meant to punish wrong doers amongst them mainly. Note these two arms of the government are endangering Indian democracy with their flagrant violations of the law and massive corruption which has undermined the confidence of the Indian state amongst its citizens. We don't see much hope that this bill will get passed but it deserves the support of every responsible citizen.

10

A Critique of The Two Lokpal Bills

We have already dealt with the details of the Government and the Civil Society's Lokpal Bill in our earlier Chapter. In the fitness of things we are not repeating it. Here we shall go into the merits and demerits of the Jan Lokpal Bill and the Lokpal Bill presented in our Parliament.

Below is a quick summary of the major differences between the drafts of Jan Lokpal Bill proposed by the anti-corruption movement led by Anna Hazare, and the government's version of the Lokpal Bill.

The summary will also make one quickly realize that

• The Government's Lokpal version gives less powers to Lokpal, but at the same time gives it more immunity from any action against the institution itself.

• The Jan Lokpal version gives more powers to Lokpal but less immunity if its own actions are found unaccountable.

ACCOUNTABILITY OF THE LOKPAL

Jan Lokpal

Any Citizen can go and complaint to Supreme Court to remove a Lokpal if the Lokpal is not found accountable in his/her action.

Government Lokpal

Only Government has the power to remove a Lokpal.

So according to government's draft, if government appoints a corrupt person as the Lokpal, then people have no way of seeking the removal of such a Lokpal. But in case of Jan Lokpal, I or you can go to the court and demand that the Lokpal be removed if we are able to provide justification for that removal.

CORRUPTION ALLEGATIONS AGAINST LOKPAL MEMBERS

Jan Lokpal

Complaints of corruption against Lokpal members will be heard by an independent authority.

Government Lokpal

Lokpal itself will hear complaints of corruption against its members!

Which is more accountable? Lokpal hearing complaints against its own members? Or an independent authority acting on these complaints?

PROBE CORRUPTION ALLEGATIONS AGAINST MPS

Jan Lokpal

Lokpal will have the power to probe into allegations of corruption by Members in Parliament like MPs taking bribe to vote as in the case of 'Cash for Votes' scandal.

Government Lokpal

Lokpal will not have any right to probe into allegations of corruption by MPs in the Parliament!

COMPLAINTS AGAINST PUBLIC SERVANTS

Jan Lokpal

Lokpal can act on complaints against any, government officer.

Government Lokpal

Lokpal can act on complaints against only "Group A" level government officers.

There are around 80 lakh state government officials and 40 lakh central government officials in the country. Of which only 65,000 are Group A level officers. So according to government's draft Lokpal or no Lokpal it makes no difference to over 99.995% of the government officers. The fact is that it is these officers below Group A level who actually cause problems to the common man. If common man cannot complain to Lokpal about problems like corruption in the Public Distribution System, corruption in his local RTO, corruption in rural employment scemes etc, then what is the use of such a Lokpal?

ACTION AGAINST GOVERNMENT OFFICERS

Jan Lokpal

If a government officer delays the work of a citizen beyond scheduled time frame then he will be deemed corrupt by Lokpal and penalized for that.

Government Lokpal

There is no penalization of government officers who do not do their duties.

The Government had earlier agreed to the proposal in Jan Lokpal on this issue. But this again is missing from the government's Lokpal draft.

CORRUPTION ALLEGATION AGAINST JUDICIARY

Jan Lokpal

Lokpal will have the authority to investigate allegations of corruption against judges.

Government Lokpal

Lokpal will not have the authority to investigate allegations of corruption against judges.

Government wants judiciary to be investigated based on a separate Judicial Accountability Bill (JAB). Anna's team is fine with that provided the the flaws in giving permission for investigations against judges are removed. In the JAB, permission to investigate allegations against a judge will be given by a three member judge team, two of whom will be judges from the same court, and even the third judge will be a retired chief justice of the same court!

CORRUPTION ALLEGATIONS AGAINST PRIME MINISTER

Jan Lokpal

Lokpal will have the authority to investigate allegations of corruption against the Prime Minister.

Government Lokpal

Lokpal will not have the authority to investigate allegations of corruption against the Prime Minister.

Government wants CBI to investigate any allegations of corruption against the Prime Minister. But the fact is that the CBI comes directly under the Prime Minister, So, unlike Lokpal, CBI is not an independent organization in this scenario.

ANTI CORRUPTION BRANCH OF CBI

Jan Lokpal

The Anti Corruption Branch of CBI will be merged with Lokpal to give it more independence.

Government Lokpal

The Anti Corruption Branch of CBI will continue to remain with CBI, which means direct government control over it, because CBI is controlled by government.

Government has now even removed CBI from RTI! So nobody knows what is going on within CBI.

DISMISSAL OF CORRUPT PUBLIC SERVANT

Jan Lokpal

Lokpal will have the power to dismiss a corrupt public servant from job.

Government Lokpal

Lokpal will have no power to dismiss a corrupt public servant. The concerned minister will decide whether to dismiss a corrupt public servant or not.

What if the minister is also a beneficiary of this corruption? Will he in such a case dismiss the corrupt public servant?

PROTECTION AGAINST FALSE COMPLAINTS

Jan Lokpal

Lokpal will impose fine to those who make false complaints or ill motivated complaints. Lokpal will decide whether a complaint is false or not.

Government Lokpal

Lokpal will send those who make false complaints to jail for a period of two to five years! The accused can also go to court against the complainant, and in this case, the legal expenses of the accused will be borne by the government, where as the complainant has to pay for the legal expenses from his own pocket.

This one clause in the government's draft is enough to ensure that nobody will dare to go and complain to Lokpal. If the corrupt who are also generally rich, are able to mute all evidences against them, then the person who complained will have to go to jail, do trips to courts, bear his legal expenses and what not.

While the minimum imprisonment for a false complaint is two years in the government's draft, the minimum imprisonment for those found guilty of corruption is only 6 months! The government's draft clearly targets the complainant than the accused.

SELECTION OF THE LOKPAL MEMBERS

Jan Lokpal

An independent search committee which consists of retired constitutional authorities (like judges, eminent IAS officers etc) will prepare the first list of eligible candidates. Then an independent selection committee comprising of two politicians, four judges and two retired constitutional authorities will do the selection. So there is no scope for government interference in the selection process of Lokpal members here.

Government Lokpal

A Panel of 10 members, 6 of whom are politicians, 5 of whom are from the ruling alliance/ruling party will select the Lokpal members. Even the search committee which searches for eligible lokpal members will be selected by the above mentioned selection committee. 5 members from ruling alliance and totally 6 politicians in a group of 10 will ensure that government will be able to appoint its own people to Lokpal!

The Government had earlier agreed to the selection committee proposed by Jan Lokpal. But this proposal is not there in the government's draft now! Instead we have what is described above in Government's version.

PERMISSION TO TAP PHONES OF THOSE ALLEGED OF CORRUPTION

Jan Lokpal

Lokpal will give permission to tap phones of people suspected to be involved in corruption.

Government Lokpal

Home Secretary will give permission to tap phones of people suspected to be involved in corruption!

What if the permission sought is against those who control the Home Secretariat? Is it fair to expect that the Home Secretary will give permission in such cases? What if Home Secretary himself is under the Lokpal scanner?

CORRUPTION BY BUSINESS ENTITIES

Jan Lokpal

If Lokpal finds that business entities are involved in corruption, then Lokpal will have the right to ban such companies from taking part in future government contracts and to black list them.

Government Lokpal

No power to Lokpal to black list any business entity found guilty of corruption.

FAST TRACK HEARING OF CORRUPTION CASES

Jan Lokpal

Lokpal can setup special benches in High Courts to speed up hearing of corruption cases.

Government Lokpal

Lokpal has no power to setup special benches like this. Which means slow hearing of corruption cases.

Justice delayed is justice denied.

PROTECTION TO COMPLAINANTS, WHISTLE BLOWERS

Jan Lokpal

Lokpal will provide adequate protection and security to complainants and whistle blowers.

Government Lokpal

No mention about any protection to those who complaint about cases of corruption.

ESTABLISHMENT OF LOKAYUKTAS

Jan Lokpal

There will also be Lokayuktas established at each state level with powers similar to Lokpal. These Lokayuktas will probe into corruption at a state government level against ministers, MLAs and state government officials.

Government Lokpal

No establishment of any Lokayuktas through Lokpal Bill

If people have any issue of corruption at a state government level, then according to the Government's Lokpal bill - forget it.

METHOD OF ENQUIRY

Jan Lokpal

Enquiry will be done just like in any other criminal case. After preliminary enquiry FIR will be registered, and after that investigations will be done, and then the trial will be held in the courts.

Government Lokpal

After preliminary enquiry, before filing FIR all evidence collected so far should be presented to the accused, and he should be asked why an FIR should not be filed against him based on that evidence! After investigations, before filing a case against the accused, again all evidences collected so far should be presented to the accused, and he should be asked again as to why a case should not be filed against him!

Now what on earth is this business of showing the evidence to the accused and asking him? Evidences are shown to the courts not to the accused. Does the government want to give an opportunity to the accused to wipe out all evidences? This would also reveal to the accused as to who complained against him, endangering the lives of the complainants and whistle blowers.

ISSUES OF CONFLICT

Jan Lokpal Bill	*The Government Lokpal Bill*
1. Prime Minister can be investigated with permission of seven member Lokpal bench.	1. PM can be investigated by Lokpal after she/he vacates office.
2. Judiciary Can be investigated, though high level members may be investigated only with permission of a seven member Lokpal bench.	2. Judiciary is exempt and will be covered by a separate "judicial accountability bill".
3. MPs can be investigated with permission of seven member Lokpal bench.	3. Can be investigated, but their conduct within Parliament, such as voting, cannot be investigated.
4. All public servants would be included.	4. Only senior officers (Group A) will be covered.
5. Anti corruption wing of Central Bureau of Investigation (CBI) will be merged into the Lokpal.	5. The CBI will remain a separate agency.
6. Removal of Lokpal members and Chair: Any person can bring a complaint to the Supreme Court, who can then recommend removal of any member to the President.	6. Any "aggricved party" can raise a complaint to the President, who will refer the matter to the CJI.
7. Removal of Lokpal staff and officers Complaints against Lokpal staff will be handled by independent boards set-up in each state, composed of retired bureaucrats, judges, and civil society members.	7. Lokpal will conduct inquiries into its own behaviour.
8. Lokayukta: Lokakyukta and other local/state anti-corruption agency would remain in place.	8. All state anti-corruption agencies would be closed and responsibilities taken over by centralized Lokpal.

9. Whistleblower protection: Whistleblowers are protected by law.	9. No protection granted to whistleblowers.
10. Punishment for corruption: Lokpal can either directly impose penalties, or refer the matter to the courts. Penalties can include removal from office, imprisonment, and recovery of assets from those who benefited from the corruption.	10. Lokpal can only refer matters to the courts, not take any direct punitive actions. Penalties remain equivalent to those in current law.
11. Investigatory powers: Lokpal can obtain wiretaps, issue rogatory letters, and recruit investigating officers. Cannot issue contempt orders.	11. Lokpal can issue contempt orders, and has the ability to punish those in contempt. No authority to obtain wiretaps, issue rogatory letters, or recruit investigating officers.
12. False, frivolous and vexatious complaints: Lokpal can issue fines for frivolous complaints (including frivolous complaints against Lokpal itself), with a maximum penalty of 1 lakh.	12. Court system will handle matters of frivolous complaints. Courts can issue fines of Rs. 25,000 to 2 1akh.
13. NGOs: NGOs not within the scope due to their role in exposing corruption.	13. NGOs are within the scope and can be investigated.

CONCLUSION

In summary, looking at the government's version of the Lokpal bill, doesn't it look like that the government wants to simply pass a bill for the namesake of it and wash its hands off from the entire issue? After 45 years of waiting, the government simply wants to create an illusion that it has passed an anti-corruption law. Do we really need another dummy institution at the tax payer's expense?

Just look at the government's draft once again and you will wonder, who actually comes under the jurisdiction of Lokpal according to the government's lokpal draft. No Prime Minister, no MPs, no judiciary, no state level Lokayuktas, no government officers other than "Group A" officers....

Rajinder Sachar, former chief justice of the Delhi high court had said that the Lokpal Bill proposed by the Government of India is shamefully toothless and meant just to give a false reassurance to the people that the government is serious in its fight against corruption.

Arvind Kejriwal had rightly called the government's draft—A Jokepal Bill. It not only has loopholes in it, it is full of potholes. Now you decide whether we want the government's version of Lokpal or the Team Anna's Jan Lokpal to become a law in this country.

11

Contentious Issues in Lokpal Bill

The Opposition spoke in unanimous voice as they urged the government to include the Prime Minister and lower bureaucracy under the ambit of lokpal and asked for more autonomy for CBI. Leaders of BJP, CPI(M), CPI, JD(U), Akali Dal, TDP and BJD participated in the public debate on Lokpal Bill at Jantar Mantar where Hazare was sitting on a one-day dharna protesting against Parliamentary Standing Committee report on Lokpal Bill. No representative of Congress was present. Most of the leaders concurred with Hazare's demands for inclusion of Prime Minister, lower bureaucracy and CBI's anti-corruption wing under Lokpal but they did not favour bringing higher judiciary under the ombudsman and argued for a separate mechanism to check corruption in it.

Accusing the Parliamentary Standing Committee of not honouring Parliament's resolution on Lokpal, senior BJP leader Arun Jaitley said there were no two opinions about having a strong Lokpal Bill. "We demand everybody who is in the government should come under the purview of lokpal. We oppose the Prime Minister's non-inclusion in the Lokpal Bill," he said.

"We are of the view that the lokpal should have a search

committee of its own and people with impeccable integrity should be its members and they should select. It is very important to take the CBI out of the government's hands. It is being misused by the Government. The CBI director should not come under the government," he said.

However, he said, as far as judiciary is concerned, it should not come under lokpal. "There should be a National Judicial Commission," Jaitley said.

"The very basic principles of having a strong lokpal should not be tampered with. Including lower bureaucracy and citizens' charter in lokpal was the sense of the house. We can differ on mechanism but not on the basic principle," he said.

Bardhan said it was unfair to keep the Prime Minister out of the lokpal ambit. "The Prime Minister is also a minister of many ministries and he is responsible for taking decisions. If the Prime Minister is not brought under the lokpal, then who will take care of the corruption in the ministries. The investigation has to be done," he said.

Alleging that CBI is being misused by the government which if it "wants to wean away a chief minister, uses CBI", he said, "This cannot keep on happening and anti- corruption wing of the CBI should be made answerable to lokpal."

"Corruption in judiciary is a very sad state of affairs and we are of the opinion that judiciary should not be brought under lokpal. The Constitution has given a special place for judiciary and that should not be disturbed. We demand that a Judicial Accountability Bill has to be brought and passed," he said.

CPI-M leader Brinda Karat said fighting graft in the corporate world was equally important because the private sector was "looting" national wealth and enjoyed freedom. "We should also focus on corruption in the corporate world. We should not forget the loot by the corporate world," Karat said.

She said licences and contracts given to private companies on the basis of corruption should be cancelled and the Lokpal should have a power to do so. "The 2G (telecom) licenses and Land mining contracts in Karnataka have not been cancelled," Karat pointed out.

She said the recommendations of the parliamentary standing committee on the Lokpal bill were weak and "are equivalent to not having the lokpal at all". "It is a weak Lokpal Bill. You are after NGOs but why leave the corporate world out," she asked.

She said the CPI-M was for the inclusion of the Prime Minister under the purview of the lokpal. Contending that the Prime Minister should be brought under lokpal, she also batted for MPs to be under the ombudsman's ambit. "Many of my colleagues here may disagree with me but we are of the opinion that MPs should also be under lokpal," she said.

"Why Group-C employees are not brought under Lokpal, we want to know. Parties keep talking about national security being affected if the Prime Minister is brought under lokpal. There are a lot of defence deals where corruption has taken place," she said.

Strongly backing Anna, JD(U) chief Sharad Yadav said his party will ensure that "not a comma or a full stop will be changed" of the 'Sense of the House' summed up by finance minister Pranab Mukherjee in August after the debate on lokpal in Parliament.

Terming "political use" of CBI as "very dangerous", he pitched for an autonomous and independent CBI, He pressed for extending the winter session of Parliament or call a special session to pass lokpal bill.

The sticky points discussed above can be summed up in the chart given below :

POINTS OF CONTENTION

The positions stakeholders may take on lokpal after the parliamentary committee finalises report on Wednesday.

	Government	*Team Anna*	*Parliamentary committee*
PM under lokpal	After the PM demits office	PM should be brought under lokpal	Let Parliament decide on it
CBI under lokpal	Present set-up should not be disturbed	CBI should be free from govt. control, political interference	CBI should not report to govt. or lokpal

Lower bureaucracy under lokpal	Group A govt. officials should be covered	Entire bureaucracy should be brought under lokpal	Lower bureaucracy should also be under lokayuktas
Accountability of judiciary	There is a separate judicial accountability bill	Corruption in judiciary should be handled by lokpal	Agrees with the govt. but wants a national judicial commission
Citizen's charter	A separate bill put out for consultations	It should be part of the lokpal bill	Mechanism to tackle grievances needed

PRIME MINISTER UNDER LOKPAL

The basic question is whether the Prime Minister should be brought under the ambit of Lokpal and be subject to its scrutiny?

Reasons for PM's Inclusion

Prime Minister ought to be brought under the purview of the Lokpal, for several reasons:

• It is important to observe that in most of the Lokpal bills, including the 2010 government draft (except the 1985 version) the Prime Minister has been within the ambit of the Lokpal.

• If MPs and Ministers are brought under the purview of the Lokpal, there is no compelling reason to keep the PM out of it.

• In our country, the PM is also minister for Atomic Energy, Space and a host of other key departments. Would immunity from the Lokpal extend to protect the PM from his actions as minister in these departments? If that is so, it is but a small matter for a malafide and adroit PM to take over sensitive and corruption prone ministries and escape examination by the Lokpal!

• In some of the other countries also the Heads of the Government have been indicted on being found guilty. In Japan, Prime Minister Kakuei Tanaka (July 1972 to December 1974) was found guilty of bribery and sentenced. In Israel, Prime Minister Ehud Olmert was indicted in corruption scandals in August 2009. In Italy, Prime Minister Silvio Berlusconi enacted, through a pliant legislature, a law by which he shielded himself from prosecution. The Italian Constitutional Court recently invalidated crucial parts of that law, which may result in his trial being revived.

• Under the Indian Constitution there is no provision to give immunity to the Prime Minister, Chief Ministers or Ministers. Under Article 361, immunity from criminal proceedings is conferred on the President and the Governor (formerly the Rajpramukh) only "during his term of office." Constitutional heads who do not directly exercise executive powers are given immunity as heads of state. But active politicians such as Prime Minister, who cannot remain aloof from the hurly-burly of electoral and party politics, ethical or unethical, honest or corrupt, are not given any immunity. They are subject to penal laws and criminal liability.

Justice A.K. Ganguly, a sitting Supreme Court judge, supports inclusion of the Prime Minister's Office within the ambit of Lokpal Bill tabled in Parliament. He says, "As a student of law, I see no substance in the debate that the Prime Minister should be outside the (Lokpal) Bill. A public office of such importance cannot shy away from public scrutiny, Pointing out that Prime Minister Manmohan Singh had himself expressed his willingness to bring the PMO under the Lokpal's scanner, Justice Ganguly said, "more efforts to keep the PM out will add to the suspicion among people."

• Even the basic structure of the Constitution clearly denies immunity to the Prime Minister.

Reasons for PM's Exclusion

While the Janlokpal insists that the Prime Minister ought to be covered, the stand of the Government so far has been that the Prime Minister ought to be excluded. The Government relies on several points of view, most of which have been articulated well in two high level reports—Justice Venkatachalaiah Commission and Veerappa Moily Commission.

• Both commissions felt that the office of the Prime Minister should be kept out of the purview of the Lokpal. Their reasoning was similar; both felt that the Prime Minister is totally accountable to

Parliament. Therefore, there is no need for separately bringing this office under the purview of the Lokpal.

• Both felt that the Prime Minister has very important executive responsibilities and in the interests of stability and continuity, should not be vulnerable to investigations commenced by the Lokpal.

• Venkatachalaiah summed up the stand of his commission, by saying that the relationship between the Prime Minister and Parliament is essentially a political one and one must resist the temptation to make legal rules to govern a political relationship.

• J.S. Verma, the former Chief Justice of the Supreme Court believes, "The simple answer is, if the Prime Minister is covered under ordinary law (the Prevention of Corruption Act), you don't need him covered under Lokpal."

• It is argued that if the Prime Minister is within its ambit, the Lokpal could be used by foreign powers to destabilize the government.

• It is argued that bringing the Prime Minister under the Lokpal's scrutiny would mean a parallel government being put in place.

• According to Pranab Mukerjee, "In this time of frenzy, anybody can write to the Lokpal and make a complaint. If the Lokpal prima facie sees merit in it...the Prime Minister will have to resign. Prime Minister is the keystone in our system and if he goes, then the entire government goes. This way you will institutionalize permanent instability."

Conclusion

In the light of discussion above it seems reasonable that the Prime Minister ought to be brought under Lokpal with a few conditions like national security and public order.

CBI UNDER LOKPAL

The views of the Standing Committee, CBI and Anna's team about bringing CBI under Lokpal are given below:

Standing Committee on CBI

The ground reality is that CBI, the premier anti-corruption investigative agency, is under the Department of Personnel and Training, which is controlled by the Prime Minister's Office (PMO). The career prospects of CBI officers and other personnel are dependent on the political executive, and all officers are subject to transfer except the Director. Thus, the investigative arm is controlled by the 'political suspects' themselves.

Besides it, the Single Directive, a secret administrative directive that was invalidated by the Supreme Court in the Jain Hawala Case in 1997 *(Vineet Narain* v. *Union of India)* has been legislatively revived. Consequently, under Section 6A of the Delhi Special Police Establishment Act, the CB1 is disabled from starting an inquiry or investigation against Joint Secretary or higher level bureaucrats without the Central government's prior approval. Therefore, the Prevention of Corruption Act is a non-starter against Ministers and high-level bureaucrats who may act in concert. Therefore, it is imperative that the CBI's anti-corruption wing be brought under the Lokpal and not under the PMO. This alone would meet the test of an independent and fearless investigative agency as enunciated by Justice Krishna Iyer.

The standing committee on Lokpal appears to have skipped the crucial issue of reducing government's say in appointing the CBI chief, something which has been exploited by regimes of the day to put a loyalist at the top of the country's premier investigating agency who can act as per the wishes of political masters.

Several strong representations were made to Parliament's standing committee on how to make the appointment of CBI director a non-partisan exercise, but the final report has fought shy of addressing the flaw in the country's anti-corruption regime. Not surprisingly, the 286-page report tabled in both Houses of Parliament is marked by strong reservations from BJP, BJD, SP, Ram Vilas Paswan's Lok Janshakti Party and Rajya Sabha member Ram Jethmalani.

Building upon the notes of dissent by seven of its members who were on the standing committee, BJP leader Arun Jaitley attacked the report for not seeking to loosen government's control over who gets to head CBI. "The appointment of CBI director should be made by a statutory collegium which should include the prime minister and the leader of opposition in Lok Sabha," Jaitley said.

The Lokpal bill is silent on changing the current scheme where the appointment of CBI chief is the privilege of the ruling dispensation; something which is seen as a power perk and has been used to reward pliant officials who have reciprocated by toeing the government line in sensitive cases.

CBI has trimmed its investigations to suit the regimes in a whole range of cases stretching from Bofors and Fodder Scam to disproportionate assets case against UP heavyweights Mulayam Singh Yadav and Mayawati, the view supported by the Supreme Court in a judgement on Mayawati's appeal on July 6, 2012.

The practice, which has stripped CBI of the credibility and respect that it once enjoyed ..and ought to have in order to function effectively, has disappointed even agency officials who feel let down. Reliable sources in the agency feel that selection of its head by a process which is objective, transparent and professional will be the best way to restore functional autonomy to government's chief anti-corruption arm.

Deposing before the standing committee, the current CBI chief said the collegium may include the PM, the leader of opposition and the head of constitutional bodies, including but not necessarily Lokpal.

With the Abhishek Singhvi-led panel steering clear of the issue, one of its prominent members Ram Jethmalani has submitted a scathing note of dissent. "The report proposes that the CBI be the main anti-corruption agency and that it be left to the administrative control of the Lokpal in the same manner in which the CVC currently has that supervisory jurisdiction. This would be totally unsatisfactory and would leave the CBI under the control of the government through its power of postings, transfer, promotions and disciplinary control. Using these powers, the governments of the day have been misusing CBI for their own political purposes despite the supervisory jurisdiction of the CVC," the eminent lawyer said.

He further said, "I am not exaggerating but I believe that I have tremendous experience of the criminal side of justice system and the way CBI has become a shameless instrument of the evil political design of the ruling government. My experience convinces me that CBI has got to be rescued from this infamy and the nation saved from the grave consequence of its misdeeds. The present system of supervision has become hopelessly inadequate and a much more effective one has to be imposed upon it."

The view was supported by BJP members on the panel. In their notes of dissent, they stressed that CBI as an institution had been "seriously compromised" because it was under the influence of the government. Endorsing the view of the CBI chief, they argued that the agency could only be made independent if the appointment of its chief was done not through the government but a collegium including PM, leader of opposition and chairperson of the Lokpal, The party also suggested that the department of personnel should only be an administrative interface of the central government.

CBI Chiefs View Point

The chiefs of the Central Bureau of Investigation and Central Vigilance Commission on Wednesday knocked on Prime Minister Manmohan Singh's door to plead that the clamour for a strong lokpal does not come^at the cost of the two institutions. The meetings came hours before the Prime Minister convened a meeting of political leaders to decide the final shape of the lokpal bill.

Central vigilance commissioner Pradeep Kumar and CBI director A.P. Singh after appearing before the Parliamentary Standing Committee felt that MPs having blamed the CBI for its inability to deal effectively with corruption, the two central anti-graft agencies could find their roles diminished once the lokpal law is passed. Singh had hinted there ,-were impediments. "The ideal situation would be that the CBI is made autonomous, independent and effective," AP Singh told the panel.

With the panel's report currently under the government's consideration, the CBI is concerned that the anti-corruption watchdog might end up becoming a super body that—and not the CBi director—will have the last word on initiating and closing investigations.

With staff strength of about 285, the CVC at present has jurisdiction over Group A officers only. The CVC, however, is worried that it might end up playing a vigilance watchdog for more than 70 lakh Group C central government employees—a job that could practically kill the commission .

Apart from asking for the elimination of partisan considerations in the appointment of the director, CBI officials also feel that increasing his tenure beyond two years could help the agency function in an unbiased manner. "It would be a strong safeguard against interference and foster more accountability," they said.

CBI's argues that the Director CBI should be made an ex-officio Lokpal member entrusted with control and investigations undertaken by Lokpal. Lokpal will exercise general supervision and control in anti corrupt ion cases through the Director CBI. In respect of corruption cases after investigation CBI will file a final report in the competent courts. Investigation and prosecution will remain in the hands of the CBI. Thus there will be no vivisection of CBI and no need for a separate investigation wing under the Lokpal. Creation of two investigating wings, namely one under CBI and one under Lokpal with the same mandate is likely to lead to overlapping of work, conflict of jurisdictions, and demand for more resources. Functional autonomy of the CBI as well as its credibility has been eroded over the years and effective steps are necessary to restore its full functional autonomy.

Anna's View Point

However, the hard fact that cannot be wished away is that no powerful and effective anticorruption body can function without an investigation wing. Otherwise, it will be a toothless tiger. The proposal to induct the Director CBI after a very careful selection as ex-officio Lokpal is likely to encounter opposition from legal and judicial fraternity and other members of the Lokpal some of whom are likely to be Justices and Chief Justices of Supreme Court and High Courts. So instead of toying with the idea of bringing the anticorruption wing of the CBI under the Lokpal a better and more pragmatic alternative will be to entrust CBI with the investigation of corruption cases referred to it by the Lokpal. This measure will ensure avoidance of the vivisection of the CBI and consequent weakening of its core competence, and at the same time insulate it from extraneous pressures, at least in respect of anticorruption cases referred to it by the Lokpal. Lokpal will closely monitor the cases investigated by the CBI. This will enable the Lokpal to utilize all the resources of the CBI towards anticorruption work and not the resources of the anti-corruption wing only. CBI's anti-corruption unit will be ineffective without the support of the other units of the CBI. For effectively combating corruption CBI and the Lokpal should act in tandem and the similar model can be replicated in respect of state Lok Ayuktas.

LOWER BUREAUCRACY UNDER LOKPAL

Team Anna thinks the corruption that common people everyday encounter would remain as it is, if the proposal for exclusion of lower bureaucracy from the ambit of the Lokpal is accepted.

"They don't indulge in corruption separately," Team Anna said in a statement, rejecting government's proposal of covering lower bureaucracy under Central Vigilance Commission and NCPRI model of police first investigating the case and not Lokpal.

If the lower bureaucracy is not brought under Lokpal, the corruption by Central and State Government employees of Group C will not be checked. Almost Rs 30,000 crore worth of ration meant for poor people is annually siphoned off by Group C employees. Thousands of crores of leakage takes place in NREGA works at the level of Group C employees. Panchayat secretary and officials are also Group C employees, huge corruption is committed by them too.

The Government argue that bringing the entire bureaucracy under Lokpal would make it unwieldy. India needs 28,500 anti-corruption staff in CVC to check corruption of 57 lakh employees. CVC has a staff of 285 employees. Does the government plan to provide 28,500 additional workforce to them? Then won't CVC become unwieldy? Morecver, CVC does not have police powers and cannot register a criminal case.

Opposing NCPRI model of first approaching police and then Lokpal, Team Anna said this may lead to delay in every investigation as it would ultimately go to Lokpal only as a complaint or an appeal.

Team Anna claims their proposal is for a decentralized system where Lokpal would set up a police station in every district and Lokayukta in every block.

The government, is opposed to the inclusion of lower bureaucracy directly within Lokpal's jurisdiction as demanded by Anna Hazare. Instead, it would like these employees to be under the Central Vigilance Commission over which the Lokpal can have supervisory role.

CITIZEN'S CHARTER

The concept of Citizen's Charter was first articulated and implemented in the United Kingdom by the Conservative Government of John Major in 1991 as a national programme with an aim to continuously improve the quality of public services for people of the country. Later on, several countries implemented similar programmes, including Australia (Service Charter in 1997), Belgium (Public Service Users' Charter 1992), Jamaica (Citizen's Charter 1994), Malaysia (Client Charter 1993), etc.

In India, at a conference of Chief Ministers held on May 24, 1997 in New Delhi, which was presided over by then Prime Minister Inder Kumar Gujral, it was decided the Central and state governments would formulate Citizen's Charter, starting with those sectors that have a large public interface. The idea was to improve service delivery, make officials more responsive towards public and introduce transparency in the functioning of government departments.

The Department of Administrative Reforms and Public Grievances (DARPG) was given the task of coordinating, formulating and operationalising Citizen's Charters. The guidelines for formulating the Charters as well as a list of dos and don'ts were communicated to all state governments. Nodal officers were appointed in states and the Union Ministries to formulate and implement their Citizen's Charters. DARPG sent a format of the charter to the states, but they were free to make changes according to their requirement. The states were also asked to set up a grievance redressal system. However, few seem to have bothered to accept these recommendations.

The Citizen's Charter, which Anna Hazare's India Against Corruption wants to be introduced, is nothing new. This exists in all Central ministries, states and several autonomous institutions for more than a decade. What is new is IAC's demand for penal provisions and empowering the Lokpal to take action in cases of violation of the charter. At present, most charters do not even include a complaint redressal system which was part of the original scheme of things.

According to the information available at goicharters.nic.in, which is an official website of GOI, at least 729 Citizen's Charters had been formulated by 24 states and Union Territories by January this year. The maximum of these were in Gujarat (293), followed by Haryana (89), Delhi (75), Goa and Rajasthan (63) each, Tamil Nadu (57), and Uttar Pradesh (41). Besides, 131 Citizen's Charters existed in various union ministries, public sector banks, boards, institutes and hospitals. The charters are available on the websites of the institutions.

The charters, although not uniform, usually include details of the functioning of the issuing department or organization, the names, addresses, salary of officers and responsibilities assigned to them; the time duration allocated for response on various applications, charges for various procedures. Basically, these are informative documents.

IAC wants the government offices should display the charter on a board which should give details of services available there and officers who deal with these. The board should specify in how many days a person will get each service. If an official fails to provide the service in specified time, the applicant could appeal to the Lokpal.

In the event of delay due to corruption, the official or his department will have to submit proof to deny corruption charges. If the official or the department fails, the Lokpal or his representative should have powers to dismiss the employee and impose penalty which should be deducted from the salary of official and paid to the applicant.

The government has introduced in Parliament a bill that is intended to prove its commitment to fighting corruption among government officers. The Right of Citizens for Time Bound Delivery of Goods and Services and Redressal of their Grievances Bill, 2011 clearly outlines the responsibilities of government departments towards citizens -and how someone who is denied the service due to them can take action. Anti-corruption crusader Anna Hazare had asked for this issue to be included in the Lokpal Bill. Though the government has not done that, it has tried to meet Team Anna halfway by suggesting that if a citizen does not get the help he or she is entitled to, the Lokpal or the Lokayukta can be appealed to as a last resort.

These are the highlights of the Bill:

Every public authority or government department has to publish a citizen's charter that clearly lists all the services that department has to render along with timelines. The bill also provides for a "grievance redressal mechanism for non-compliance of citizen's charter."

The Bill sets up a central public grievances redressal commission - and an equivalent in every state.

There is a designated authority i.e. an officer who is not from the department against .which the complaint has been filed. This officer is selected by the government and has to be above the rank of the Grievance Redressal Officer.

Citizen's charter has to clearly explain the complaint redressal system for that office—like which officer in that department the complaint should be registered with every government department or public authority shall create an "information and facilitation centre"—that could include a customer helpline or helpdesk to deliver services and to handle complaints.

Every public authority will appoint or designate Grievance Redress Officers whose contact information will be clearly shared with the public. The Grievance Redress Officer shall provide the public with all necessary assistance in filing complaints. Within two days of the complaint being registered, the citizen who has filed a complaint will receive—by SMS or mail—a unique complaint number and a time frame within which the complaint will be handled. That time frame cannot exceed 30 days from when the complaint was received.

The Grievance Redress Officer has to ensure that the person who made the complaint is informed in writing with an Action Taken Report of how his or her complaint was handled. If this does not happen, the citizen can appeal to a Designated Authority. This officer can summon others and ask them to testify under oath.

The Designated Authority has to ensure the appeal is acted upon within 30 days. He or she can fine the officer concerned and compensate the citizen, if appropriate.

If a citizen is not happy with the Designated Authority's response or decision, he or she can take their complaint to the State Public Grievance Redressal Commission (assuming that the complaint is against a government department that is under the jurisdiction of the state government). Each state shall set up this body. It will have a Chief Commissioner and a maximum of ten other commissioners. They will be appointed by a committee consisting of the Chief Minister, the Leader of the Opposition in that state, and a sitting judge of the High Court. The commissioners will have a term of five years.

For citizens who are unhappy with a service provided to them from a government office that is under the jurisdiction of the central government, they can finally appeal to the Central Public Grievance Redress Commission. This body with have a Chief Commissioner and a maximum often other commissioners who will be appointed by the President after they are chosen by a committee of the PM, the Leader of the Opposition and a sitting judge of the Supreme Court.

If citizens are unhappy with the decision of the Central or State Commissions, they can appeal to the Lokayukta or Lokpal.

JUDICIAL ACCOUNTABILITY

Team Anna might consider dropping the contentious demand to bring the judiciary in the anti-corruption ombudsman's jurisdiction if the government delivers on a strong judicial accountability bill. The inclusion of higher judiciary has been opposed by both the government and main opposition party BJP on the ground that it would affect the independence of the judiciary.

WHO STANDS WHERE

	PM under lokpal	*CBI under lokpal*	*Lower bureaucracy under lokpal*	*Single Bill for lokpal, lokayuktas*	*Citizen's charter as part of lokpal bill*
BJP (Sushma Swaraj)	Yes, except in matters of national security and public order.	It should be autonomous with separate probe and prosecution wings.	Yes, Group C staff should be under lokpal, but an appropriate mechanism required.	Yes.	With govt's separate bill, solution now is for an authority to hear complaints under lokpal.
JD(U) (Sharad Yadav)	No. this can create serious problems.	We support BJP stand.	Yes.	No Federal structure of constitution should not be disturbed.	Yes, It should be under lokpal.
CPI-M (Sitaram Yechury)	Yes, exceptions can eb worked out.	It should be given autonomy. It can report to lokpal on corruption cases.	Yes.	Quiet on the issue.	Since cabinet has cleared the bill, it should go ahead with a separate bill.
BSP (Satish Mishra)	Yes, with certain safeguards.	Yes, it should be under lokpal.	Yes.	Such a bill should not disturb federal structure.	No objection to putting it under lokpal.
SP (Mohan Singh)	Yes, with safeguards.	Yes, it should be under lokpal.	Yes.	No.	Keep it under lokpal.

WHO STANDS WHERE

The chart given below gives in brief the views of different political parties on the contentious issues discussed above.

CONCLUSION

In the light of arguments on various contentious issues and the party positions on various issues it seems that there is a consensus on most of the issues. But the ruling alliance is adament on PM's non-inclusion under Lokpal jurisdiction and not allowing autonomy to CBI. The bill is likely to hang in balance in the absence of compromizing posture by the Government.

12

Parliamentary Drama

At the Congress Parliamentary Party (CPP) meeting on Dec. 21,2011, Sonia Gandhi was emphatic and assertive in listing out the action taken by the government to combat corruption. And her remarks to journalists after emerging out of the CPP meeting that "she will fight for Lokpal and women reservation bills" triggered an aggressive posturing by Congress leaders against the Team Anna.

Sonia Gandhi attacked the Opposition for its "obstructionist tactics" and also critisized Anna Hazare and his team—for spreading "deliberate and malicious misinformation" against the government.

The government was set to introduce the lokpal bill in the Lok Sabha on Thursday, December 22, 2011 with a combative UPA chairperson Sonia Gandhi coming out strongly in support of the government on this issue. What is more, the government was also likely to move another bill to give the watch-dog a constitutional status.

The draft was sealed late on Wednesday, December 21, 2011 evening after the government removed minorities from the list of categories that will get 50% representation in the lokpal panel, as the Constitution did not allow reservation on the basis of religion.

The bill, to be taken up for discussion and passing on December 27, 28 and 29, was tabled for the second time this year and the 10th time in 43 years. Proposing the creation of both the lokpal in the Centre and lokayuktas in states, it will replace the one that was tabled on August 4, 2011.

DRAMATIC INTRODUCTION OF THE BILL

10.55 am - RJD Chief Lalu Prasad Yadav enters with a copy of the Bill, goes to the Congress Chief Sonia Gandhi and points out to deletion of minorities from the Lokpal panel.

11.00 am - SP, BSP and JD(U) members join Lalu as the House assembles. Sonia requests them to allow introduction of the Food Security Bill.

11.20 am - As House takes up a Constitution Amendment Bill on cooperatives, Lalu again raises the issue with Sonia, who refers him to Pranab Mukherjee.

12.10pm - Lok Sabha adjourns till 2.00 pm, soon after Lalu, Hyderabad MP Assaduddin Owaisi, Congress members Sandeep Dixit and Raj Babbar and AIUDF leader Badruddin Ajmal meet PM and demand inclusion of minorities in Lokpal panel. JD(U) Chief Sharad Yadav also meets PM, who assures that their concerns will be addressed.

1.00 pm - Congress core group meets. Besides group members, ministers Kapil Sibbal, Salman Khurshid and V. Narayansamy also attend meet.

1.58 pm - Core group meeting ends with decision that minorities will be brought in Lokpal panel.

2.00 pm Lok Sabha meets again and adjourned amid rucus.

3.30 pm - A corrigendum incorporating the provision is circulated and the bill is introduced, followed by an hour long discussion.

FEATURES OF THE BILL

The following are the salient features of the proposed anti-graft Lokpal bill introduced by the government in the Lok Sabha:

Lokpal and its role

The bill proposes to establish autonomous and independent

institutions called Lokpal at the central level and and Lokayukta for states. These shall have powers of superintendence and direction for holding a preliminary inquiry, causing an investigation to be made and prosecution of offences in respect of complaints under any law for the prevention of corruption.

Structure

The Lokpal will consist of a chairperson and a maximum of eight members of which fifty percent shall be judicial members.

Fifty per cent of members shall be from amongst Scheduled Caste (SC), Scheduled Tribe (ST) and Other Backward Classes (OBC), minorities and women.

It has an inquiry wing for conducting the preliminary inquiry and a separate independent prosecution wing.

Officers of the Lokpal will include the secretary, director of prosecution, director of inquiry and other officers.

Process of selection

The selection of chairperson and members of Lokpal shall be through a selection committee consisting of prime minister, Lok Sabha speaker, Lok Sabha leader of opposition, chief justice of India or a sitting Supreme Court judge nominated by chief justice.

Eminent jurist to be nominated by the president of India.

A search committee to assist selection committee in the process of selection. Fifty per cent of members of search committee shall be from amongst SC, ST, OBCs, minorities and women.

Jurisdiction

Prime minister has been brought under the purview of the Lokpal with specific exclusions, Lokpal can not hold any inquiry against the prime minister if allegations relate to international relations, external and internal security of the country, public order, atomic energy and space.

Any decision of Lokpal to initiate preliminary inquiry or investigation against prime minister shall be taken only by the full bench with a 3/4th majority. Such proceedings shall be held in camera.

Its jurisdiction to include all categories of public servants including Group 'A', 'B', 'C' and 'D' officers and employees of government.

On complaints referred by Lokpal, the Central Vigilance Commission (CVC) will send its report in respect of Group 'A' and 'B' officers back to Lokpal for further decision. With respect to Group 'C' and 'D' employees, the CVC will proceed further in exercise of its own powers under the CVC act subject to reporting and review by Lokpal.

All entities receiving donations from foreign sources in the context of the Foreign Contribution Regulation Act (FCRA) in excess of Rs.10 lakh per year are brought under the jurisdiction of the Lokpal.

Lokpal will not be able to initiate suo moto inquiries.

OTHER SIGNIFICANT FEATURES OF THE BILL:

No prior sanction shall be required for launching prosecution in cases enquired by Lokpal or initiated on the direction and with the approval of Lokpal.

Provisions for confiscation of property acquired by corrupt means, even while prosecution is pending.

Lokpal to be final appellate authority on all decisions by public authorities relating to provision of public services and redressal of grievances containing findings of corruption.

Lokpal to have power of superintendence and direction over any investigation agency including Central Bureau of Investigation (CBI) for cases referred to them.

The bill also lays down clear time lines. For the preliminary enquiry, it is three months extendable by three months and for investigations it is six months extendable by six months. The trial will have a one year period extendable by one year.

DEBATE IN LOK SABHA

The Lokpal Bill was passed in the Lok Sabha by voice vote late on Tuesday night, December 28, 2011 even as the Left parties, the BJD and the AIADMK walked out.

Leading the attack, Leader of the Opposition Sushma Swaraj said the Bill should be sent back to the Parliamentary Standing Committee for further discussion to make it "effective and strong." "Accept our amendments or withdraw the Bill... Send it back to the Standing Committee for further discussion," she said.

The UPA allies, the Trinamool Congress and the DMK and supporting parties such as the RJD and the SP maintained that the provisions to create the Lokayuktas through a central legislation would impinge on the powers of the States and said it should not be rushed through under Team Anna's pressure.

Rejecting the Opposition's charge that the UPA government showed "undue haste" in bringing in the Lokpal and Lokayuktas Bill, 2011, Leader of the House and Union Finance Minister Pranab Mukherjee said in the Lok Sabha that the Bill was a "collective draft," based on a number of suggestions received from political parties, civil rights activists and others.

Defending the Bill introduced in the House last Thursday, he said it also reflected the August 27 "sense of the House" resolution that called for bringing a citizen's charter, introducing a single piece of legislation for establishing the Lokpal and the Lokayuktas and bringing the lower bureaucracy under the Lokpal.

He said the government had been debating the draft of the Bill for the past six months even as the issue was being debated outside Parliament by social activists.

Touching upon the consultation process the government had initiated, Mr. Mukherjee said the process of dialogue with political parties was initiated at the all-party meeting. "A large number of suggestions were received from different parties and groups. The Bill was not produced from the hat of a magician. It is high time that we took action against corruption."

Mr. Mukherjee said the government had written to 25 Chief Ministers and leaders of all political parties, urging them to give their suggestions. As for Bharatiya Janata Party president Nitin Gadkari's communication, Mr. Gadkari's response was that they are "decision-makers and not suggestion-givers."

He rubbished the charge that those appointed to high offices by the executive shed their independence. Citing the example of the Chief Election Commissioner and the Comptroller and Auditor-General (CAG), Mr. Mukherjee said these functionaries were working independently. "We have an independent judiciary. We have to respect institutions in a parliamentary democracy," he said, warning that parliamentary democracy had collapsed in several countries where such institutions came under attack.

Rejecting the charge that the Bill was an attack on federalism, Mr. Mukherjee said the "sense of the House" resolution had called for bringing in a single piece of legislation for establishing the Lokpal and the Lokayuktas.

Earlier, the Bill was described by the Opposition and other parties in the Lok Sabha as being "weak, deficient and inadequate" even as Prime Minister Manmohan Singh said it contained a "judicious blend of functional autonomy and accountability of the Central Bureau of Investigation."

Although the UPA has passed its version of the Bill itself, it has, however, failed to pass the Bill for making the Lokpal a Constitutional body, like the Election Commission. This is because this needed a Constitutional amendment, which itself requires a majority of two-thirds of those present and voting, and a simple majority of the overall strength of the House. The UPA failed to muster the required numbers on both parameters. Thus, a proposal that would actually have made the Lokpal a more independent body was not carried through.

The government made several significant concessions to the Opposition over the final form of the Lokpal Bill that was passed on December 27, 2011, a day of high-pitched though cogent debate in the Lok Sabha,. It withdrew some of the requirements for presenting reports on enquiries against MPs to the Lokpal. It agreed to remove the Armed Forces from the jurisdiction of the Lokpal.

It also countered the BJP's argument that including Lokayuktas in the Bill would violate the Constitution since this was a state matter and not a central one by including a clause specifying that the State Governments would continue to have the final say on whether to implement the Lokayukta. However, it is believed to be this very issue over which the proposal to make the Lokpal a Constitutional Body may have fallen through.

HOW THE BILL WAS PASSED

The Lokpal and Lokayukta Bill, 2011 was passed by the Lok Sabha on Tuesday even as the Left Front, Samajwadi Party and the Bahujan Samaj Party staged a walk out. The Bill was passed by a voice vote after several amendments to the Bill. However, the Bill to give Constitutional status to the Lokpal, which required two-third majority in the House, was defeated.

While Leader of the Lok Sabha and Finance Minister Pranab Mukherjee said that the defeat of the Bill giving Lokpal a constitutional status was a "sad day for democracy; Prime Minister Manmohan Singh said that "such things happen".

Before the Lokpal Bill as put to vote the Government decided to drop the provision that enabled the setting up of Lokayuktas by the states, Section 24, the provision to keep armed forces and coast guard personnel under its ambit. The Government also amended the requirement of three-fourth of members of Lokpal to approve inquiry against the Prime Minister was changed to two-third.

The provision in the Lokpal Bill enabling the setting up of Lokayuktas by the states had been a contentious issue with the Opposition as well as several allies of the Congress opposing it.

Section 24 had given the right to Speaker of the Lok Sabha and Chairman of the Rajya Sabha to take action against MPs even if the trial by the Lokpal was on. The exemption time of former MPs was also increased from five to seven years after vociferous protests by the members.

Abstentions

The Bharatiya Janata Party (BJP) abstained from voting on the amendment moved by Basudeb Acharya on bringing corporate houses and the act of the Prime Minister signing commercial agreements under the Lokpal.

Just before the voting started the Samajwadi Party and the BSP MPs walked out of the Lok Sabha.

"We could not have gone with the BJP, so we walked out," said Samajwadi Party chief Mulayam Singh Yadav.

Since our amendments were not accepted, we walked out," said BSP MP Dara Singh Chauhan.

A number of amendments moved by Opposition to bring the media and NGOs receiving donations were also defeated.

Prime Minister's Intervention

During the animated over 10-hour debate, Prime Minister Manmohan Singh asked parties to "rise above partisan politics" to demonstrate to the people of the country that "this House means business" in its effort to combat corruption.

He said a "holistic" approach was needed to deal with the "cancer" of corruption but rejected demands for bringing the Central Bureau of Investigation (CBI) under the purview of Lokpal as he warned that no entity should be created inconsistent with the Constitutional framework.

Capping the 10-hour animated debate during which several parties, including BJP, Biju Janata Dal (BJD), Janata Dal (United), Rashtriya Janata Dal (RJD), Samajwadi Party, Telugu Desam Party (TDP) and Left Front said the Bill was weak and wanted it withdrawn, Finance Minister Pranab Mukherjee rejected the contention that the legislation had been brought in "haste" or under pressure.

Allaying fears of several parties, including UPA constituents Trinamool and Dravida Munnettra Kazhagam (DMK), that the provision for setting up Lokayuktas was an "attack" on federal structure, he said the government had made amendments stating that notification would not be issue without the consent of state governments.

The amendment, along with some others, was decided during an emergency meeting the Prime Minister held with Congress President Sonia Gandhi and other senior leaders ahead of the voting in view of opposition by allies.

This is the ninth Lokpal Bill introduced in government in a series that started as early as 1968 and ended in 2001. Seven of them lapsed with the dissolution of the Lok Sabha while one was withdrawn.

"There are some very special moments in the life of a nation. This is one such moment. The nation awaits with bated breath how the collective wisdom of this House will be reflected in the vote at the end of the debate on the Lokpal and Lokayuktas Bill, 2011," Singh said.

Noting that the broad provisions of this Bill have been vigorously debated both in the public domain and by political parties, he underlined that the task of legislation was "very serious business and must eventually be performed by all of us who have been constitutionally assigned this duty."

In an apparent message to Hazare who has been pressing his demands with regard to Lokpal, Singh said, "others can persuade and have their voices heard. But the decision must rest with us."

He warned that "no entity should be created inconsistent with our constitutional framework and charged with onerous executive responsibilities without any accountability... Let us not create something that will destroy all that we cherish all in the name of combating corruption. Let us remember that the road to hell is paved with good intentions."

He said, "today we are given to believe that a Government that is directly elected by the people and accountable to it cannot be trusted but a body that will not derive its legitimacy from the people directly or be accountable to it could be trusted to wield its immense powers with honor and trust."

Poor Floor Management by Congress Party

At least 15 Congress members and close to a dozen belonging to UPA allies were not present at the time of voting, contributing to the defeat of the idea first proposed by Rahul Gandhi- who had termed it a "game-changer"-in August. The government needed an aye vote from 288 out of the 432 members present in the House. It could manage only 249, though there were 275 UFA members present in the Lok Sabha in the morning. The defeat led BJP leader Yashwant

Sinha to demand that the government quit as it had lost moral authority. "Say bye, not aye," he quipped.

The government was able to get the Lokpal bill itself through thanks to its accommodative stance and the surprise decision of the BSP, SP and RJD not to participate in voting: something which brought down the effective strength of the House and eased the task of the government's managers to rustle up numbers.

Although the absence of 26 UPA MPs was an important factor for the defeat, the government accused the opposition of seeking to weaken the fight against corruption. "We have the majority but we don't have the two-thirds majority", said Mukherjee, putting the onus of the Bill's defeat on the opposition.

After a wait of 43 years and an intense 11 hour-debate that lasted almost till the stroke of the midnight hour, the Lokpal and Lokayukta Bill was passed by the Lok Sabha by a voice vote after the government agreed to 10 amendments. It also secured the passage of the Whistleblowers Bill. But a legislation designed to confer constitutional status on the anti-corruption watchdog fell through, as the government failed to get two-thirds support for it-prompting finance minister Pranab Mukherjee to lament, "a sad day for India, a sad day for democracy".

Congress Party's Attack on Opposition

The Constitution (116th Amendment) Bill, 2011 was crafted to give effect to Rahul Gandhi's proposal that the proposed ombudsman should have constitutional status. The Congress general secretary's suggestion had led Parliament's standing committee to recommend it although the issue was not on Team Anna's "wish list".

Other Congress members also lost no time in raising the chorus of accusations against the opposition for denying the Lokpal constitutional status. The opposition hit back by saying that the UPA was trying to cover its own failure. "It seems certain sections in government were not happy with the proposal and they sabotaged it. Now they are trying to score propaganda points against the opposition", said CPM leader Sitaram Yechury.

BJP's Yashwant Sinha also accused the government of deliberately losing the vote in order to pin the blame on the opposition, particularly the BJP. The failure of the Constitutional Amendment Bill means that Rajya Sabha will on Wednesday debate only the Lokpal Bill and the Whistleblowers Bill. The Lokpal Bill faces a tough task in the Upper House as the UPA does not have a majority there and will find it difficult to get the legislation passed even if SP, BSP and RJD repeat their walkouts. Opposition will have more success in getting its amendments accepted in the Upper House. In a worrying development, Trinamool indicated late on Tuesday night that it was unhappy with the concession on compulsory setting up of Lokayukta. It will decide how to vote in the RS on Wednesday morning.

The amendments agreed to important concessions and helped government placate some of the restive supporters. It accepted the demand that states should not be compelled by a central law to set up Lokayuktas: a tweak which helped them to neutralize two UPA partners Trinamool Congress and DMK who had joined the Opposition in criticizing the original provision which would have made it mandatory for States to have Lokayuktas.

The attack on the Opposition was part of government's strategy to occupy the high moral ground in the fight against corruption. In the debate, Congress leaders accused Opposition of blocking the landmark because they were not sincere in fighting corruption. They said that the House should not let go of the moment to pass the landmark legislation, a far cry from the days when large sections in the government chafed at being pushed by the civil society to set up Lokpal.

Government also accepted BJP leader Sushma Swaraj's amendment to dilute the provision which required 3-4ths of Lokpal to agree on starting proceedings against Prime Minister. Now the requirement has been reduced to an agreement among two-thirds of the anti-corruption body. Section 24 which required presiding officers of legislatures to report to Lokpal action taken on reports compiled against their members has been done away with. So has been the provision which put the armed forces within Lokpal's purview.

KEY AMENDMENTS

1. Lokayuktas in states will not be notified without the consent of state assemblies.

2. Instead of three-fourths of the nine-member Lokpal needing to approve an inquiry against PM, the approval of two thirds will now be required. Approval made less stringent.

3. Armed Forces excluded from purview of Lokpal. They are covered under specific statutes as also civilian and criminal laws.

4. Parts of Section 24 giving presiding officers of legislatures power to act against members on the basis of a Lokpal or Lokayukta report for corruption deleted. This means action cannot be taken before trial.

STICKING POINTS REMAIN

The following sticking points continued even after the passage of the Bill by Lok Sabha.

- **Reservation**

At least 50% of the members of the Lokpal should be from scheduled caste, scheduled tribe, other backward classes, women and minorities.

Opposition: The BJP and Shiv Sena said including minorities is against the basic spirit of the constitution which doesn't allow reservation along religious lines. The BJP also said the Congress was confused on the issue as it first included minorities, then excluded and again included. It also charged the Government of introducing more than 50% reservation in a Law that was against the constitutional norms.

Support: The Congress, SP, RJD, BSP, DMK, LEFT PARTIES and the Trinamool Congress said it is within the framework of the constitution and everyone should be included in the fight against corruption. They also claimed that the minorities couldn't be treated as groups but a class who can get benefit of reservation. Leader of the House, Pranab Mukherjee said the Parliament had legislative competence to formulate a law and its review should be left to the higher judiciary.

- **Lokayukta**

One law to setup Lokpal at the central level and Lokayuktas in the states.

Opposition: The BJP, ADMK, DMK, TDP and BJD said it would disturb the federal structure and trample the right of the states to frame laws. Having Lokayukta in a Central law will mean existing Lokayukta laws will have to be scrapped. It will create confusion for state governments.

Support: The Government said the issues can be addressed when the Bill is taken up for discussion next week. And if the members want they can bring in the requisite amendments.

- **Prime Minister**

Lokpal to investigate the office of the Prime Minister except on issues related to international relations, external and internal security, public order, atomic energy and space.

Opposition: The RJD, SP, ADMK and Shiv Sena did not want the PM to come within the purview of Lokpal saying that the PM is not only a leader of a party but the entire country. An inquiry against the PM will show the entire country in bad light.

Support: The CPM and BJP said the fight against corruption has to cover all top levels of governance including the Prime Minister.

- **Constitutional Validity**

Under which article of the Constitution can the Government introduce the Bill?

Opposition: The BJP said the Bill should have been introduced under article 52 of the Constitution, which would have made it patently valid.

Support: The Government defended introduction of the Bill under article 53, saying it has the power to bring in law covering the Centre and the state under this provision. On the legality of the article, the Government said review should be left to the higher judiciary.

DEBATE IN RAJYA SABHA

Here are some of the views expressed in Rajya Sabha by the leaders of various political parties including ruling party alliance.

Leader of Opposition in the Rajya Sabha Arun Jaitley

"If you are creating history, let us not create bad history. We will be leaving a lot of task for the next generation to do. Let us create an institution which is constitutionally possible. Why are you creating a constitutional havoc? The government is trying to make constitutional cocktail. You wanted to create a phoney lokpal and create a smokescreen that you are giving a constitutional status."

Congress leader Abhishek Manu Singhvi

"If you don't want to pass the bill, say so, and have the courage and don't hide behind excuses. We would have invited Jaitley to help gift us a strong lokpal as a birthday present. But BJP (Bharatiya Janata Party) is parsimonious in giving birthday presents. So don't do it for our sake but join us in passing a lokpal bill for the sake of the nation. You are using conditionally as a pretext not to pass the bill. If you don't want to pass the bill, say so. Have the courage of your convictions."

Communist Party of India-Marxist leader Sitaram Yechury

"Supremacy of the constitution cannot be violated. Spirit of constitution is that India comprises of states. Corporates need to be brought under lokpal, if you don't cover supply side and only demand side, it (corruption) will not be cured. All matters under Prevention of Corruption Act taken by CBI should be brought under superintendence of lokpal."

Bahujan Samaj Party leader Satish Chandra Mishra

"We all know how CBI is being misused by the central government. So we want the CBI to be independent and not under the administrative control of government."

Trinamool Congress Sukhendu Sekhar Roy

"Previously it was only 'lokpal bill', suddenly and surprisingly it became the 'lokpal and lokayukta bill'. It is an attack on federal structure which is unacceptable."

Cornered, as its biggest ally Trinamool Congress insisted on deleting the lokayukta provision from the lokpal bill, the government postponed voting in the Rajya Sabha after an 11 -hour-long debate on Thursday.

But before that, the government, in its efforts to save the situation, negotiated with the SP and BSP for abstention from voting, as they did in the Lok Sabha. That, too, was not to happen.

With the Lok Sabha passing the bill on Tuesday, the earliest the Upper House can now take it up for passing is during the budget session beginning in February.

On Thursday, in a virtual replay of the Lok Sabha debate two days ago, every leader -except those from the Congress - found fault with the lokayukta provisions.

The tone for the day was set by leader of the Opposition Arun Jaitley, who tore into the bill, saying the government was trying to wreak "constitutional havoc" on the country by bringing a bill which would be vulnerable, if challenged in a court.

"If you are creating history, let us not create bad history. We will be leaving a lot of task for the next generation to do," he said.

As numbers and allies stacked unfavorably, the exit route from defeat in the Upper House came, ironically, in the form of a disruption of proceedings by two RJD members, Rajniti Prasad and Ramkripal Yadav, even as their leader Lalu Prasad - a member of the Lok Sabha - watched it from the gallery.

Prasad and Yadav interrupted the reply by minister for personnel V. Narayanasamy. Yadav even snatched papers from the minister.

Narayanasamy's reply soon deteriorated into chaos, with accusations flying thick and fast, forcing an adjournment at 11.28 pm for 15 minutes.

When the House reassembled at 11.43, Parliamentary Affairs Minister Pawan Bansal said given the 187 amendments moved in the Rajya Sabha, the government would like more time to consider them.

"An unprecedented situation of everyone trying to out shout each other has arisen," House chairman and vice-president Hamid Ansari said declaring adjournment of the House 12.07 am.

Immediate reply from Jaitley was: "No sir, there is a desire to avoid the vote (by the government)."

Agitated opposition MPs shouted slogans soon after the national anthem was over, and marched out of the building. Even Trinamool leaders said outside the House that it was an orchestrated move to disrupt the House.

"A government that is afraid of facing a vote has no right to stay," Jaitley said.

"This debate and the disruption are choreographed by a minority government to ensure that no voting takes place."

Taking a swipe at the government over its lack of the required numbers in the House, Jaitley offered it the BJP's support in case it was prepared to amend key provisions of the Bill.

The Bill hangs in the air once again to be taken up once again in the Budget Session after Assembly Elections of the five States.

13

The Flame Still Blazing

After the Parliamentary Drama in Rajya Sabha, a few important developments took place subsequently reflecting upon the present Government's attitude towards corruption, black money and its earnestness in the passing of Lokpal Bill. The important developments that deserve special attention are :

- Violations of model code of conduct in Assembly Elections 2012.
- White Paper on Black Money presented in the Parliament.
- Dramatic referring of the Lokpal Bill to the Select Committee
- The Budget session and Lokpal
- New tiff between Team Anna and Government
- Team Anna alleges Prime Minister and ministers for corruption
- Anna and Ramdev join hands

VIOLATIONS OF MODEL CODE OF CONDUCT

What can the public expect from the Government that flogs them for their genuine protests against corruption and black money whereas its ministers flout the constitution and disobey the constitutional poll panel, wilfully violating the Model Code of Conduct for personal and party gains.

EC raps Salman Khurshid

The Election Commission censured Minister for Law and Minority Affairs, Salman Khurshid for violating the model code of conduct for elections by announcing that Congress would carve out 9% of the OBC quota exclusively for minorities. Khurshid, who was campaigning for his wife Louise, the Congress nominee for Farrukhabad seat in the UP polls, had also indicated in his January 10 speech that Muslims would benefit from the proposed move because of their sizeable population.

The Election Commission, which had asked for an explanation from the law minister following a complaint by the BJP, had rejected Khurshid's defence that the announcement was not aimed at a particular community, as well as that he had merely reiterated the commitment in Congress's manifesto for 2009 polls. He had also argued that he made the announcement as a member of Congress and not as a central minister.

Expressing "deep anguish and disappointment" over the violation of model of conduct, the poll watchdog had said, "The commission has come to the inescapable conclusion that Khurshid made a new promise to a distinct targeted group of the electorate among the minorities that 9% of seats would be reserved for them out of the overall quota of 27% for the other backward classes. The commission is also satisfied that the above promise was made by Khurshid as Union minister for law and minority affairs. Thus, Shri Salman Khurshid has violated the model code of conduct by making the above said promise."

Chief election commissioner S.Y. Quraishi, along with the two election commissioners V.S. Sampath and H.S. Brahma, reminded Khurshid that his job as the Union law minister made it all the more important for him to stay on the right side of the list of don'ts that the commission has laid down to ensure that the ruling party does not get an unfair advantage.

"As a Union minister for law and minority affairs, he has an added responsibility of ensuring that the model code of conduct is observed in letter and spirit so that elections are conducted in a free and fair manner and all political parties enjoy a level playing field in the matter of their election campaign," it said.

Rejecting Khurshid's argument that he only articulated an existing policy of the government, Quraishi and his colleagues noted that the law minister "failed to show to the commission any manifesto of his party where the party has made any announcement to the effect that 9% of seats would be reserved for minorities out of the abovementioned 27% quota for OBCs either as on that day or on later".

More significantly, it also noted that the quota was not mentioned either in Congress's manifesto or the vision document for UP polls, highlighting a rethink by the party on the issue which BJP has turned into one of its main campaign themes in UP.

Beni Prasad Verma also dares EC

Just two days after law minister Salman Khurshid regretted his 'Muslim quota' remark, another Union minister Beni Prasad Verma belonging to UP dared the Election Commission to act against him for saying that reservation for Muslims would be increased if Congress came to power.

"Reservation for Muslims will be increased and if EC wants, it can now issue notice to me," steel minister Verma had said while addressing a rally in Khurshid's Lok Sabha constituency of Farrukhabad. Khurshid and Congress general secretary Digvijay Singh, who had criticized EC's censure of the law minister, were present when Verma chose to defy the poll watchdog. In fact, Khurshid's wife Louise is among the Congress candidates in the Farrukhabad fray.

The remark immediately attracted the charge of "serial offence" against Congress, with rival BJP and ally Trinamool Congress accusing it of violating the model code of conduct, and drawing EC's scrutiny into the affair. The EC had censured Khurshid for a similar comment and even sought presidential intervention against him, forcing him to buy peace by writing a regret letter.

Poll Panel Writes to President

Taking strong objection to Salman Khurshid's comments after his censure on his minority quota remarks, the Election Commission wrote to President Pratibha Patil against the 'defiant and aggressive' law minister and sought her immediate decisive intervention.

The EC said the defiance by a union minister of the Constitutional body was "unprecedented" and his "improper and unlawful action" has put a strain on the delicate balance of functions between Constitutional authorities.

The strongly-worded two-page letter was written to the President after an emergency meeting of the full Commission in the wake of Khurshid's statement earlier in the day that he would continue to pursue the line on nine per cent sub-quota for minorities 'even if they hang me'.

The EC had earlier censured him for the same statement made on January 8, 2012 while campaigning in Uttar Pradesh elections, holding that it was violative of the Election Model Code of Conduct.

"The Commission is shocked that instead of being remorseful about the violation of the Model Code, that carries the consensus of all political parties and the sanction of the Supreme Court, the Minister has chosen to be defiant and aggressive. This is unprecedented," the EC letter said.

Addressing an election rally in Khatakpur locality last night, the law minister said that Election Commission had censured him, but even if the "Commission hangs him or does anything else, he would ensure that people of Pasmanda community get their rights".

"Can't I even say that Pasmanda Muslims would get their due?" he said, adding that Congress was set to hoist the tricolour in the state assembly after 22 years.

The Commission had censured Khurshid for his remarks on sub-quota for minorities, finding them to be a violation of the model code of conduct for elections.

The EC said the defiance by a union minister of the Constitutional body was "unprecedented" and his "improper and unlawful action" has put a strain on the delicate balance of functions between Constitutional authorities.

"The Commission is shocked that instead of being remorseful about the violation of the Model Code, that carries the consensus of all political parties and the sanction of the Supreme Court, the Minister has chosen to be defiant and aggressive. This is unprecedented," it said.

"The Commission is approaching you with serious dismay and a deep sense of urgency that requires your kind intervention in the midst of the poll process in the state of Uttar Pradesh," said the EC letter to President.

The EC cited "certain statements and announcements" made by Khurshid during the course of his campaign in UP, one of which was to the effect that the Congress would provide a quota of 9 per cent reservation to the minorities within the existing quota of 27 per cent for OBCs.

"He (Khurshid) also indicated that Muslims having a sizeable population will be benefited from this move," the letter noted.

The EC pointed out that it had censured Khurshid for these statements but today he said he would continue to pursue that line "irrespective of whatever the Commission directs",

The EC found "the tone and tenor of the Union Minister dismissive and utterly contemptuous about the Commission's lawful direction to him, besides the fact that his action is damaging the level playing field in the election," the letter said.

Underlining that the "response of a union minister and that too, the law minister, to the Commission's decision in a MCC (Model Code of Conduct) case has created a disturbing situation", the EC said, "we find the immediate need to draw attention of the Executive to the fact that the onus of holding free and fair polls falls on all organs of the State."

The Commission said it is "quite concerned that the delicate balance of functions between constitutional authorities has come under a strain, because of the Minister's improper and unlawful action."

The Election Commission "finds it necessary and unavoidable to turn to you at this juncture for immediate and decisive intervention so that the ongoing general election to the Uttar Pradesh assembly is conducted, and this Commission discharges its functions, in accordance with the Constitution and the law," the letter to the President said.

In its letter, the Commission also referred to its earlier order passed two days back holding that Khurshid had indeed violated the Model Code of Conduct.

In its earlier order, the Commission had said it "cannot help expressing its deep anguish and disappointment over his (Khurshid's) violation of Model Code of Conduct."

"As a union minister for law and minorities affairs, he has an added responsibility of ensuring that the Model Code of Conduct is observed in letter and spirit so that elections are conducted in a free and fair manner and all political parties enjoy a level-playing field in the matter of their election campaigns."

"In the above circumstances, the Commission hereby censures Sh. Salman Khurshid and ....hopes and expects that such violations of model code of conduct would not be repeated by him in future."

Congress Mum on EC Step Against Khurshid

Congress wilfully avoided commenting on the Election Commission's letter to President Pratibha Patil seeking "immediate decisive" action against a "defiant and aggressive" law minister Salman Khurshid for his remarks on job quotas for minorities.

"We have not gone through the letter written by the EC to the President, We will get back to you after we go through it," Congress spokesman Rashid Alvi said.

"Ask Salman," was the pithy remark of a senior Congress leader when reached by the pressmen for comments on the poll authority's unprecedented step against the law minister. A number of phone calls and text messages to Khurshid remained unanswered.

EC's Notice on Sriprakash Jaiswal for 'President Rule' Comments

Holding prima facie that his comments on imposition of President's Rule in Uttar Pradesh a threat to voters and violation of Model Code of Conduct, the Election Commission slapped a show-cause notice on Union Minister Sriprakash Jaiswal asking why action should not be initiated against him.

"The commission is, prima facie, satisfied that Shri Sri Prakash Jaiswal, by making the aforesaid uncalled-for statement has attempted to threaten the voters of districts going for poll in 6th and 7th phases either to vote for his party i.e. INC, or face imposition of President Rule in Uttar Pradesh and has thus violated the aforesaid provisions of the Model Code of Conduct," the EC notice served on him said.

The commission asked the coal minister to explain his position on the matter by 2 pm on Monday, February 27, failing which it will decide the matter without giving any further opportunity to him.

The commission discussed the matter at its meeting attended by Chief Election Commissioner SY Quraishi and Election Commissioners VS Sampath and HS Brahma and decided to issue a show cause notice to Jaiswal on his comments.

The EC action comes in the wake of complaints received by it from BJP and Samajwadi Party, charging Jaiswal with violating the Model Code and for threatening the voters of Uttar Pradesh.

FIR against Rahul Gandhi for Violating Code of Conduct

An FIR had been filed against Congress General Secretary Rahul Gandhi for alleged model code of conduct violation by not taking up the route it had prescribed to the leader for his road campaign in Kanpur. The case had been filed in Kanpur for violating Section 144. Kanpur District Magistrate Hari Om on Monday said that Rahul stuck to his route, despite having been assigned an alternative route by the Election Commission, "We had allotted a separate route for Rahul's roadshow considering he would have faced traffic," the official said.

"The route of the road show would have ended in a traffic jam. We had given them an alternate route. It was for the safety of Rahul

Gandhi as well. But he did follow our orders and carried on his road show. This is violation of rules. We will see what action needs to be taken. We may take action against Rahul Gandhi as well," he said.

The UP assembly elections reveal the real character of the Congress party, its undemocratic stance and its utter disrespect for the Constitution and the constitutional institutions of India. The Congress and its ministers had the arrogance off throwing to the wind the Election Commission's Model Code of Conduct and showing its utter unconcern to the Presidential reference on the Commission's complaint to the President makes it very clear. Above all, Rahul Gandhi, whom the Party is projecting as the future Prime Minister, unscrupulously violating Prohibitory Orders during campaigning for the party seems to convey that such orders are meant for the opposition parties and the people in general and not for those in power. There can be no greater mockery of democracy than all this. How glibly can the Congress talk about its being a secular Party in the light of religious utterances of its leaders in UP Assembly elections and condemning others as communal!

THE WHITE PAPER ON BLACK MONEY

A White Paper on a subject is issued by the government, presumably to give a definitive view on it and inform the public of an important issue. The White Paper on black money presented by Pranab Mukherjee in Parliament does nothing of the sort. The Opposition had made a demand for it in the light of a large number of scams that have been in the news. But the paper hardly throws light on any of them.

The Finance Minister in his preface admits that he is presenting "...this document now in response to an assurance given to the Parliament." The implication is that he is not giving anything definitive. He also says that he would have been happier if he "... could have included the conclusions of reports of three premier institutions that have been tasked to quantify the magnitude of black money." It is surprising that these three institutions are only looking at the magnitude rather than the gamut of issues surrounding the black economy. Thus, even after these reports are presented, we may not have a better understanding of the problem. After all, knowing the quantum of black money in the country is not the same thing as analyzing how to deal with the problem.

Quotes Old Data

The White Paper consists of five chapters and several appendices spread over about 100 pages. This seems like a lot. But it flatters to deceive.

The title itself is incorrect. What is estimated is the annual generation of black incomes in an economy and not how much black money there is in the economy. The various estimates mentioned are of black income and not black money. The definition of "black money" given is itself erroneous, with money confused for assets. Even an elementary economics or commerce textbook suggests that money is only one part of the portfolio of assets that an economic agent may own. Hence referring to the whole by a part is not appropriate. The definitional confusion is made worse when it is stated that "the term black money would also include income that is concealed from public authorities." Even then, the report does not give an estimate but simply quotes estimates from reports that were written more than 25 years ago, ignoring later literature that has also brought about greater clarity in the matter. The first chapter ends with the title, "Need for more research." Why state the obvious? The earlier reports that this Paper relies upon had pointed to how big the problem already was. So why has the government not studied it since then?

It quotes the Global Financial Integrity (GFI) report of 2010 on how much illicit flow has taken place from India since independence. That report mentions that its figure is a gross underestimate. It is convenient to quote from the GFI report because it gives a low figure but why has the government not made the effort in the last year-and-a-half to remove deficiencies in the GFI methodology and use the data collected by its intelligence agencies and other departments to arrive at a better estimate?

One service that the Paper does is to list many agencies involved in dealing with the problem. So far so good, but why have these agencies failed in the task they should have been performing, namely, checking the growth of the black economy? What are the problems they have faced? Why does prosecution fail most of the time whether it relates to the income tax department, or the police or the Central Bureau of Investigation (CBI)? Is that the reason for the law has been treated with contempt by the powerful people and for the increase in the number of people resorting to illegality resulting in the growth of the black economy?

Functioning of Judiciary

A large number of laws to check the black economy are mentioned but there is no analysis of why they have been ineffective in controlling the problem. A law on paper differs substantially from its practice. Much space is devoted in the Paper to international treaties and efforts at the global level. This is convenient since the black wealth held outside is small compared to what is held in the country. Further, it is far more difficult to get at the black wealth held abroad compared to tackling what is held in the country. Thus, it becomes convenient to discuss the former rather than the latter.

Most of the wealth held abroad illegally would not be in the names of the actual beneficiaries but in the names of shell companies, and most of it cannot be tracked to an Indian entity.

No wonder the data on deposits in Swiss Banks given in the Paper indicates that Indians have only between 0.13 and 0.29 per cent of the deposits. There is no analysis of this problem or of how money is transferred out of the country. We could have been enlightened if information with the intelligence agencies about tax havens and the modus operandi of taking funds out of the country or of generating incomes outside India were revealed.

Vulnerable Sectors

The interface between the judiciary and the investigative agencies is an important aspect of non-implementation of the laws of the land and the contempt they have come to be held in by the public. That is the cause of the judicial delays with four crore cases pending. Even routine matters that should be decided in a few months drag on for years. This encourages perpetrators of the black economy. The functioning of the judiciary needed to be dissected that has not been done.

The paper lists the real estate, bullion and jewellery sectors as vulnerable to black money generation. This again reflects a definitional confusion. Activities in these sectors constitute transfers of black savings from one individual to another, and as such circulate black incomes but do not generate them.

In the chapter "Way Forward," strategies are listed but again no new ground is broken. As has been pointed out earlier, the Double Taxation Avoidance Agreement (DTAA) and the Tax Information Exchange Agreement (TIEA) are about declared incomes abroad and not black savings held abroad. Similarly, voluntary disclosure schemes have been discredited in the past. The Comptroller and Auditor General (CAG) of India has said the scheme turns people into habitual tax offenders.

Nexus and Political Questions

The paper skirts the most important question, namely, why laws do not get implemented. It avoids mentioning the nexus between politicians, officials and businessmen that drives the black economy, and how criminals have entered this nexus. Why have steps taken in the past to control the black economy not worked?

The answer to why there are so many omissions in the Paper lies in the fact that the existence and the control of the black economy are political questions. Dealing with the black economy is not a narrow technical question that can be tackled by a few more laws or a few steps here and there, or strengthening of a few provisions of the law or through computerization. Whether it is the ruling party or the opposition, national or regional parties, all of them have been mired in the black economy. The question is one of political will. Should the Paper not have called a spade a spade rather than avoiding the difficult question all together?

But then a White Paper is a political document and not a technical one. It helps the government whitewash its image and diverts attention from the difficult questions. It is not an instrument that can generate the political will to action—a task that only public agitations and the political process can accomplish.

THE BUDGET SESSION AND LOKPAL BILL

In yet another twist, the controversial Lokpal and Lokayuktas Bill was referred to the select committee of the Rajya Sabha, further delaying the setting up of the anti-graft ombudsman that has been hanging fire for 42 years.

The bill, on which debate had remained inconclusive in the Rajya Sabha during the last winter session, was referred to the select committee through a motion soon after Minister of State for Personnel V. Narayanasamy moved it for consideration and passage.

With consensus on the Lokpal Bill proving elusive, the government on May 22, 2012 referred the proposed legislation to a select committee of the Rajya Sabha. The move spells further delay for the bill that has failed to make it to the law books since it was first introduced in 1942.

The select committee has been given three months to submit its report on the Lokpal Bill. Minister of state for personnel V. Narayanasamy expressed the hope that the panel would finalize its recommendations by the last week of the monsoon session.

The motion for referring the Lokpal Bill to the select committee was passed by voice vote but not without giving some tense moments to the government. The Opposition objected to a "friendly" party of UP A, the Samajwadi Party, taking the lead in bringing the motion. Even after the government agreed to move the motion itself, parties such as BJP and BSP questioned the hurry in referring the bill to a select committee without a discussion in the House.

BJP, BSP and Left joined hands in questioning the government's "clever" ploy to use a Samajwadi Party member. Soon after Narayanasamy moved the Lokpal Bill for passage, SP's Naresh Agrawal got up and sought to bring a motion for referring the bill to a 15-member select committee of the Rajya Sabha.

He proposed that the panel be given three months to submit its recommendations. He even went on to identify the members of the committee - Shantaram Naik, Satyavrat Chaturvedi, Arun Jaitley, Rajiv Pratap Rudy, S.C. Mishra, K.N. Balagopal, Shivanand Tiwari, D. Bandopadhyay, Tiruchi Siva, D.P. Tripathi, Ram Gopal Yadav, V. Maitreyan, Kantilal Bhuria, Bhupender Yadav and Ashok Ganguly.

The proposal from Agrawal made the Opposition benches to suspect that he was only reading from a script prepared by the UPA managers keen to avoid the perception that the government had anything to do with delaying the Lokpal Bill. BJP leaders Ravi Shankar Prasad and Rajiv Pratap Rudy raised points of order arguing that rules allowed only the member in charge of legislation, Narayanasamy in this case, to move the motion for referring the bill to a select committee. Besides, they argued that it was for the House to decide on membership of the committee.

Leader of Opposition Arun Jaitley, during his intervention, objected to the government bringing the bill for passage in the Rajya Sabha on the penultimate day of the budget session. Not only this, the proposal to refer it to the select committee said Jaitley, had put the credibility of the parliamentary institution at stake.

"The debate (on Lokpal) started in the sixties and since it was introduced 42 years ago, the government has been dribbling the ball," alleged Jaitley.

Referring to the decision of the chair to adjourn the House just before the bill was to be voted upon on December 29 last year, Jaitley said the nearly 190 amendments, which had made the government jittery, really boiled down to four broad heads - control of the investigative agency, appointment and removal of Lokpal chairman and members, who all were covered under Lokpal and whether Lokayuktas should be part of the Central legislation.

"On December 29, had a vote been taken, some of the amendments would have gone through," he noted. Wondering if the government wanted a Lokpal or not, Jaitley alleged that enough time had passed since December 29 to enable the government to consult the political parties and take a call on the bill.

Also, objecting to the government's proposal to hive off the Lokayuktas' provisions and leave the states to enact their own Lokayukta laws based on a model Act to be circulated by the Centre, Jaitley said the right course would have been to enact a model Lokayukta legislation under Article 252 of the Constitution, based on resolution by two state assemblies.

Jaitley also criticized the government for choosing to fire from the shoulder of a friendly party while proposing a select committee to examine the Lokpal Bill. The sentiments were echoed by the Left and BSP, who argued that it was for the government to move the motion on the select committee. "Let Naresh Agrawal give the names, on which we can agree or disagree," said CPM leader Sitaram Yechury, who also put his wit to use by warning the government against bringing "loose motions" to the House,

At this point, a seemingly chastened Narayanasamy relented and moved the motion for referring the bill to a select committee of the House saying that it should be allowed to submit its report by the last week of monsoon session. He also endorsed the constitution of the committee proposed by Naresh Agrawal.

As the government gave in to Opposition pressure, BSP leader Mayawati could not resist taking pot shots at the treasury benches. "This is against parliamentary rules. The honorable minister brought the motion for the select committee as a second thought, after having tried to ride piggyback on a friendly party... The minister and the government did not act responsibly," she told the House.

After the government moved the motion to refer the bill to the standing committee, the Chair declared the motion moved by Naresh Agrawal as infructuous. The government motion was subsequently passed by voice vote.

NEW TIFF BETWEEN TEAM ANNA AND GOVERNMENT

Team Anna's Allegations

On May 26, 2012 Team Anna came out with set of graft charges against 15 ministers including the Prime Minister. Many of the charges followed media reports of Comptroller and Auditor General's draft report supposedly claiming irregularities in the allocation of coal mining blocks to private companies when Manmohan Singh was in charge of coal ministry between 2006 and 2008.

Veteran social activist Anna Hazare intensified his attack on the Prime Minister, saying if Dr. Manmohan Singh is honest, then he should be ready to face any kind of probe. "The inquiry into charges against the Prime Minister should be headed by a former judge," he told a leading English news channel. Hazare, however, asked for time to study the allegations against the Prime Minister. "I always saw the Prime Minister as a non-corrupt personality. I need time to study the allegations against the Prime Minister," he said.

Hazare's key aide Arvind Kejriwal had earlier said they would be extremely delighted if the allegations levelled against the Prime Minister are found to be false. "We will be most happy if the allegations levelled against the Prime Minister are found false. But how will it be proved? For that, we need to have an independent investigating agency to probe it," said Kejriwal. We want to tell him that it was not we who levelled these allegations but the CAG, which is a Consitutional body," he added.

Supreme Court lawyer and Team Anna member Prashant Bhushan had earlier criticized the Prime Minister, saying that the ruling Congress Party had been using his honest credentials as a 'shield' while perpetrating corruption with brazen impunity. Bhushan questioned the Prime Minister's perceived hesitancy in dealing with corrupt minister and coalition allies.

"The Congress party repeatedly hails the honesty of the Prime Minister. He is projected as an honest leader of the government. So, I had said the Congress party was trying to use the Prime Minister and his clean image as a shield, just like the character of Shikhandi was used in the Hindu epic Mahabharata," he said. Bhushan further called for the establishment of an independent panel to probe the allegations of graft levelled against senior cabinet ministers.

Dissociating himself from allegations, Justice Santosh Hegde, who has worked closely with Team Anna in the past, to allow an inquiry to prove his innocence. "I myself am finding it very difficult to believe that there could be any charge or allegation of corruption against Manmohan Singh, I am finding it extremely difficult to believe, but at the same time, the things are happening in this country in such a way that at least let him clear himself of this allegation. I think some enquiry should be conducted," he said.

Ministers' Responses

Replying to Team Anna's allegations Manmohan Singh said that the allegations levelled against him were baseless, unfortunate and irresponsible. "There have been reports about the allocation of coal blocks based on leaked portions of a draft report on the issue. We have also received a letter on the same subject. The Coal Minister has given factual details in response to these allegations and the Coal Ministry has put up all the information on its website (on May 17th), We have not yet received the CAG report," Dr. Singh told media on-board press interaction enroute from Yangon to New Delhi "When we do, the Government will submit its detailed factual response before the Public Accounts Committee as per Constitutional procedure. Uninformed allegations and discussions based on leaked drafts are unfortunate. It is unfortunate that irresponsible allegations are being made without confirming the facts," he added. Dr. Singh also said that if it was found that he had done something wrong, he would not hesitate to quit public life,

Union Law and Justice Minister Salman Khurshid had, however, hit out at Team Anna for demanding an independent probe into charges against the Prime Minister, saying it seems that the underlining urge of the civil society activists is that either bring the Lokpal Bill of our choice or be ready to face the accusations.

Commenting on the allegations made by Team Anna against senior Cabinet ministers, including the Prime Minister, Khurshid said India is a country where the rule of law prevails, and emphasized that there is a system that has to be followed.

"Of course, they are making the allegations. We all read those allegations and we see those allegations. I don't think we can have trials for anybody, forget about ministers and certainly the Prime Minister, we can't have media trials, and we can't have street trials. We are a country where the rule of law prevails. There is a system. They are the same people, who have gone to the Supreme Court and the various High Courts; and they have got matters investigated," said Khurshid.

"So, nobody stops them from going to institutions that are available. It seems to me that the underlying intention is that please give us Lokpal and give us the Lokpal of the kind that we want, otherwise we will keep accusing you of all kinds of things," he added.

Union Coal Minister Sriprakash Jaiswal said to NDTV that there was no question of a probe into the allegations of Team Anna against the PM. "The nation benefited with these coal block allocations. There is no question of an investigation," Mr Jaiswal said.

Congress spokesperson Rashid AM also rejected Team Anna's demand for an independent probe into the charges, saying "it is not possible that anybody makes allegation and you set up an inquiry.

But the question is how much moral authority can be attached to what the Law Minister says who himself flouted the Moral Code of Conduct, Election Commission and the Constitution during UP election.

ANNA AND RAMDEV JOIN HANDS

The day-long fast by Ramdev and Hazare was called to mark one year of Ramdev's last agitation at Ramlila ground, from where he was arrested in the middle of the night between June 3 and 4, 2012.

Addressing the huge crowd on a hot and sweltering day, Ramdev said he would continue exerting pressure on the government bring back the black money stashed in foreign banks. Ramdev targeted the prime minister for inaction over widespread corruption in his government.

"The nation respects you for being an honest individual, but you should also be honest politically. The country sees you as the person holding the highest constitutional post. Your personal honesty is not enough... Keep your cabinet honest," he said.

Arvind Kejriwal took the attack a notch further, saying that parliament would never pass the Lokpal bill as long as 'MPs like Lalu Prasad, A. Raja and Suresh Kalmadi were present'. He also made a direct attack on the prime minister, saying coal block allocations were made to 'underwear makers, cassette makers, gutka (tobacco makers)' when the prime minister was looking after the ministry between 2006 and 2009.

Extending the base of his agitation Anna Hazare in his speech made a strong pitch for the right to reject and said people with criminal cases pending against them should be kept out of parliament using the clause. He said that he was on a tour in Maharashtra and had come as he had promised to support Ramdev. 'If I hadn't shown up, people would have again said that there is a rift with Ramdev,' he said.

At the end of the day-long fast, Ramdev asserted that he would return again on Aug 9 to launch a larger movement against corruption.

The Congress, in its usual way, was quick to rubbish allegations against Manmohan Singh in coal block allocations and accused Ramdev and Team Anna of a pro-BJP bias. Congress spokesperson Raashid Alvi said the allegations were 'baseless' and while names of leaders of several parties were taken in context of corruption, none of them were from the BJP. Taking a dig at the joint fast by Hazare and Ramdev, Samajwadi Party leader Shahid Siddiqui said their alliance would 'not yield any result'. But one thing is clear from this that the congress is trying to form a political nexus to subvert the Lokpal Bill.

A few important inferences emerge from these developments:

One, the assembly elections 2012 reveal the real character of the Congress party that continues to patronize the British policy of 'divide and rule till date. It brands BJP as communal party whereas we saw the most naked communal dance of the Congress in this election when it carved out 4.5% reservation out of the OBC quota for the Muslims a [0] couple of days before the Model Code of Conduct laid down by the Election Commission came into operation. The matter did not end there, the Union Law Minister Salman Khurshid, Union Beni Prasad Verma, Union Coal Minister Sriprakash Jaiswal and Rahul Gandhi flouting the constitution and the constitutional body. Mr. Khurshid and Mr. Verma continued playing the communal card under the umbrella of party manifesto with a promise to raise it further to 9% if Congress came into power. In spite of repeated warnings from the Election Commission they kept on daring the Commission that it had to write to the President and PM who cold shouldered it. So insensitive are the Government and the party towards the violation of the constitution that they don't take seriously even the strictures from the higher judiciary and waste time in undeserved appeals and judicial reviews. All this shows the Government's dictatorial attitude in governance considering itself above the constitution and the constitutional authorities caring a fig for Election Commission, Judiciary, CAG and parliamentary procedures, fiddling with them for personal and party gains ignoring the national interests.

Two, the government is least interested in curbing corruption and initiating action against those who hold accounts in tax havens. The so called 'White Paper on Black Money' recently presented to the Parliament by Pranab Mukherji hides more than it reveals belittling the cry of the opposition parties and the public in general. It seems to have been done simply to complete the formality of answering the very long standing demand of the opposition parties for white paper on the issue.

Three, the handling of the Lokpal Bill in the winter session of the parliament in Rajya Sabha on the last day of the winter session, its taking up at the end of the budget session and referring it to Select Committee in a dramatic way clearly hints at the non seriousness of the Government about the Bill and reining on corruption. This Government's indifference towards matters relating to black money and corruption and blaming the forums creating awareness about them is underestimating the public wrath against the Government. Dilly dallying about the Bill raises doubts about the sincerity of the government in this regard.

Four, the Team Anna's frustration with the Government and its realization that the corrupt Government cannot pass a Lokpal Bill against itself prompted it to directly allege 15 ministers including the Prime Minister. The credibility of the Government being at the lowest ebb, the onus of proving them not guilty through an independent investigating agency lies on the Government. Although the Government has ordered CB1 inquiry but it cannot be an impartial one as CBI reporting to the Prime Minister cannot be unbiased.

The June 3, 2012 joint dharna by Baba Ramdev and Team Anna should be wake up call for the Ministers and the Parliamentarians to take up the issues relating to corruption and black money seriously. Sitting in the temples of democracy they cannot claim immunity for their ignoble action flouting the public will in a princely manner. It's high time that instead of finding fault with the crusaders the Government take appropriate measures to restore its credibility and the glory of the democratic institutions.

But the Prime Minister's utterances at the CWC Meet on June 4, 2012 seems that his Government is not I mood to tackle seriously the problems corruption and black money. The Congress party seems to be more interested in the blame game as revealed by the PM's and the Sonia Gandhi's following statements.

"Canards and falsehoods being spread" he said, describing the people behind the allegations as "disparate, desperate elements unified only by their opposition to our government." Dr. Manmohan Singh

"In a democracy, it is the job of the Opposition to oppose but the manner in which Opposition and some anti-Congress elements are, as part of a conspiracy, levelling baseless allegations against the Prime Minister, the UPA government, the party and some of our colleagues, is a matter of regret," said Sonia Gandhi.

Whatever be the allegations of the Congress Party against the Opposition, the fact of the matter is that its intentions are in doubt and it doesn't seem to be very serious about the passage of the Bill. Witch haunted by its own alliance partners, the Congress somehow wants to stick to power caring a fig for the governance and the economy.

ONCE AGAIN TEAM ANNA BEGINS FAST

After waiting for a long time for the passage of a strong Lokpal Bill and repeated dilly dallying by the government, Team Anna began a fresh round of agitation on 25th July 2012 at Jantar Mantar in New Delhi, in support of a stronger Lokpal Bill, with three members launching an indefinite hunger strike. Arvind Kejriwal, Manish Sisodia and Gopal Rai were the three members on an indefinite hunger strike. Anna Hazare, the leader of the Team, joined the fast from July 29th onwards, as there was no response from the government to the agitation. "The aim is to campaign for a Lokpal Bill... the government is only giving us assurances, but takes no action," Hazare said.

Apart from the demand for a strong Lokpal, the Team wanted a

Special Investigative Team to probe charges of corruption against 15 serving ministers. Pranab Mukherjee, who figures in the list, is now the President of India. However, Arvind Kejriwal said that the Team would continue to target him. Mukherjee was the Defence Minister when the Scorpene Scam took place. Other demands included transferring cases of corruption against party chiefs to the SIT and the setting up of a fast track court to try cases against Members of Parliament.

Baba Ramdev, who has been acting in tandem with Team Anna over issues of corruption, also joined them for a day.

Public Request to End Fast

On August 2, 2012 Anupam Kher, who read out the statement of solidarity from 22 prominent citizens of the country said the government was not responding to the fast and was not paying heed to the protest. "The government has turned its back to the agitation and has also not shown political will to punish corrupt people. The opposition also does not fare well on the issue. Do not expect anything from this political class," the letter said.

"We request Anna Hazare and other fasting activists to channelize their efforts in setting up a political alternative, to give a responsive, democratic and non-violent system. Indian democracy needs a new direction. We request the people who are fasting to accept this historical challenge and call off their fast," it added.

Responding to the request Anna Hazare said that he and his team members would end their fast on August 3 and added that his aides want feedback from public within 48 hours on whether they should form a political party. Asserting that power should rest with the people in a true democracy, Hazare reiterated that there is nothing wrong in forming a political party. He said that power should be with the people of the country.

"In a true democracy, power should be in the hands of the people. The power must be given to the public. Village land, village water belongs to the village. There is a government in Delhi, but in the village, we are the government. Village has the right over coal, water in the village," he said. Hazare asked his supporters to dislodge those leaders, who don't give in to people's demand. He, however, said that he himself would not enter politics.

"I will not get into politics. I will fight from the outside. You have to think who goes into a party. Do they have a good character? Such people only should be given a ticket. If you want to change the nation, form a party. But see who is going into that party. How will you monitor them? You have to think about that," said Hazare.

The 75-year-old social activist also reiterated that the government is not serious on bringing a strong anti-graft bill to combat rampant corruption in the country. The government, however, hit back at Team Anna, saying that they have always been power-hungry and must contest elections to prove its claim of representing the will of the people.

Team Anna Dissolved

Two days after Team Anna ended its indefinite fast at Jantar Mantar, social activist Anna Hazare disbanded the nearly 18-month-old core committee of India Against Corruption, and said that he would travel across the country to pick "good candidates" for the coming Lok Sabha elections.

Hazare, who left for his village, Ralegan Siddhi in Maharashtra, after two days of discussions with key members of his team—Arvind Kejriwal, Prashant Bhushan, Kiran Bedi, Kumar Vishwas, Manish Sisodia and Gopal Rai—wrote in a blog post reiterating that he would travel across the country, seeking views of "every gram sabha and every municipal local body to choose good candidates" for the 2014 Lok Sabha elections. Hazare said he had selected 12 "people's candidates" in the past in Maharashtra for the assembly elections and eight of them got elected. "The same pattern would be repeated." This is the last chance for the country to elect a corruption-free government, he said.

However, the decision to dissolve the committee did not go down well with all members of the team. Devender Sharma, a member of the committee who was kept out of the meetings, said that he came to know about the development through television. "If this is a sample of the democracy they propose to bring in to politics, then people are better off without it," he said. Santosh Hegde, Medha Patkar, Arvind Gaur, Sunita Gorada and Akhil Gogoi, all among those who supported Hazare's movement, were also upset with his latest decision.

BABA RAMDEV TAKES UP THE RELAY

Baba Ramdev seems to have taken up the relay from Anna Hazare. Yoga Guru Baba Ramdev on August 9, 2012 made a cautious start to his agitation at Ramlila Maidan to bring back black money stashed abroad. With Team Anna's just-concluded anti-graft stir finding little support, Ramdev also sought to distance himself from Team Anna's methodology and announced that he would not vilify any political party nor did he intend to challenge the government. However, unlike the previous occasion, the issue of Lokpal Bill figured in his charter of demands as also he welcomed Anna Hazare to join his protest.

Treading cautiously, the Yoga Guru said he would fast for three days and later decide on the future course of action. "There will be no indefinite fast or protest. We will go without food and water for three days in support of our demands. After that, we will decide on our future strategy. We will be pleased if the Government accedes to our demands but we will also not be displeased if it refuses to heed. We will fight for it," said Ramdev to the cheers of thousands who had swarmed at Ramlila Maidan from across the country on the first day of his protest.

But the Government cold shouldered his demand and Ramdev extended his fast by one day, threatening a big stir if steps were not taken by the Government to pass a strong Lokpal and bring back black money. Apart from demanding that the Indian money lying abroad be declared as national property and brought back, Ramdev was also batting for a stronger Lokpal Bill. Other demands by him included a transparent process in naming heads of the Central Bureau of Investigation and the Election Commission.

Baba Ramdev kept extending his fast and intensifying his protest by writing to the PM to take cognizance of his demands and giving call to 'gherao' Parliament, on which he and thousands of his followers were arrested and put in Ambedkar Stadium that had been converted into jail and released after some time.

Baba Ramdev left Ambedkar Stadium very much on his own terms after keeping the police waiting overnight, winning the endorsement of all political parties except the Congress, and serving notice to the Prime Minister and his party about his plans to ensure that the Congress is defeated in the next general election.

THE FLAME STILL BLAZING

In the blog post, however, Anna Hazare said the struggle for the Lokpal would continue. "We will continue our struggle for the Lokpal through selection of good candidates in the Lok Sabha elections. Such an opportunity won't come again. If people don't support now, the loss will be their not mine."

He added he would neither form a party nor contest elections. However, he implied that his fellow activists in IAC would form a political party and run it like a struggle. First it was the struggle for a Lokpal. And now it will be a struggle for a clean government with candidates selected for that purpose. Once such government comes into power, its motive would be to pass legislation to enable the Lokpal, right to reject, right to recall and rural self-rule, Hazare wrote in the post.

For the first time, social crusader Anna Hazare on September 18, 2012 spoke publicly of the differences between him and Arvind Kejriwal over formation of a political party, saying he would stick to his apolitical movement against corruption while Kejriwal was free to chase his political ambitions.

Hazare met prominent Pune citizens and activists to discuss the way forward for his movement. He is scheduled to have similar consultations in New Delhi and other cities over the next few days, including meetings with Kejriwal, Kiran Bedi and other former Team Anna members.

Asked if there was a rift between him and former Team Anna members led by Kejriwal over the formation of a political party, Hazare said, "It is obvious, despite the rift, we have one single aim. This (rift) is not like what happens with political parties. He (Kejriwal) will go his way and I will go mine. I have always stated that I don't want to form a political party and contest elections. My path is different. I had made it clear at Jantar Mantar."

After a marathon eight hour meeting with his former colleagues on September 20, 2012, Anna Hazare completely cut off his ties with the political wing of Arvind Kejriwal of India Against Corruption saying that his name or photo should not be used during any political campaign.

Anna Hazare rejected the online SMS poll conducted by the IAC on the issue of forming a political party, saying, "Internet and Jantar Mantar cannot determine the outcome of the country,"

Anna Hazare feels that joining politics would take him away from his goals of serving the nation and society. "Politics is not service. It is all about selfishness," he said. "I told them (core committee members) we have one common aim—to have a corruption-free nation. If you want to start a political party, go ahead and contest elections. I will go back to the people and continue with my work. I will not support all candidates nominated by Arvind's party. I will check their background and character and support a few appropriate ones."

CONCLUSUION

But the insensitive Government does not seem to buzz as the entire system created by them during the last 65 years seems to have made them so strong that it has the audacity to bow down the public will to their nefarious designs to shield the corrupt. However the time will show how firm and strong is the people's desire to bring about the change. Now it depends on the public how sincerely it executes its will through the ballot and demonstrate their potent rage in the coming elections through their ballot power.

14

Epilogue

It is well neigh impossible to cover up the detailed dynamics of the kaleidoscopic socio-cultural, political and economic complexion of the great nation, that is India, within the frame work of a book. But we have tried in this book to keep our focus on the growth of black money and corruption in India in the light of growing public discontentment about it and the political will to counter it. Since Independence the Governments expressed their awareness about it, but the malady seems to be achieving alarming dimensions in the face of the tall claims of the Government's attempts to curb it.

THE EXISTING MODEL

The history of corruption in post-Independence India starts with the Jeep scandal in 1948, when a transaction concerning purchase of jeeps for the army needed for Kashmir operation was entered into by V.K. Krishna Menon, the then High Commissioner for India in London with a foreign firm without observing normal procedure. Contrary to the demand of the opposition for judicial inquiry as suggested by the Inquiry Committee led by Ananthsayanam Ayyangar, the then Government announced on September 30, 1955 that the Jeep scandal case was closed. Union Minister G.B.Pant declared "that as far as Government was concerned it has made up its mind to close the matter. If the opposition was not satisfied they can make it an election issue." Soon after on February 3, 1956 Krishna Menon was inducted into the Nehru cabinet as minister without portfolio.

In 1950, AD Gorwala, an eminent civil servant was asked by Government of India to recommend improvements in the system of governance. In his report submitted in 1951 he made two observations: "One, quite a few of Nehru's ministers were corrupt and this was common knowledge. Two, even a highly responsible civil servant in an official report as early as 1951 maintained that the Government went out of its way to shield its ministers."

Corruption charges in cases like Mudgal case (1951), Mundra deals (1957-58), Malaviya-Sirajuddin scandal (1963) and Pratap Singh Kairon case (1963) were leveled against the Congress ministers and Chief Ministers, but no Chief Minister resigned.

The Santhanam Committee, which was appointed by the Government in 1962 to examine the issue of corruption in its report submitted in 1964 observed: "There is widespread impression that failure of integrity is not uncommon among ministers and that some ministers, who have held office during the last sixteen years have enriched themselves illegitimately, obtained good jobs for their sons and relations through nepotism and have reaped other advantages inconsistent with any notion of purity in public life."

The following comments of Nehru on the memorandum of charges against Pratap Singh Kairon submitted to the President of India by the non-Communist opposition in Punjab suggest his approach on corruption: "The question thus arises as to whether the Chief Minister is compelled to resign because of adverse findings on some questions of fact by Supreme Court. The ministers are collectively responsible to the legislature. Therefore, the matter was one, which concerned the assembly. As a rule therefore, the question of removing a minister would not arise unless the legislature expressed its wish by a majority vote."

Thus, we find that while Nehru's tolerance of corruption among his ministers legitimised this malady, his daughter Indira Gandhi institutionalised it by holding both the posts of the Prime Minister and Party President. By doing so she was herself controlling the party funds, which gave birth to the money power in politics. The famous V.P.Malhotra (Chief Cashier of State Bank of India) case in which he got a telephone call believing from Indira Gandhi to pay Rs. 60 lakh to one Nagarwal remained a mystery. Corruption cases like Fairfax, HBJ, Pipeline, and HDW Submarine deal came up since then. The famous Bofor's deal is well known. Narsimha Rao was the first Prime Minister being prosecuted in corruption charges. Cases like Rs.2500 crore-Airbus A-320 deal with France involving kickback (1990), Harshad Mehta security scam (1992), Gold Star Steel and Alloys controversy (1992), JMM bribery case, Hawala scam of Rs. 65 crore and Urea scam (1996) also came up during the period of Narsimha Rao Government.

Criminalization of politics is another facet of corruption. N.N.Vohra, Union Home Secretary in his report (1995) on this issue observed: "A network of mafias is virtually running a parallel Government pushing the state apparatus into irrelevance." Quoting some 'DIB' sources, he added, "...there has been a rapid spread and growth of criminal gangs, armed senas, drug mafias, smuggling gangs and economic lobbies in the country, which have over the years developed an intensive network of contacts with bureaucrats, government functionaries at local level, politicians, media persons and strategically located individuals in non-state sector. Some of these syndicates have also international linkages including the foreign agencies."

Former Prime Minister Rajiv Gandhi, in 1985, had said, "Of every rupee spent by the government, only 17 paise reached the intended beneficiary."

"I remember my father who had once said that only 17 paise out of a rupee reach the people; now the situation is much worse, I have seen that not even five paise out of a rupee reach here," said Rahul Gandhi addressing a public meeting in Jhansi.

Prime Minister Manmohan Singh admitted 'leakage' of funds earmarked for development works, but said it was 'not as big' as was mentioned by Rajiv Gandhi.

All these stand to support that since independence till date all the Congress Governments had complete knowledge about the prevalence of corruption in the Government. The Prime Ministers who are wholly responsible for their governments not only ignored it but willfully protected the corrupt that amounts to promotion of corruption by them. Even in the present Government, Dr. Manmohan Singh, who might be Mr. Clean, openly comes out to protect the ministers alleged for mishandling of public funds with the intra government and otherwise evidences, make it clear that there is an utter lack of political will to check corruption.

Political parties other than the Congress cannot be completely absolved of their responsibility in this regard. They too have not done much that was expected from them in overcoming corruption, they too lagged behind. But we have overlooked their role for a few genuine reasons. One, Congress was almost a single party, rather a single family dictatorship while the opposition had only nominal existence for a sufficiently long time. Two, they had weak political saleability as compared to the Congress during the transitional phase. They had short-lived governments struggling for existence with little time left to them for controlling corruption. Three, they had only one full term Government to their credit with so many things to do and learn.

The recommendations and findings of democratic institutions like CAG, Joint Parliamentary Committees, judiciary etc. substantiating the corruption and carelessness have been overlooked by the Government. When it comes to the genuine protests by the public, in the name of the constitution they are put on hold. Open defiance of the constitution by the political parties in power has become the rule of the day. The party is above the nation and above the constitution for them. Their thrust is more on protecting their corrupt ministers and partymen rather than protecting the country from corruption. When it comes to toppling the other political Party's Governments in the states they set aside the law and the constitution, the CrPC does not come in their way. But the rightful and peaceful protests of the poor public and the farmers are dealt with lathis, and guns in the midnight hours and the broad day light by the police.

The Systemic Betrayal

A minority of people, especially the clever business people of India, take full advantage of government-sponsored corruption as we witnessed in 2G and other gigantic scandals. Without exception these are the people who pay hefty bribes to both—politicians and bureaucrats to get whatever they want, let the nation be damned. They could amass a vast amount of black money because they could silence bureaucrats of the Internal Revenue Service by properly greasing their palms. They are totally ignorant as to how that ill-gotten money would destroy their children and grandchildren. We read in newspapers on regular basis how a son or a daughter of a filthy rich man is involved in criminal behaviour, or a drunk-driving accident in which innocent people were killed or maimed. Today, thousands of corrupt businessmen are busy bailing out their fat, waywardly children from one disaster or another caused by their unethical behaviour. The corrupt police are busy making a fortune from these misfortunes of the filthy rich and their poor victims. The bottom line is that India now has a parasitic nexus of politicians, bureaucrats and businessmen sucking away its blood.

The vast majority of common people, however, cope with corruption by paying bribes to the callous officials even for small services such as getting death certificate of a parent or a license to drive a motorcycle. They suppress and repress their helplessness, powerlessness and rage (stuff it into their hidden mind) and 'adjust to the reality of corruption' by paying bribes. This 'adjustment' is not acceptance or self-deception. If someone reminds them of the corruption one could get a glimpse of the rage within them. They would say something like, "Well, this is India. Here nothing happens unless you pay bribes to officials. You have to set aside your principles if you want to survive. I hate this system, but there is nothing we can do. These officials could destroy lives." They are not happy about corruption, but they feel helpless and fearful to do anything about it.

The Impotent Rage

The helplessness and powerlessness that simmers in the hearts of overwhelming people is what is called *impotent rage.* This is the kind of rage women feel when someone kidnaps them and rapes them repeatedly, and they could do nothing about it. Stuffing impotent rage in the hidden mind has serious long-term consequences. In individuals such repressed painful emotions could lead to behavioural changes, or they could suddenly resurface triggered by an event. For example, a woman being physically, emotionally and sexually abused by her husband for years might cope with her predicament by hiding painful emotions in her hidden mind. She could express her hidden rage by means of *passive-aggressive behaviour* such as putting dog poop in her husband's sandwich. Or, one fine morning even a minor event could shake up her soda bottle, spew-up all buried emotions into her conscious mind (balloon) resulting in her becoming severely sick; or, blowing her husband's brain off in a fit of rage

When impotent rage is *shared by a large number of people,* triggered by a symbolic event it could suddenly and furiously resurface resulting in a revolution such as the one we saw in Tunisia and Egypt. In Tunisia, unable to cope with his impotent rage against government-sponsored corruption, a young man finally decided to *do something.* He set himself on fire in public. This *precipitating event* triggered spewing up of *shared impotent rage* of people into the conscious mind of the Tunisian society with such fury that it exploded into a revolution. And the frightened dictator fled the country. The same thing happened in Egypt, but not before the dictator took the lives of over eight hundred brave people who insisted on his departure. These cataclysmic events in Tunisia and Egypt, in turn, shook-up the soda bottles of millions of people in other authoritarian countries, such as Libya, Bahrain, Yemen and Syria resulting in widespread protests.

In India we saw this phenomenon in non-violent demonstrations in many cities voicing support to Anna Hazare's and Baba Ramdev's crusade against corruption and black money. Even though India claims to be a democracy, the truth is that the government has its subjects by the throat and everyone feels stifled.

GANDHI EMERGES FROM ASHES

We witnessed this *resurfacing-of-impotent-rage* phenomenon in India in the first week of April 2011. When Anna Hazare went on fast unto death demanding that half the members of Lokpal Bill Drafting Committee should be from the 'Civil Society,' this sensory input shook up the soda bottle of millions of people, and brought up into their balloon *shared impotent rage* related to the chronic stress of government-sponsored corruption. The fury of this resurfacing impotent rage was such that all over India they spontaneously rose as one and held public rallies expressing their outrage over the corruption at the highest level of the government. We witnessed how one selfless man, who identified with people's shared impotent rage, could galvanize them by deciding to *do something* against the abominable nexus of bureaucrats and politicians. His principled stand against official corruption resonated so profoundly with people that they instinctively identified with him ("I am Anna Hazare!") and spontaneously gave vent to the simmering rage in their hearts. When a T.V. reporter asked a young demonstrator whether he had personal experience with bribery, he said shamefacedly, "When I refused to pay the R.T.O., they failed me in the driving test. Then I had no choice but to pay the bribe. I am ashamed that *I had to do this"*

The Satyagraha method Hazare applied to force the apathetic government's hand was absolutely appropriate in view of the fact that Dr. Singh ignored his and other concerned citizen's repeated pleas to address this serious issue. Dr. Singh was simply hiding behind his clean image, or more likely behind someone else's sari. Something drastic had to be done to shake up the *laissez faire* attitude of the government. Since Hazare already had the image of a selfless activist who practiced Gandhian philosophy of Truth and Non-violence, people spontaneously rallied behind him. People, who accuse Hazare of blackmail, are ignorant of the fundamental tenets of Satyagraha or fundamental duty of every citizen. They are ignorant of the timeless adage:

All that is necessary for the triumph of evil in this world is for enough good men (and women) to do nothing.

Government's Gimmics

At first the government indulged in much self-deception and gave all kinds of flimsy excuses why they could not meet Hazare's simple demand. These people, who had little regard for the constitution, even gave 'constitutional reasons' why they could not agree to the demand. As expression of outrage spread like wild fire they gave in to Hazare's demand, but not before letting Hazare fast for five days, perhaps to punish him, or to show that the government did not yield without a good fight. Privately, though, the ministers are not scared of the Lokpal Bill at all. They have enough devious ways and means to neutralize the civil society members in the drafting committee *before* the Bill is tabled in the Parliament, and the Lokpal system *after* it is set up. Playing dirty tricks, denying adequate funding for the bureaucracy, infiltrating it with their own people and delaying implementation of the Bill, and discrediting Lokpal by false documents, ignoring his directives etc. are but some of the many tactics the vested interests could use to make the Lokpal system almost impotent. We have seen some of these tactics practiced against Lokpal in Karnataka by the BJP government.

After the dramatic show off by a joint committee with the Civil Society, the Government cleverly tabled a Lokpal Bill in the Parliament threatening the public and devoid of the soul of Jan Lokpal without any real powers to him. It was going to carry through the Bill in a huff, but for Anna Hazare's Ramlila Ground protests that was at first handled shabbily by the Government but later succumbing to the three demands of Hazare by accepting them as the 'Sense of the House' and sending a publicly read letter from the Prime Minister by one of his ministers in Ramlila Grounds. But the revised Lokpal and Lokayukta Bili was not as per the 'Sense of the House' and was torn into pieces with the mockery of giving Lokpal a constitutional status, whereas the party in power itself is challenging the constitutional institution of Election Commission and flouting its 'code of conduct' repeatedly in recent U.P. elections. The Bill is still hanging in balance, because it was misconceived by the Government while throwing its onus on the opposition, especially on its rival party BJP to gain electoral advantages.

We have seen that the Indian constitution is not able to resolve all these problems. It has become a tattered motley coat on which so many diverse patches have been put that it has lost its original texture that needs to be discarded lest the largest democracy should stink.

The steps like institution of Lokpal, electoral reforms, right to recall etc. might serve as good stepping stones, but we shall have to think beyond them in the long run to bring about a systemic change to get rid of demagogy and restore democracy in which interests of the largest and the meanest are taken care of. It needs an understanding of the weaknesses of the existing system and a complete restructuring of the political system.

WEAKNESSES OF THE SYSTEM

Non-Gandhian Approach

We have to accept that Gandhiji was the son of the Indian soil. Therefore, he knew the ground realities and had practical solutions to resolve them. On the other hand, Nehru was ambitious and brought up in western culture and thought, having little knowledge of the 80% of India that lived in villages. But Gandhi died too soon after Independence and Nehru tried to implant the western system on the Indian soil that was carried on by Indira, Rajiv, Nasimah Rao and Manmohan Singh, giving rise to distorted growth. In the whole process India seems to have lost its way.

The British Constitution

The second tragedy was that we adopted the British model of constitution that was meant for a small country with strict adherence to conventions whereas India is a vast country with ethnic and cultural diversity. As a result it turned into non-participative democracy alienating the people from the Government.

Colonial Administration

Nehru and his family rule have learnt the Governance from Mountbatten whose general rule was to suppress dissent by hook or crook disallowing the participative democracy. The whole history of more than 50 years of the Congress rule is replete with such examples.

Central Bias

Dictatorial tendencies through concentration of authority in one hand gave rise to high headedness, corruption and public upsurge.

Expensive elections

Expensive elections have become the game of the rich and the mafia in which public is distanced from the politicians.

Economic model

Except for the First Five Year Plan our model has been of a non-agrarian and affluent economy—corporate growth and political corruption—inequitable growth ignoring the basic needs of the common man rotting food, hungry people and flooded villages.

Lack of transparency

Transparency is a cornerstone of good governance as it allows citizens everywhere to hold institutions and governments accountable for their policies and performance. In India, a country that ranks low on the Transparency International Index and is known for high levels of corruption, one such step taken so far under civil society's pressure, has been the Right to Information Act, 2005. We have already discussed the increasing levels of corruption in Government. There has been a recent surge of activity from Civil Society Organisations leading to a new consciousness among citizens about their role in a democracy. It needs to be carried further.

GANDHIAN SOLUTIONS

Gandhiji explained his vision in 1946:

"Independence begins at the bottom... A society must be built in which every village has to be self sustained and capable of managing its own affairs... It will be trained and prepared to perish in the attempt to defend itself against any onslaught from without... This does not exclude dependence on and willing help from neighbours or from the world. It will be a free and voluntary play of mutual forces... In this structure, composed of innumerable villages, there will be ever widening, never ascending circles. Growth will not be a pyramid with the apex sustained by the bottom. But it will be an oceanic circle whose centre will be the individual. Therefore, the outermost circumference will not wield power to crush the inner circle, but will give strength to all within and derive its own strength from it."

He further said, "It may be taunted with the retort that this is all Utopian and, therefore not worth a single thought... Let India live for the true picture, though never realizable in its completeness. We must have a proper picture of what we want before we can have something approaching it."

Gandhi's model of Swaraj was almost entirely discarded by the Indian government. He had wanted a system of a classless, stateless direct democracy. In what is known as his *Last Will and Testament,* Gandhi suggested the disbanding of the Congress as a political forum.

He said, "Its task is done. The next task is to move into villages and revitalize life there to build a new socio-economic structure from the bottom upwards." He wanted the Congress party to change into a constructive work organisation—Lok Sewak Sangh was the name he proposed—to awake the conscience and mobilize the people to work and struggle for Swaraj. However, none of these objectives were achieved when India became independent. India, although a federation, got a strong central government. Representative democracy, rather than direct democracy, was adopted. The Congress Party was not disbanded. Rather, it went on to become one of the front runners in running the government of India. Additionally, modern India has kept in place many aspects of British (and Western) influence, including widespread use of the English language, common-law, industrialization, liberal democracy, military organization and bureaucracy.

It was unfortunate that by ignoring the vastness of our country and the existing diversity of our culture, we adopted the British constitutional model meant for a small country that has turned India into a non-participative democracy. The colonial style of governing through crooks, that the Congress inherited from Mountbatten, has now infested the entire political system of the country. The ancient Indian literature is replete with the styles of good governance and politics, but our pioneers in the post independence era had an infatuation for the West and we seem to have lost our best in their quest for the West.

While the freedom struggle was in progress, Gandhi was working on ideas of a new social order for post-colonial India. He believed that there would be no point in getting rid of the British without getting rid of the centralised, exploitative and violent system of governance and the economics of greed that they pursued. Gandhi designed a new trinity to achieve his vision of a new non-violent social order.

The first of this trinity was Sarvodaya, Upliftment of All. The western system of governance is based on the rule of the majority and is called democracy. This was not good enough for Gandhi. He wanted no division between the majority and the minority. He wanted to serve the interests of each and everyone, of all. Democracy is also limited to care for the interests of the human beings. Democracy, working with capitalism, favours the few who have capital. Democracy, together with socialism, favours the majority, but is still limited to humans. Sarvodaya includes the care of the earth, of animals, forests, rivers and land. For Gandhi, life is sacred, so he advocated reverence for all life, humans as well as other than humans.

The second aspect of the Gandhian trinity is Swaraj, the Self Government. Swaraj works to bring about a social transformation through small-scale, decentralized and participatory structures of governments on the one hand. On the other, Swaraj implies self-transformation, self-discipline and self-restraint. "There is enough in the world for everybody's need, but not enough for anybody's greed", said Gandhi. So a moral, ethical, ecological and spiritual foundation is necessary to build good governance.

The third part of the trinity is Swadesi, Local Economy. Gandhi opposed mass-production and favoured production by the masses. Work for him is as much a spiritual necessity as it is economic. So he insisted on the principle that every member of society should be engaged in manual work. Manufacturing in small workshops and adherence to arts and crafts feeds the body as well as the soul, professed Gandhi. He believed that long-distance transportation of goods, competitive trading and relentless economic growth would destroy the fabric of human communities as well as the integrity of the natural world.

The Problem of Unemployment, Labour and Strikes

"I suggest that we are thieves in a way. If I take anything that I do not need for my own immediate use and keep it, I thieve it from somebody else. Nature produces enough for our wants from day to day without exception. If only everybody took enough for himself and nothing more, there would be no pauperism in this world. There would be no man dying of starvation. In India we have got many millions of people who have to be satisfied with one meal a day." (This reminds me of a four-year old boy, the youngest of five children of a tricycle driver telling me that he eats rice with a bit of water and salt. There must be a million others like him in our country.)

"Sparsely populated America may have need of machinery, India may not need it at all. Where there are millions and millions of idle labour, it is no use of thinking of labour saving devices. The reason of our poverty is the extinction of our local cottage industries and our consequent unemployment."

Economics and Ethics

"The masters care only for the service they get. What becomes of the labourer does not concern them. All their endeavors are generally confined to obtaining maximum service with minimum payment. The labourer on the other hand tries to hit upon all tricks whereby he can get maximum pay with minimum work. The result is that although the labourers get an increment there is no improvement in the work turned out."

"A satisfactory solution of the condition of labour must include the following: the hours of labour must leave the workmen some hours of leisure; they must get facilities for their own education; provision should be made for an adequate supple of food, clothing and necessary education for their children; there should be sanitary dwellings for the workmen; and they should be in a position to save enough to maintain themselves during their old age.

Regional Planning

Most developing nations adopted Soviet type centralized planning. Under it, the national and state governments controlling most of the resources, allocate funds for various social, environmental and economic programmes, including social and physical infrastructure, and allocate them to local governments in the from of schemes with preconceived conditions and stipulators often not suiting local needs. This leads to wastage, heavy overheads and application of resources often not suiting local requirements. Centralized planning is linked with development economics. Development economics is a fake discipline that imposes programmes and schemes on local communities thus alienating them from the decision-making processes.

The only scientific method of planning is regional planning. Regional planning takes the available resources into consideration to prepare plans covering socio-economic infrastructure and environmental issues, expressed in analytical, quantitative and special plans. These plans are reiteratively coordinated at the local, state and national levels. Satellite imagery and geographic information systems now facilitate such planning. This type of planning was practised by many traditional societies. India has such a full-fledged scientific planning discipline called vastu shastra. Colonial rule disrupted India from its traditional knowledge base and, in the name of modernity, insensitive leadership continued to pursue centralized systems.

Development economics, based on centralized planning, is a fake discipline. What we need is housewife economics—local governments handle housekeeping while state and national governments provide higher level infrastructure and coordination, but cannot interfere in housekeeping. Effective transparency mechanisms covering the sovereign rights of the people to information, consultation, participation and referendum prevent wasteful bureaucratic overheads, abuse of authority, corruption and wastage.

It is only through such true democracy that local communities can educate themselves, use the environment in a sustainable manner, and ensure adequate health-care to contain the population. It can also generate adequate resources to enable the state and national governments to provide higher level infrastructure including transportation. Needless to say, resource management should be through scientific regional planning, now facilitated through satellite imagery and geographic information systems.

Four-tier Government

A government with a Central bias with concentration of authority at the top has a tendency to turn dictatorial grossly losing peripheral perceptions resulting into neglecting the welfare of states, districts and the villages. It does not end there, it also alienates the government from the public and gives rise to costly electoral process giving rise to corruption and criminal politics. Therefore, decentralization of authority and the government at your door step are the need of the day to achieve the Gandhian objectives of Self Rule and Sarvodaya. In this process the decision making and executive powers have to be vested with the Village Governments while the District and the State Governments have to act as coordinating administrative agencies. The role of the Central Government should be mainly focused on Defense, Foreign Affairs, Monetary Management etc.

Village Governments

Within local governance, Gandhi laid great emphasis on village governance since being at the grassroots level it constitutes direct democracy whereas all others are representative democracy. According to Indian scriptures, the village parliament consisting of all adult men and women control all village resources, officials and decision-making. Women have thus been franchised in India for 4,000 years whereas they got enfranchised in the West only in this century. The village parliament elects the village head and councilors for day to day work, usually for a year, and can remove them any time for misconduct. Counselors are held in high esteem but if the community finds that any one of them has abused authority, he can be summarily removed through simple majority.

The village government gives land and other environmental resources on lease for specific use. The community thus prevents misuse of land and protects the interests of the weak. Such grassroots empowerment regenerates the spiritual energies of the people for self-development as they are involved in day to day decisions about the community and the environment.

In contemporary times, industrial proposals will need the approval of village governments. This will nurture an environment in which industry functions in trusteeship of society, producing goods and services useful for society, investing the surplus for common good, and avoid ostentatious consumption. Such industry can also support social services such as education and health-care to supplement the programme of the village and district governments.

District Governments

Nation-states are often created through wars and mergers whereas district or counties are generic. They generally form mini-catchments in which people have cultural links and can traverse within a reasonable time. They constitute the highest level of local governance.

They provide professional support to and coordinate village governments.

An intermediate level government is often provided as a link between district and village governments. Large cities have autonomous city governments.

Most social and environmental matters are in the exclusive jurisdiction of local governments. Social or environmental conflict at the grassroots level should be mediated at the intermediate and finally at the district or city level. The state and national governments should have no jurisdiction over such issues.

History has shown that communities have lived in harmony with each other at the local level, and that it is higher level politics, priesthood and feudal interests that have divided them. Gandhi was convinced that once control over local resources and decision-making is restored at the local level, most social and environmental issues and all social ills and discords will gradually give way to social harmony and economic self-reliance.

Ethnic conflicts are becoming a major global concern the world over. True democracy provides the framework for enrichment of every ethic identity.

State Governments

State governments will control resources to handle state level infrastructure such as state level armed police, highways, water systems, state-grid power generation and distribution, industry, minerals, higher education, referral hospitals and heritage sites. It will be accountable to the people of the state through effective transparency laws covering the sovereign rights of the people to information, consultation, participation and referendum.

The state governments will ordinarily not be dependent upon the national government for support. It will deal with Resource Management, a part of the revenue from identified environmental resources and some sources of taxation and/or share in tax revenue, shall be assigned to state governments. This is to enable them to provide (1) state level infrastructure, (2) support to local entities with inadequate resources, and (3) coordination, but not interfere in local jurisdictions.

Central Government

The national government will control resources to handle national level infrastructure such as external relations, defence, national reserve police, national highways, national water systems, national power generation and distribution, national level minerals, selected higher education, selected referral hospitals and inter state heritage sites. It will be accountable to the people of the nation through effective transparency laws covering the sovereign rights of the people to information, consultation, participation and referendum.

It will deal with Resource Management, a part of the revenue from identified environmental resources and some sources of taxation and/or share in tax revenue shall be assigned to national governments. This will be to enable it to provide (1) national level infrastructure, (2) support to states with inadequate resources, and (3) coordination, but not interfere in state and local jurisdictions. Its main concerns will be Defense, Foreign Affairs, Monetary Management etc.

The Political System

The political system is an important component of democratic governance. It needs to be properly structured so that it nurtures responsible politics and enable the society to prevent self-seekers and the corrupt from holding public offices. Political parties seem to have become indispensable in the present context, but they seem to have done more than good to the society and the system. They divide the society, create narrow loyalties and promote orthodox thinking. They are in the genre of a caste system that generates a new sort of political unsociability. Otherwise also most of the precious time of the legislatures is wasted in mudslinging on and by the party in power and the real issues are lost. Therefore, the best thing is to do away with them so that we may have a conflict free political system, no wastage of man hours in legislatures and coherent governance. However, if it sounds Utopian to begin with initially, we should try to reduce them to two. It also requires a fair electoral system that ensures direct accountability of the Government to the people.

Roles and Jurisdictions

There shall be elected governments at the local, state and national levels each having exclusive jurisdiction over local, state and national matters. To take democracy close to the people, the local level may be further divided into local, sub local and grassroots. The grassroots government will be most important from the perspective of the people being direct democracy while all others are representative democracy.

In grassroots governments, the parliament consisting of all adult men and women shall be the supreme authority. All other governments shall have an elected chief executive, a parliament and judiciary, all accountable to its people. The chief executive and his deputy shall be directly elected. The chief executive and the ministers appointed by him shall not be members of any parliament. The parliament shall consist of an elected assembly. It shall approve the budget, perform watchdog functions and approve the appointment of the political ministers and professional departmental heads selected by the chief executive.

Electoral Process

The electoral system should combine the chief advantages of both direct and indirect elections. The election should be direct in the village and it should enjoy maximum local autonomy. As the functions of the higher bodies will be mainly advisory and coordinative, indirect election would be the most suitable method. It will avoid colossal waste of national energy, time and money involved in direct elections especially in a vast country like India. The unhealthy growth of political parties and communal feelings will also be automatically checked to a great extent. Since indirect elections will be confined to a few responsible individuals, there will be hardly any room for bribery and corruption.

Besides, the representatives of the upper bodies will not be in a position to 'forget' their constituencies because they would owe their delegation to the lower panchayats. According to the proposed constitution, the president of the lower panchayat shall be the ex officio member of the next higher panchayat. Thus, even the president of the All-India panchayat shall be the president of his own village panchayat as well; he shall, at the same time, be a member or president of the taluka, district and provincial panchayats. He will, therefore, be fully conversant with and alive to the difficulties and requirements of the masses; he cannot be a mere 'armchair' politician. If any member of the highest body does not discharge his civil duties towards the people satisfactorily, he would stand no chance at the next elections; he might even be 'recalled' by his own village panchayat, thus, compelling him to resign his membership of all the other higher bodies. Since the village constituencies will be small and there will be direct and intimate knowledge of the candidates seeking election, the scope for electioneering frauds would be eliminated root and branch.

Sovereign Rights Commission

Power having got centralized, the political system is not willing, nor able to restore it to local governments and the community, nor institute effective transparency mechanisms. Thus, most constitutions instituted in the name of the people, have become a Frankenstein that is destroying its creator, the people, and the people apparently can do nothing about it. Centralisation can lead to further centralization, not to democracy. All talk of people's participation begs the question.

'People are the first' has conceptualised a legitimate process of reforms. Through lateral thinking, it has conceptualized that contemporary democracy needs apart from the familiar institutions such as parliament and judiciary, a new institution, Sovereign Rights Commission with authority to direct referendums, except on issue fundamental to democracy or the integrity of the nation. There can, for example, be no referendum on making the state theocratic or a region seceding.

MN Venkatachaliah, former Chief Justice of India, Chairman of the recently constituted Commission for Review of the Working of the Constitution, also endorsed referendum as the supreme sovereign right of the people, intrinsic to democracy. He has also praised the concept of Sovereign Rights Commission as providing a legitimate, non-violent process for transforming the society.

Transparency

"Even as we recognise and celebrate the efficacy and effectiveness of the RTI Act, we must take a critical look at it. There are concerns that need to be discussed and addressed honestly," the PM said. The remarks were made at the Sixth Annual Convention of Information Commissioners in Delhi, which also marks six years of the enactment of the RTI Act in 2005.

First, he said the government was being flooded with RTI requests having no bearing on public interest. This situation was 'undesirable' as it was stretching the limited time and resources available with the government.

He said that honest bureaucrats felt discouraged from expressing their views. "We need to remember that a point of view brought under public scrutiny and discussion in an isolated manner may sometimes present a distorted or incomplete picture of what really happened in the process of making the final decisions. We must take a critical look at the exemption clauses in the RTI Act to determine whether they serve the larger good and whether a change is needed in them," Singh said. He said there were "certain grey areas" on the privacy issue as well.

His remarks come against the backdrop of the controversial 2G memo of the Finance Ministry which was released by the Prime Minister's Office (PMO) following an RTI application. The internal memo had brought P. Chidambaram under the scanner in the 2G case and created a deep political crisis in the government.

Aruna Roy countered the PM's position. "I think that the PM has this feeling that RTI will bring down the government's efficiency. However, RTI has only exposed the government's inefficiency. Nothing has been stalled or made less effective by the RTI. Accessing file notings has not harmed anyone," she said.

According to Roy, the only thing that has harmed the government is the 2G scam. The RTI Act only imposes a standard of performance and there is resistance to that in the government. "Simple access to records is a problem for this government," Roy said. Rights activist Medha Patkar, who was also at the conference, said the ambit of the RTI Act should actually be widened for the sake of transparency rather than diluting it. "Bureaucrats will be scared of writing anything on a file only if they are doing something illegal or favoring a person," Patkar said.

Prominent RTI activist Subhash Chandra Agrawal said UPA Chairperson Sonia Gandhi should intervene to prevent any dilution of the RTI Act. "Union Ministers like Veerappa Moily and Salman Khurshid have been a cause of embarrassment for the government first on the Lokpal Bill issue and now for talking of the dilution of the RTI Act, which has been indirectly hinted at by the Prime Minister." Agrawal said the correspondence between the PM and former Telecom Minister A. Raja in 2007 on 2G, revealed through an RTI petition, had drawn the attention of the Supreme Court.

Had there been any dilution of the provisions of the Act, similar correspondence related to major scams would not have come to light, he said. "File notings have been instrumental in exposing the irregular appointment of P.J. Thomas as the Central Vigilance Commissioner," Agrawal said.

Bibek Debroy of the Centre for Policy Research said that diluting the RTI Act would be a public relations disaster for the government as it has been the UPA's big success story.

Transparency is absolutely needed for accountability and good governance. It keeps a check on mismanagement and corruption, inspires public confidence and permits informed participation of citizens but for national security perspective. Thus transparency is one indicator of a government that is citizen-focused and service-oriented. Transparency depends on good records and clear procedures. It implies a proactive effort to make information accessible to citizens.

Summing up, we can say that secrecy breeds corruption. In this electronic age the administration, the government, the legislation and the judiciary should be open to the electronic screen except in matters pertaining to national defense.

CONCLUSION

Materialization of this utopian dream is going to be a long journey. But this does not mean that Anna Hazare's agitation for Lokpal and

Baba Ramdev's agitation against black money have been frustrating steps in this direction. They might have had little impact upon the insensitive double tongued Government that talks of constitutional status for Lokpal on one hand and in the recent elections to the five state assemblies cared a fig for the Code of Conduct laid down by the Election Commission of India, a constitutional institution. Despite little impact of these crusaders on the Government so far they have started making the people conscious that they are the masters and the Prime Minister, the ministers, the legislators and the bureaucrats are their servants, accountable to them as they are the pay masters through taxes to the public exchequer. The masses should know that they will have to give up the slave mentality and the lax attitude towards laws made to protect their rights. Otherwise, neither Jan Lokpal nor any other strong law will be able to solve the problem of corruption and black money. No doubt Lokpal might help to solve the problem of corruption and black money to some extent, however, the complete resolution of the problems of our system needs Gandhian solutions as suggested earlier in this chapter.

Let us pledge to dedicate our lives to reconstruct India of Bapu's Dream... free from, exploitation, corruption, poverty, ignorance and disease.

Let the verse of Swami Vivekanand resound in the minds of our people: Arise, awake and stop not till the goal is reached.

Appendices

APPENDIX-ONE

JAN LOKPAL BILL 2011

A Bill to establish an independent authority to investigate offences under the Prevention of Corruption Act, 1988 to detect corruption by expeditious investigation and to prosecute offenders and to ensure timely redressal of certain types of public grievances and to provide protection to whistleblowers.

Be it be enacted by Parliament in the Sixty! first Year of the Republic of India as follows:

CHAPTER I

PRELIMINARY

1. (1) This Act may be called the Jan Lokpal Act, 2011.

(2) It shall come into force on 120th day of its securing assent from the President of India.

2. Definitions:

In this Act, unless the context otherwise requires:

(a) "Board" means the Chairman and the other members of the Lokpal Collectively.

(b) "Complaint" means an allegation of corruption or a request by whistleblower for protection and appropriate action.

(c) "Lokpal" means and includes.

(i) Benches constituted under this Act and performing functions under this Act;

(ii) Any officer or employee performing under this Act,

(iii) The Board in rest of the cases;

(d) "Lokpal Bench" means a Bench of 2 or more members of the Lokpal acting together in respect of any matter in accordance with the regulations. Each bench shall have a member with legal background.

(e) "Act of corruption" includes :

(i) anything made punishable under Chapter IX of the Indian Penal Code or under the Prevention of Corruption Act, 1988; which would also include any offence committed by an elected member of a house of legislature even in respect of his speech or vote inside the house.

(ii) willfully giving any undue benefit to any person or obtaining any benefit from any public servant in violation of any laws or rules.

(iii) victimisation of a whistleblower or a witness.

(iv) repeated violation of citizen's charter by any public servant.

(f) "Full bench" means a bench with seven members with or without the Chairperson

(g) "Government Servant" means a public servant, who is not an elected representative or a judicial officer,

(h) "Grievance" means a claim by a person that he could not get satisfactory redressal according to a citizens' charter despite approaching a Grievance Redressal Officer of that Department;

(i) "Judicial officer" means the officers appointed under section 22 of this Act.

(j) "Penalty" under this Act means punishment of dismissal, removal or reduction in rank

(k) "Public authority" means any authority or body or institution of self governance established or constituted—

(i) by or under the Constitution; or

(ii) by or under any other law made by the Parliament, or a state legislature

(iii) by notification issued or order made by the Government, and includes any body owned, controlled or substantially financed by the Government;

(l) "Public servant" shall have the same meaning as defined in section 2(c) of Prevention of Corruption Act 1988.

(m) "Whistleblower" means any person, who provides information about corruption in a public authority or is a witness or victim in that case or who faces the threat of:

(i) professional harm, including but not limited to illegitimate transfer, denial of promotion, denial of appropriate perquisites, departmental proceedings, discrimination or

(ii) physical harm, or

(iii) is actually subjected to any harm;

because of either making a complaint to the Lokpal under this Act, or for filing an application under the Right to Information Act, 2005 or by any other legal, action aimed at preventing or exposing corruption or mal-governance.

3. Notwithstanding anything in any other Act or Law the provisions of this Act shall prevail and to the extent that the provisions of this Act are repugnant to any other provision in any other Act or law, the provisions in other Acts or laws shall stand amended to the extent of such repugnancy.

CHAPTER II

ESTABLISHMENT OF LOKPAL

4. (1) Immediately after the commencement of this Act, the Central Government by a Notification shall establish an institution known as Lokpal, who would have administrative, financial and functional independence from the government.

(2) The Lokpal shall consist of a Chairperson and 10 other members and various officers under them at different levels to perform such functions as are assigned to them under this Act.

(3) The Chairperson and the 10 members of the Lokpal shall be appointed by the President on the recommendation of a Selection Committee.

(4) The following shall not be eligible to become Chairperson or Member of Lokpal:

(a) Any person, who is not a citizen of India, or

(b) Any person, against whom charges were ever framed by any court of law for any offence involving moral turpitude, or

(c) Any person, who is less than 45 years in age, or

(d) Any person, who was in the service of any government and has remitted office within the last two years, either by way of resignation or retirement.

(5) At least four members of Lokpal shall have a legal background.

Explanation: "Legal Background" means that the person should have held a judicial office in the territory of India for at least ten years or should have been an advocate in a High Court or the Supreme Court for at least fifteen years.

(6) The Selection Committee shall consist of the following:

(i) The Prime Minister of India, who will be the Chairperson of the Selection Committee.

(ii) The Leader of the Opposition in the Lok Sabha

(iii) Two judges of Supreme Court of India and two permanent Chief Justices of the High Courts selected by collegium of all Supreme Court judges

(iv) The Chief Election Commissioner of India

(v) The Comptroller and Auditor General of India

(vi) All previous Chairpersons of Lokpal.

(7) The Selection Committee shall select the Chairperson and the other members of the Lokpal from out of a short list prepared by the Search Committee. The Chairperson shall be a person with extensive knowledge of law.

(8) A Search Committee shall consist of 10 members. 5 of its members shall be selected by the Selection Committee from amongst the retired Chief Justices of India, the retired Chief Election Commissioners and the retired Comptroller and Auditor Generals with impeccable reputation of integrity, who have not joined any political party after retirement and who are not holding any office under any government. The 5 members so selected shall, through consensus, coDopt another 5 members from the Civil Society in the search committee.

(9) The Search Committee before preparing the short list will invite nominations from such eminent individuals or such class of people, whom they deem fit, for the position of Chairperson or the members of the Lokpal.

(10) Only persons with impeccable integrity and record of public service particularly in the field of fighting corruption shall be eligible for being considered for nomination.

(11) The recommendations about nominees should, interalia, contain details of any allegations faced by that candidate under any law, details of his work against corruption in the past, reasons why that person is suitable for the job and any other material that the search committee may decide.

(12) The search committee, using any other means, shall collect as much information about the background and past achievements of these candidates.

(13) Such nominations as are received shall be put on a web site for inviting comments from the people with regard to the suitability or otherwise of the nominees.

(14) The Search Committee after taking into consideration the comments/information received from the public shall prepare, preferably through consensus, the short list of 3 times the number of persons to be appointed as members of the Lokpal.

(15) Any nominations to which objections are raised by any 3 members of the Search Committee shall not be included in the short list.

(16) Before sending the short list to the Selection Committee, the Search Committee will get the names of the short listed persons put on a public web site to enable people to send any relevant information/comments about the shortlisted persons.

(17) The Selection Committee shall, after considering all relevant information about the short listed candidates, select the required number of persons preferably through consensus. However, a person shall not be selected if 3 members of the Selection Committee disapprove such names.

(18) The Selection Committee after selecting the persons to be appointed as members or Chairperson of the Lokpal shall ascertain their willingness to serve as members or Chairperson, as the case may be, before recommending the names to the President.

(19) The Government shall fill up a vacancy of the Chairperson or a member 3 months before the member or the Chairperson is due to retire. If the vacancy arises due to unforeseen reasons, it shall be filled within three months of such vacancy arising.

(20) The Officers in the Lokpal shall be appointed by the Board or any other authority designated by the Regulations whether on a permanent basis or on a temporary basis.

(21) The Chairperson or members of Lokpal shall not be serving member of either the Parliament or the "Legislature of any State and shall not hold any office of'profit (other than the office as Chairperson or member) or carry on any business

or practice any profession and accordingly, before he enters upon his office, a person appointed as the Chairperson or member of Lokpal shall :

(i) if he holds any office or profit, resign from such office;

or

(ii) if he is carrying on any business, sever his connection with the conduct and management of such business; or

(iii) if he is practicing any profession, suspend practice of such profession, or

(iv) if he is associated directly or indirectly with any other activity, which is likely to cause conflict of interest in the performance of his duties in Lokpal, he should suspend his association with that activity.

Provided that if even after the suspension, the earlier association of that person with such activity is likely to adversely affect his performance at Lokpal, that person shall not be appointed as a member or Chairperson of Lokpal.

(22) A person appointed as the Chairperson or member of Lokpal shall hold office for a term of five years from the date on which he enters upon his office or upto the age of 70 years, whichever is earlier; Provided that,

(a) the Chairperson or member of Lokpal may, by writing under his hand addressed to the President, resign from his office;

(b) the Chairperson or member may be removed from office in the manner provided in this Act.

(23) There shall be paid to the Chairperson and each member a salary equal to that of the Chief Justice of India and that of the judge of the Supreme Court respectively;

(24) The allowances and pension payable to and other conditions of service of the Chairperson or a member shall be such as may be prescribed by the government;

Provided that the allowances and pension payable to and other conditions of service of the Chairperson or a member shall not be varied to his disadvantage after his appointment.

(25) The Chairperson and members of Lokpal shall not be eligible for appointment to any position in the Government of India or the government of any State or any such body which is funded by any of the Governments or for contesting elections to Parliament, State Legislature or local bodies.

5. The Lokpal shall select and appoint a Secretary to the Lokpal who will have the rank of Secretary to the Government of India. He shall be competent to authenticate all orders passed by the Lokpal.

CHAPTER III

POWERS AND FUNCTIONS OF THE LOKPAL AND ITS OFFICERS

Functions of Lokpal:

6. The Lokpal shall have the following functions and powers

   (a) to exercise superintendence over the investigation of offences involving any act of corruption.

   (b) to give directions to the investigating officers for the purpose of proper investigation of such offences.

   (c) after completion of investigation in any case involving an allegation of an act of corruption, to impose punishment of dismissal, removal or reduction in rank against government servants after giving them reasonable opportunities of being heard.

   (d) to ensure that the public grievances covered by this Act are redressed in a time bound manner

   (e) to initiate prosecution before a Special Court established under the Prevention of Corruption Act, 1988

   (f) to ensure the proper prosecution of cases before a Special Court established under the Prevention of Corruption Act, 1988.

(g) to provide by rules for the terms and'conditions of service including the allowances and pension payable to the officers and staff of the Lokpal.

(h) to authorize a Bench of the Lokpal to issue letters Irogatory in relation to any case pending investigation under this Act.

(i) to receive complaints from whistle blowers.

(j) to receive complaints against any officer or staff of Lokpal.

(k) to recruit investigating officers and other officers and staff and get them trained in modern methods of scientific investigation.

(l) to appoint judicial officers, prosecutors and senior counsels.

(m) to acquire modern equipment necessary for proper investigation.

(n) to attach property and assets acquired by corrupt means and to confiscate them in certain cases as provided under this Act.

(o) to recommend cancellation or modification of a lease, license, permission, contract or agreement, if it was obtained by corrupt means and to recommend blacklisting of a firm, company, contractor or any other person, involved in an act of corruption. The public authority shall either comply with the recommendation or reject the same within a month of receipt of recommendation. In the event of rejection of its recommendation, the Lokpal may approach appropriate High Court for seeking appropriate directions to be given to the public authority.

(p) to ensure due compliance of its orders by imposing penalties on persons failing to comply with its orders as provided under this Act.

(q) to initiate suo moto appropriate action under the Act on receipt of any information from any source about any corruption.

(r) to make recommendations to public authorities, in consultation with them, to make changes in their work practices to reduce the scope for corruption and whistleblower victimization. The concerned authority shall send its compliance report to Lokpal within two months specifying detailed reasons, wherever they choose to reject any of the recommendations.

(s) to prepare a sentencing policy for the offences under Prevention of Corruption Act and revising it from time to time.

(t) to ensure that the time limits mentioned in this Act are strictly adhered to.

(u) to ensure the integrity of its functionaries and impose punishments of dismissal, removal and reduction in rank against

(v) to require any public authority to render any specific help required by the Lokpal.

(w) to prepare an appropriate reward scheme to encourage complaints from within and outside the government to report acts and evidence of corruption.

Provided that the total value of such reward shall not exceed 10% of the value of the loss recovered or loss prevented.

(x) to inquire into the assets declaration statements filed by all successful candidates after any election to any seat in any House of the Parliament.

(x) Such other functions as may be necessary for the proper implementation of this Act.

Powers of officers under Lokpal

7. (1) The Investigating Officers of Lokpal authorized to investigate

offences under the Prevention of Corruption Act 1988 shall have all the powers which are vested in a Police Officer while investigating offences under the Code of Criminal Procedure, as well as the powers conferred on the director of enforcement under the Foreign Exchange Management Act, 1999 as well as under the Prevention of Money Laundering Act, 2002.

(2) The members of Lokpal or any officer under the Lokpal while exercising any powers under the Act shall have the powers of a civil court trying a suit under the Code of Civil Procedure, 1908, and in particular, in respect of the following matters :

(a) summoning and enforcing the attendance of any person from any part of India and examining him on oath;

(b) requiring the discovery and production of any document;

(c) receiving evidence on affidavits;

(d) requisitioning any public record or copy there of from any court or office;

(e) issuing commissions for the examination of witnesses or other documents; and

(f) any other matter which may be prescribed

(3) All members of the Lokpal and all officers of the Lokpal superior in rank to an Investigating Officer may exercise the same powers as may be exercised by such Investigating Officcr.

(4) A Lokpal bench may punish a public servant with imprisonment up to 6 months or with fine or both, if he fails to comply with its order for ensuring their compliance

(5) If during the course of investigation into a complaint, the Lokpal feels that continuance of a government servant in that position could adversely affect the course of investigations or that the said government servant is likely to destroy or tamper with the evidence or influence the witnesses or is likely to continue with corruption, the Lokpal may issue appropriate directions including transfer of that government servant from that position.

(6) The Lokpal may, at any stage of investigation under this Act, direct by an interim order, appropriate authorities to take such action as is necessary, to prevent the public servant from secreting the assets allegedly acquired by him by corrupt means;

(7) While investigating any offence under Prevention of Corruption Act 1988, Lokpal shall be competent to investigate any offence under any other law in the same case.

(8) If during any investigation under this act, the Lokpal is satisfied that any preventive action is necessary in public interest to prevent the ongoing incidence of corruption, it may make any recommendation to the public authority concerned to stay the implementation or enforcement of any decision or take any such action as is recommended by the Lokpal. The public authority shall either comply with the recommendation of the Lokpal or reject the same within 15 days of the recommendation thereof. In the event of rejection of its recommendation, the Lokpal may approach the appropriate High Court for seeking appropriate directions to be given to the public authority.

8. For the purposes of investigation of offences related to acts of corruption, the appropriate Bench of the Lokpal shall be deemed to be designated authority under Section 5 of the Indian Telegraph Act empowered to approve interception and monitoring of messages of data or voice transmitted through telephones, internet or any other medium as covered under the Indian Telegraph Act read with Information and Technology Act 2000 and as per rules and regulations made under the Indian Telegraph Act 1885.

Issue of search warrants:

9. (1) Where, in consequence of information in his possession, the Lokpal (a) has reason to believe that any person -

(i) to whom a summon or notice under this Act, has, been or might be issued, will not or would not produce or cause to be produced any property, document or thing which will be necessary or useful for or relevant to any inquiry or other proceedings to be conducted by him;

It may by a search warrant authorize any officer not below the rank of an Inspector of Police to conduct a search or carry out an inspection in accordance therewith and in particular to, enter and search any building or place where he has reason to suspect that such property, or document, is kept;

(2) The provisions of the Code of Criminal Procedure, 1973, relating to search and seizure shall apply, so far as may be, to searches and seizures under sub-section (1),

(3) A warrant issued under sub-section (1) shall for all purposes, be deemed to be a warrant issued by a court under section 93 of the Code of Criminal Procedure, 1973.

CHAPTER IV PROCEEDINGS OF LOKPAL

10. (1) The Lokpal may regulate the procedure for the transaction of its business or that of its officers as also allocation of its business amongst the different benches of Lokpal.

(2) No act or proceeding of the Lokpal shall be invalid merely by reason of:

(a) any vacancy in, or any defect in the constitution of Lokpal;

(b) any defect in the appointment of a person acting as a member of Lokapl; or

(c) any irregularity not affecting the merits of the case.

(3) All policy level decisions including formulation of regulations, assignment and delegation of functions and powers shall be taken by the Board in accordance with regulations.

(4) A complaint by any person may be made in the form of a First Information Report (FIR) as provided under the Code of Criminal Procedure which will not require any payment of fee or affidavit and could be sent to any office of the Lokpal and shall not be rejected merely on the basis of motive or intention of the complainant.

(5) The investigation in any case shall not be closed by the investigating officer without recording reasons for such closure.

(6) The hearings in any proceedings before the Lokpal shall be held in public except in exceptional circumstance where it is not in public interest to do so and the reasons for the same shall be recorded in writing before those proceedings are held in camera. The hearings held in public shall be video recorded and shall be made available to the public on payment of copying cost.

CHAPTER V

ACCOUNTABILITY OF LOKPAL

Removal of Chairperson or members of Lokpal:

11. (1) The Chairperson or any other member of the Lokpal shall only be removed from his office by the President, on the recommendation of the Supreme Court on any of the following grounds after the Supreme Court, on the complaint of any person, held an inquiry and found that he could on such ground be removed :

(a) that he has been guilty of misbehaviour; or

(b) that he is unfit to continue in his office by reason of infirmity of mind or body; or

(c) is adjudged an insolvent; or

(d) engages during his term of office in any paid employment outside the duties of his office.

(2) In any such proceeding the Supreme Court may also direct the suspension of such Chairman or member.

(3) On receipt of recommendation from the Supreme Court, the President shall forthwith remove the Chairperson or the member, as the case may be.

(4) Supreme Court shall, as far as possible, make its recommendations within 3 months of receipt of complaint under this section.

(5) If the complaint is frivolous or has been made with malafide intentions, Supreme Court may impose a fine or an imprisonment upto one year or both on the complainant.

Appeals against the orders of Lokpal:

12. Any orders passed by any bench of the Lokpal or any officer of the Lokpal shall be subject to the writ jurisdiction of the High Court under Article 226 of the Constitution of India. Ordinarily, High Courts shall not stay the order. However, if it does, it will have to decide the case within two months, else the stay would be deemed to have been vacated after two months and no further stay in that case could be granted.

Audit of Lokpal:

13. (1) The CAG shall conduct an annual financial and performance audit of the Lokpal.

(2) A Parliamentary Committee shall do an annual appraisal of the functioning of Lokpal. The Lokpal shall submit a compliance report, mentioning detailed reasons where it does not accept the recommendations of this committee, to the Parliament. It shall be placed on the table of the two Houses of Parliament.

Reports of Lokpal:

14. (1) The Chairperson of Lokpal shall present annually a consolidated report in the prescribed format on its performance to the President.

(2) On receipt of the annual report, the President shall cause a copy thereof together with an explanatory memorandum to be laid before each House of the Parliament.

(3) The Lokpal shall publish every month on its website the list of cases received during the previous month, list of cases disposed with brief details of each such case, outcome and action taken or proposed to be taken in that case, list of cases which are pending and minutes and records of Board meetings.

CHAPTER VI

ACCOUNTABILITY OF OFFICERS OF LOKPAL

Independent Complaints Authority:

15. (1) In each State, one or more complaints authority would be established by the Lokpal to entertain any complaints against any officer or staff of the Lokpal.

(2) Such complaints authority shall consist of 5 members to be selected and nominated by a Committee of 3 persons consisting of:

(i) The Chief Justice of the High Court of the State;

(ii) The Chairman of the State Lokayukata;

(iii) The Chairman of the State Human Rights Commission.

(3) The Complaints Authority shall be chaired by a retired High Court judge and shall have two retired civil servants and two members of civil society.

(4) The complaints received against any officer or staff of the Lokpal shall be inquired into by the Complaints Authority in a public hearing and shall be decided within 2 months of the receipt of the complaint. The officer or staff of the Lokpal shall be given proper opportunity to tender his defence. If the officer or member is found guilty of misbehaviour or dishonest investigation or corruption, the authority may order his dismissal, removal or reduction in rank.

(5) The final orders passed by the Complaints Authority will be subject to the writ jurisdiction of the High Court under Article 226 of the Constitution.

(6) In suitable cases it would also be open to the complaints authority to direct suspension of the officer or staff of the Lokpal.

(7) Lokpat shall provide for the expenses related to the functioning of complaints authority.

(8) Complaints authority shall work in benches in accordance with regulations made under this Act.

Transparency within Lokpal:

16. The Lokpal shall maintain complete transparency in its functioning and shall ensure that full records of any investigation or inquiry conducted under this Act after its conclusion is made public by being put on a public website.

CHAPTER VII

INVESTIGATION AND PROSECUTION AGAINST HIGH FUNCTIONARIES

17. (1) No investigation or prosecution shall be initiated without obtaining permission from a 7 Member Bench of the Lokpal against any of the following persons:

(i) The Prime Minister and any other member of the Council of Ministers;

(ii) Any judge of the Supreme Court or any High Court;

(iii) Any Member of the Parliament.

CHAPTER VIII

POWERS OF LOKPAL TO MAKE REGULATIONS

18. (1) The Lokpal may by notification make regulations consistent with this Act to carry out the provisions of this Act.

(2) In particular and without prejudice to the generality of the power contained in sub section (1) any such regulations may provide for all or any of the following matters, namely:

(a) the creation of different wings in the Lokpal to deal with different subjects like investigation, prosecution and grievances;

(b) the conferment of authority on officers at different levels to exercise powers under the Act and to lay down the procedure for any inquiries including those relating to complaints against its officers or members of staff;

(c) periods within which the investigations and inquiries have to be completed;

(d) To provide for the taking of certain decisions by appropriate benches of the Lokpal by circulation only;

(e) Work norms for each category of officers and staff of Lokpal.

(3) The regulations framed by the Lokpal under this Section shall be laid, as soon as may be after they are issued or made, before each House of Parliament.

CHAPTER IX

REMOVAL OF DIFFICULTIES

19. (1) If any difficulty arises in giving effect to the provisions of this Act, the Central Government may, on the recommendation of the Lokpal, by order, not inconsistent with the provisions of this Act, remove the difficulty provided that no such order shall be made after the expiry of a period of 2 years from the date of commencement of this Act.

(2) Every order made under this section shall be laid before each house of Parliament.

CHAPTER X

TIMELY COMPLETION OF INVESTIGATION AND TRIALS FOR CORRUPTION

20. (1) Every investigating officer shall endeavour to complete the investigation of an offence within a period of 6 months but when necessary he may obtain extension of time from a Bench of the Lokpal. In any case the period of investigation shall not extend 18 months.

(2) Every effort will be made by the special courts trying an offence under the Prevention of Corruption Act to complete the trial within a maximum period of 12 months.

(3) To achieve the objective of a speedy trial the Lokpal shall make an annual assessment of the number of special courts required for this purpose and shall make a recommendation to the Government for creating a specific number of special

courts which recommendations shall be binding on the Government.

(4) The Chief Justices of High Courts will constitute such number of special benches in respective High Courts to hear cases under this Act, to ensure that an appeal in any case is decided as expeditiously as possible and not later than six months.

(5) The judges of Special Courts and the appellate benches set up by High Courts to hear cases under this Act will deal only with cases under this Act.

CHAPTER XI

WHISTLE BLOWERS

21\. (1) Any public official or any other person having information of any corruption in any public authority would be encouraged to send the information confidentially to the Lokpal; and it shall be the duty of the Lokpal to get an inquiry made into such information and if necessary get an investigation made under the Prevention of Corruption Act.

(2) It shall be the duty of the Lokpal to provide full protection to whistle blowers from any physical harm or administrative harassment Identity of such whistle blowers shall also be protected if the whistle blower so desires.

(3) For achieving this objective it shall be competent for the Lokpal to give suitable direction to any security agencies for providing security as well as to any other authority to ensure that no harassment is caused to such whistle blower.

(4) Orders under this section shall be passed expeditiously and in any case within a month of receipt of complaint. Immediate action will be taken in cases involving a threat of physical victimization.

(5) The investigations in complaints by whistleblowers facing physical or professional victimization shall be fast tracked and completed within three months of receipt of the same.

CHAPTER XII

PENALTIES AND PUNISHMENTS AGAINST CORRUPT PUBLIC SERVANTS

Penalties:

22. (1) After the completion of an investigation against any government servant the Lokpal may either initiate prosecution against such public servant or may initiate proceedings for imposition of penalty or both.

(2) Lokpal shall appoint such officers, who may be retired judges or retired civil servants or such others as may be provided, to act as judicial officers for the purpose of this section, at such terms and conditions as may be provided in regulations.

(3) A bench of judicial officers will conduct an inquiry against such government servant for imposition of penalty in which full opportunity to show cause would be given to such government servant. After conclusion of the inquiry the bench shall also determine the penalty, if any, to be awarded to that public servant. The decision of the bench will be subject to approval by a higher authority prescribed by the Lokpal by through regulations.

(4) The recommendations so approved shall be binding on the appointing authority.

Punishments:

23. (1) For any act of corruption, the punishment shall not be less than six months of rigorous imprisonment and may extend up to imprisonment for life.

(2) The Special Court may take into consideration the higher rank of an accused person to inflict a more severe punishment.

(3) If the beneficiary of an offense is a business entity, in addition to the other punishments provided for under this Act and under the Prevention of Corruption Act, a fine of up to five times the loss caused to the public shall be recovered from the accused and the recovery may be made from the assets

of the business entity and from the personal assets of its Managing Directors, if the assets of the accused person are inadequate.

(4) If any company or any of its officer or Director is convicted for any offence under Prevention of Corruption Act, that company and all companies promoted by any of that company's promoters shall be blacklisted and be ineligible for undertaking any government work or contract in future.

(5) If a public servant is convicted under the Prevention of Corruption Act, such public servant shall stand removed from his office.

24. Wherever Lokpal directs imposition of financial penalty on any officer under this Act to be deducted from his salary, it shall be the duty of the Drawing and Disbursing Officer of that Department to implement such order, failing which the said Drawing and Disbursing Officer shall make himself liable for similar penalty.

CHAPTER XIII

GRIEVANCE REDRESSAL SYSTEM

25. (1) Each public authority shall prepare a specific charter within a reasonable time not exceeding one year from the coming into force of this Act.

(2) Every citizens' charter shall enumerate the public authority's commitments to the citizens which are capable of being met within a specific time limit and shall designate the officer whose duty would be to fulfill the commitment of the public authority.

(3) If any public authority does not prepare its citizen's charter within a year, Lokpal shall notify the citizen's charter on its own after consulting the public authority and the same shall be binding on that authority.

(4) Each public authority shall make an assessment of the resources required to implement the citizen's charter and the government shall provide such resources.

(5) Each public authority shall designate an official called Public Grievance Redressal Officer in each station where the public authority has an office, to whom a complaint could be made for any violation of the citizens' charter.

(6) The Senior most officer of that public authority in that office will be designated as the Public Grievance Redressal Officer.

(7) It shall be the duty of the Grievance Redressal Officer to get the grievance redressed within a period of 30 days from the receipt of the complaint.

(8) In the event of even the Grievance Redressal Officer not getting the grievance redressed within the specific period of 30 days a complaint could be made to the Lokpal.

(9) The Lokpal after hearing the Grievance Redressal Officer would impose suitable penalty not exceeding Rs. 500/- for each day's delay but not exceeding Rs. 50,000/- to be recovered from the salaries of the Grievance Redressal Officer.

(10) Apart from levying the penalty on the Grievance Redressal Officer, the Lokpal may also in suitable cases recommend to the appropriate authority to have departmental punishment imposed on the Grievance Redressal Officer.

(11) The Lokpal will also issue a direction to an appropriate authority to get such grievances redressed within the time to be fixed by the Lokpal.

(12) Every public authority shall review and revise its Citizens Charter at least once every year through a process of public consultation to be held in the presence of a representative of Lokpal.

(13) Lokpal may direct any public authority to make such changes in their citizens' charter as are mentioned in that order and that public authority shall make such changes within a month of the receipt of such order. Provided that such changes shall have to be approved by at least a three member bench of Lokpal.

(14) There shall be at least one officer of the Lokpal in each district to receive grievances who shall be called an Appellate Grievance Officer. However, in such places where there is more concentration of central government offices, there shall be more Appellate Grievance Officers as may be required.

(15) A social audit of each Appellate Grievance Officer shall take place every six months, in which he shall present himself before the public, present the data related to his functioning, respond to public queries and incorporate suggestions from public in his functioning. The public hearing shall be attended by a senior officer from Lokpal.

(16) No case can be closed by Appellate Grievance Officer till the citizen's grievance is redressed or the case is rejected by the Appellate Grievance Officer.

CHAPTER XIV
BUDGET OF LOKPAL

26. (1) All expenses of the Lokpal shall be charged to the Consolidated fund of India.

(2) The Board shall finalise the Lokpal's budget in such a manner that it is less than ¼ % of the total revenues of the Government of India.

(3) Lokpal shall not need any administrative or financial sanction from any government agency to incur expenditure.

CHAPTER XV
SEIZURE AND CONFISCATION OF PROPERTY AND RECOVERY OF COMPENSATION FROM CORRUPT GOVERNMENT SERVANTS

27. (1) After a public servant has been found guilty by the Special Court of having committed an offence under the Prevention of Corruption Act, the Court would also determine the assets and properties which have been acquired by such accused person by his corrupt acts.

(2) The Special Court will pass an order for the confiscation of all the assets and properties which it has found to have been acquired by the corrupt acts of the convicted public servants as well as the subsequent accruals on these assets.

(3) The Special Court would also determine whether apart from the above the accused person by his corrupt acts has also caused any loss to the exchequer or any other person and determine the amount of loss so caused. The Court shall make an order levying a fine on the accused persons so convicted for the recovery of the entire loss which his corrupt acts have caused and shall also apportion this amount among the various convicted accused persons to be recovered from them as fines.

(4) During the course of investigation if the Investigating Officer finds any property or asset which appears to have been acquired by the corrupt acts of an accused person who is being investigated, it shall make an order of attachment of those assets so that they are available for confiscation at the time of the conviction of such accused persons. In case the accused person is ultimately acquitted, these attached assets and properties will be restored to him.

CHAPTER XVI

PUBLIC SERVANTS PROPERTY STATEMENTS

28. (1) Every public servant shall within 3 months after the commencement of this Act and thereafter before the 30th June of every year submit to the Head of that public authority in which the said public servant is functioning or to such other authority as may be prescribed, a statement of his assets and liabilities and those of the members of his family which shall include their sources of income, in the format prescribed by the Lokpal.

Explanation : In this Section family of a public servant means the spouse and such children and parents of the public servant and such other people as are dependent on him.

(2) The Head of each public authority shall ensure that all such statements are put on the website by 31st of August of that year.

(3) If it is found that the public servant owns some property which was not disclosed in his statement of assets, that property would be liable to be confiscated by the Lokpal.

(4) If the public servant is found to be in possession or enjoyment of any property which is not shown in his statement of assets, it shall be presumed that it was owned by him unless he proves to the contrary.

CHAPTER XVII

APPLICABILITY AND MODIFICATIONS OF THE PROVISIONS OF CERTAIN OTHER ACTS

29. (1) Section 19(1) and 19(2) of the Prevention of Corruption Act shall be deleted.

(2) Section 6A of the Delhi Special Police Establishment Act shall not be applicable to the proceedings under this Act.

(3) Section 197 of Cr. PC shall not applicable to any proceedings under this Act.

(4) The provisions of sections 105C to 1051 of Cr. PC shall apply to offences under the Prevention of Corruption Act whether or not they are transnational in nature.

(5) Section 389(3) of Cr. PC shall not apply to offences under Prevention of Corruption Act.

(6) The right to file appeals under section 377 or 378 of Cr. PC shall be exercised by Lokpal.

(7) Under section 372 of Cr. PC, the power to file an appeal shall be with the complainant as well.

(8) Notwithstanding anything contained in Section 397 of Cr. PC, no court shall ordinarily call for records in cases related to trial of offences in Prevention of Corruption Act during any trial by a special court.

Provided that if the court calls for records, the same shall be returned within a month.

(9) Any permission which is required under any law for initiating investigation or initiating prosecution under any Act shall be deemed to have been granted once the Lokpal has granted permission to initiate investigation or prosecution for any offences under the Prevention of Corruption Act.

(10) The power of the Lokpal to investigate offences under the Prevention of Corruption Act shall be with the Lokpal notwithstanding any provision in the Money Laundering Act, 2002.

(11) The jurisdiction of the special courts under the Prevention of Corruption Act, 1988 to try offences under such act shall be with the Special Court notwithstanding any provision in the Money Laundering Act, 2002.

(12) The appropriate Bench of the Lokpal shall be deemed to be the designated authority under Section 5 of the Indian Telegraph Act empowered to approve interseption and monitoring of messages or data or voice transmitted through telephones, internet or any other medium as covered under the Indian Telegraph Act read with Information and Technology Act 2000 and as per rules and regulations made under the Indian Telegraph Act 1885.

(13) Section 4 (4) of Prevention of Corruption Act shall be amended as- "Notwithstanding anything contained in the Code of Criminal Procedure, 1973 a Special Judge shall hold the trial of an offence on day-to-day basis, and shall not grant adjournment for any purpose unless such adjournment is, in its opinion, necessary in the interests of justice and for reasons to be recorded in writing"

CHAPTER XVIII

MISCELLANEOUS PROVISIONS

Punishments for false complaints:

30. (1) Notwithstanding anything contained in this Act, if someone

makes any complaint under this Act, which lacks any basis or evidence and is held by Lokpal to be meant only to harass certain authorities, Lokpal may impose such fines on that complainant as it deems fit, but the total fine in anyone case shall not exceed Rs. one lakh.

Provided that no fine can be imposed without giving a reasonable opportunity of being heard to the complaintant.

Provided further that merely because a case could not be proved under this Act after investigation shall not be held against a complainant for the purposes of this section.

Provided that if such complaint is against the staff or officers of Lokpal, Lokpal may sentence the complainant to three months of simple imprisonment in addition to fine.

(2) Such fines shall be recoverable as dues under Land Revenue Act.

(3) A complaint or allegation once made under this Act shall not be allowed to be withdrawn.

Provisions to prevent corruption:

31. (1) No government official shall be eligible to take up jobs, assignments, consultancies, etc. with any person, company, or organisation that he had dealt with in his official capacity.

(2) All contracts, public private partnerships, transfer by way of sale, lease, and any form of largesse by any public authority shall be done with complete transparency and by calling for public tender/auction/bids unless it is an emergency measure or where it is not possible to do so for reasons to be recorded in writing. Any violation of this shall make the contract/ largesse void. The details of all such transactions would be put up by the public authority on a public website.

(3) All contracts, agreements or MOUs known by any name related to transfer of natural resources, including land and mines to any private entity by any method like public/private partnerships, sale, lease or any form of largesse by any public authority shall be put on the website within a week of being signed.

Merger of anti-corruption branch of CBI into Lokpal:

32. (1) The part of the Delhi Special Police Establishment, dealing with investigation and prosecution of offences under the Prevention of Corruption Act, 1988, shall stand transferred, alongwith its employees, assets and liabilities to the Lokpal. The Central Government shall cease to have any control over the transferred part and its personnel.

(2) Such part of Delhi Special Police Establishment, which has been transferred above, shall form part of the Investigation Wing of Lokpal.

(3) The salaries, allowances and other terms and conditions of services of the personnel transferred above shall be the same as they were immediately before the commencement of this Act.

(4) All cases which were being dealt by that part of Delhi Special Police Establishment, which has been transferred, shall stand transferred to Lokpal.

Immunity to bribe giver in certain cases:

33. Any bribe giver may be granted immunity from prosecution by the special court if he voluntarily and gives timely information to the Lokpal about the giving of bribe by him with entire evidence for the purpose of getting the concerned bribe taker/public servant caught and convicted, provided he also relinquishes all the illegitimate benefits which he had received by the giving of that bribe. If the information provided by such bribe giver is subsequently found to be false, the immunity could be withdrawn by the special court. (This draft provides only for the Lokpal for central public servants. Similar provisions for Lokayuktas in the States to deal with public servants of the State will have to be incorporated in the bill).

APPENDIX-TWO

LIST OF PRIME MINISTERS OF INDIA

No.	Name (Birth-Death); Constituency	CM	Term of office		Elections (Lok Sabha)	Political Party (Alliance)	Refs.
1.	Jawaharlal Nehru (1889-1964) MP from Phulpur	1. 2. 3.	15 August 1947	27 May 1964	1952 (1st) 1957 (2nd) 1962 (3rd)	India National Congress	(1)
		Indo-Pakistani War of 1947; created Planning commission of India and initiated Five-year plan to increase government investment in agriculture and industry; launched programmes to build irrigation canals, dams and spread the use of fertilizers to increase agricultural production; oversaw widespread poverty and unemployment, even with improvements in agriculture and infrastructure; oversaw establishment of All India Institute of Medical Sciences, Indian Institutes of Technology and Indian Institutes of Management; criminalized caste discrimination and increased the legal rights and social freedoms of women; pioneered the policy of non-alignment and co-founded the Non-Aligned Movement; Sino-Indian War; signed the Indus Waters Treaty; granted asylum to the Dalai Lama; oversaw liberation of Goa.					

No.	Name (Birth-Death); Constituency	CM	Term of office		Elections (Lok Sabha)	Political Party (Alliance)	Refs.
—	Gulzarilal Nanda (1898-1998) MP from Sabarkantha	—	27 May 1964 *(int)*	9 June 1964	-(3rd)	India National Congress	**(2)**
		Served as caretaker Prime Minister until the election of Lal Bahadur Shastri.					
2.	Lal Bahadur Shastri (1904-1966) MP from Allahabad	4	9 June 1964	11 January 1966	-(3rd)	India National Congress	**(3)**
		Indo-Pakistani War of 1965; pushed for Green Revolution in India and Operation Flood; The National Dairy Development Board was formed; died from a heart attack at a summit in Tashkent.					
—	Gulzarilal Nanda (1898-1998) MP from Sabarkantha	—	11 January 1966 *(int)*	24 January 1966	-(3rd)	India National Congress	**(2)**
		Served as caretaker Prime Minister once again, until Indira Gandhi was chosen as the new leader.					

No.	Name (Birth-Death); Constituency	CM	Term of office		Elections (Lok Sabha)	Political Party (Alliance)	Refs.
3.	Indira Gandhi (1917-1984) MP from Rai Bareli	5 6	24 January 1966	24 March 1977	-(3rd) 1967 (4th) 1971 (5th)	India National Congress	(4)
		Nationalised banks; won the Indo-Pakistani War of 1971, which resulted in the formation of Bangladesh; signed the Shimla Agreement; tested the first nuclear weapon with Smiling Buddha; initiated Green Revolution in India; imposed state of emergency 1975-1977.					
4.	Morarji Desai (1896-1996) MP from Surat	7	24 March 1977	28 July 1979	1977 (6th)	Janata Party	(5)
		Ended the state of emergency initiated by Indira Gandhi; improved relations with Pakistan, China and the United States; softened its relationship with the Soviet Union; launched Sixth Five-Year Plan, aiming to boost agricultural production and rural industries; the plan proved unsuccessful leading to resurging inflation, fuel shortages, unemployment and poverty; lost many MPs from Janata Party, including his rival Charan Singh, which led to his resignation.					

No.	Name (Birth-Death); Constituency	CM	Term of office		Elections (Lok Sabha)	Political Party (Alliance)	Refss
5.	Charan Singh (1902-1987) MP from Baghpat	8	28 July 1979	14 January 1980	—(6th)	Janata Party (Secular) with Indian National Congress	(6)
		Initiated high level diplomatic relations with Israel; list support of Congress, which led to his resignation without even a single session of Lok Sabha.					
(3)	Indira Gandhi (1917-1984) MP from Rai Bareli	9	14 January 1980	31 October 1984	1980 (7th)	Indian Natiolnal Congress (Indira)	(7)
		Operation Blue Star, which subsequently led to her assassination.					
6.	Rajiv Gandhi (1944-1991) MP from Amethi	10	31 October 1984	2 December 1989	1984 (8th)	Indian Natiolnal Congress	(8)
		1984 anti-Sikh riots; significantly reduced License Raj; expanded telecommunications in India; signed the Indo-Sri Lanka Peace Accord; Bofors scandal; nullified the Supreme Court's judgement on Shah Bano case.					

No.	*Name (Birth-Death); Constituency*	*CM*	*Term of office*		*Elections (Lok Sabha)*	*Political Party (Alliance)*	*Refs.*
7.	V.P. Singh (1931-2008) MP from Fatehpur	11	2 December 1989	10 November 1990	1989 (9th)	Janata Dal *(National Front)*	(9)
		Negotiated terriorist kidnapping of Mufti Mohammad Sayeed's daughter; vitited Golden Temple to ask for forgiveness for Operation Bluestar; withdrew IPKF from Sri Lanka; initiated fixed quota/reservation for all public sector jobs as per recommendation from Mandal Commission; Ram Janmabhoomi agitation and subsequent loss of vote of no confidence because of it.					
8.	Chandra Shekhar (1927-2007) MP from Ballia	12	10 November 1990	21 June 1991	—(9th)	Samajwadi Janta Party *with Bharatiya Janata Party*	(10)
		Resigned due to accusations of spying on former Prime Minister Rajiv Gandhi, and subsequent withdrawal of Congress' support; Assassination of Rajiv Gandhi.					
9.	P.V. Narasimha Rao (1921-2004) MP from Nandyal	13	21 June 1991	16 May 1996	1991 (10th)	Indian National Congress	(11)
		Initiated Economic liberalization in India; SEBI Act 1992; formation of National Stock Exchange of India; 1993 Bombay bombings; introduced TADA; Demolitionl of Babri Masjid.					

No.	Name (Birth-Death); Constituency	CM	Term of office		Elections (Lok Sabha)	Political Party (Alliance)	Refs.
10.	Atal Bihari Vajpayee (1924-) MP from Lucknow	14	16 May 1996	1 June 1996	1996 (11th)	Bharatiya Janata Party	**(12)**
		Hung parliament. Was in power for only 13 days, after BJP could not gather enough support from other parties to form a majority.					
11.	H.D. Deve Gowda (1933-) MP from Hassan	15	1 June 1996	21 April 1997	1996 (11th)	Janata Dal *(United Front)*	**(12)**
		Hung parliament. After a failed attempt of forming a BJP government, Congress refused to form a government and instead supported a minority United Front coalition led by Janata Dal. President of China Jiang Zemin begins the first visit by a Chinese head of state of India; initiates President's rule in Gujarat.					
12.	Inder Kumar Gujral (1919-) MP (Rajya Sabha) from Bihar	16	21 April 1997	19 March 1998	- (11th)	Janata Dal *(United Front)*	**(13)**
		Fodder scam; Jain Commission.					

No.	Name (Birth-Death); Constituency	CM	Term of office		Elections (Lok Sabha)	Political Party (Alliance)	Refs.
(10)	Atal Bihari Vajpayee (1924-) MP from Lucknow	17 18	19 March 1998	22 May 2004	1998 (12th) 1999 (13th)	Bharatiya Janata Party *(National Democratic Alliance)*	(14)
		Pokhran nuclear tests; Kargil War; National Highway Development Project; Pradhan Mantri Gram Sadak Yojana; expanding ties with Israel; POTA; Sarva Shiksha Abhiyan; 2001 Gujarat earthquake; 2002 Gujarat violence; National Technical Research Organisation.					
13.	Dr. Manmohan Singh (1932-) MP (Rajya Sabha) from Assam	19 20	22 May 2004	Incumbent	2004 (14th) 2009 (15th)	National Congress *(Inited Progressive Alliance)*	(15)
		2006 Indian anti-reservation protests; Indo-US civilian nuclear agreement; won the 2008 Lok Sabha vote of confidence; US $1 Trillion Economy milestone reached; expanding ties with Israel; Economic crisis of 2008; National Rural Employment Guarantee Act (NREGA); Right to Information Act; revoking of POTA; 2008 Mumbai attacks and the implementation of Unlawful Activities (Prevention) Act; First visit by Indian PM since 1982 to Saudi Arabia; National Investigation Agency (India); 2G spectrum scam; Adarsh scam; NTRO Scam; Commonwealth Games Scam; Unique ID; Right of Children to Free and Compulsory Education Act; Anna Hazare's Jan Lokpal agitation.					

APPENDIX-THREE

LIST OF PRESIDENTS OF CONGRESS PARTY

Name of President	*Life Span*	*Year of Presidency*	*Place of Conference*
Narasinha Mudholkar			
Nawab Syed Muhammad Bahadur	?- 1919	1913	Karachi
Bhupendra Nath Bose	1859-1924	1914	Madras
Lord Satyendra Prasanna Sinha	March 1863-1928	1915	Bombay
Ambica Charan Mazumdar	1850-1922	1916	Lucknow
Annie Besant	1 October 1847-1933	1917	Calcutta
Pandit Madan Mohan Malaviya	25 December 1861-1946	1918	Delhi
Syed Hasan Imam	31 August 1871-1933	1918	Bombay (Special Session)
Pandit Motilal Nehru	6 May 1861- 6 February 1931	1919	Amritsar
Lala Lajpat Rai	28 January 1965- 17 November 1928	1920	Calcutta (Special Session)
C. Vijavaraghavachariar	1852- 16 April 1944	1920	Nagpur
Hakim Ajmal Khan	1863- 29 December 1927	1921	Ahmedabad
Deshbandhu Chittaranjan Das	5 November 1870- 16 June 1925	1922	Gaya
Maulana Mohammad Ali	10 December 1878- 4 January 1931	1923	Kakinada
Maulana Abul Kalam Azad	1888- 22 February 1958	1923	Delhi (Special Session)
Mahatma Gandhi	2 October 1869- 30 January 1948	1924	Belgaum
SarojiniNaidu	13 February 1879- 2 March 1949	1925	Kanpur
S. Srinivasa Iyengar	September 11, 1874- 19 May 1941	1926	Gauhati
Dr. M.A. Ansari	25 December 1880- 10 May 1936	1927	Madras
Pandit Motilal Nehru	6 May 1861- 6 February 1931	1928	Calcutta

Name of President	*Life Span*	*Year of Presidency*	*Place of Conference*
Pandit Jawaharlal Nehru	14 November 1889- 27 May 1964	1929 & 30	Lahore
Sardar Vallabhbhai Patel	31 October 1875- 15 December 1950	1931	Karachi
Pandit Madan Mohan Malaviya	25 December 1961-1946	1932	Delhi
Pandit Madan Mohan Malaviya	25 December 1861-1946	1933	Calcutta
Nellie Sengupta	1886-1973	1933	Calcutta
Dr. Rajendra Prasad	3 December 1884- 28 February 1963	1934 & 35	Bombay
Pandit Jawaharlal Nehru	14 November 1889- 27 May 1964	1936	Lucknow
Pandit Jawaharlal Nehru	14 November 1889- 27 May 1964	1936 & 37	Faizpur
Netaji Subhash Chandra Bose	23 January 1897- 18 August 1945?	1938	Haripura
Netaji Subhash Chandra Bose	23 January 1897- 18 August 1945?	1939	Jabalpur
Maulana Abul Kalam Azad	1888- 22 February 1958	1940-46	Ramgarh
Acharya J.B. Kripalani	1888- 19 March 1982	1947	Delhi
Dr Pattabhi Sitaraimayya	24 December 1880- 17 December 1959	1948 & 49	Jaipur
Purushottam Das Tandon	1 August 1882- 1 July 1961	1950	Nasik
Pandit Jawaharlal Nehru	14 November 1889- 27 May 1964	1951 & 52	Delhi
Pandit Jawaharlal Nehru	14 November 1889- 27 May 1964	1953	Hyderabad
Pandit Jawaharlal Nehru	14 November 1889- 27 May 1964	1954	Kalyani
UN Dhebar	21 September 1905-1977	1955	Avadi
UN Dhebar	21 September 1905-1977	1956	Amritsar
UN Dhebar	21 September 1905-1977	1957	Indore
UN Dhebar	21 September 1905-1977	1958	Gauhari
UN Dhebar	21 September 1905-1977	1959	Nagpur
Indira Gandhi	19 November 1917-31 October 1984	1959	Delhi

Name of President	*Life Span*	*Year of Presidency*	*Place of Conference*
Neelam Sanjiva Reddy	19 May 1913- 1 June 1996	1960	Bangalore
Neelam Sanjiva Reddy	19 May 1913- 1 June 1996	1961	Bhavnagar
Neelam Sanjiva Reddy	19 May 1913- 1 June 1996	1962 & 63	Patna
K. Kamaraj	15 July 1903- 2 October 1975	1964	Bhubaneswar
K. Kamaraj	15 July 1903- 2 October 1975	1965	Durgapur
K. Kamaraj	15 July 1903- 2 October 1975	1966 & 67	Jaipur
S. Nijalingappa	10 December 1902- 9 August 2000	1968	Hyderabad
S. Nijalingappa	10 December 1902- 9 August 2000	1969	Faridabad
Jagjivan Ram	5 April 1908- 6 July 1986	1970 & 71	Bombay
Dr. Shankar Dayal Sharma	19 August 1918- 26 December 1999	1972-74	Calcutta
Dev Kant Baruah	22 February 1914- 1996	1975-77	Chandigarh
Indira Gandhi	19 November 1917- 31 October 1984	1978-83	Delhi
Indira Gandhi	19 November 1917- 31 October 1984	1983-84	Calcutta
Rajiv Gandhi	20 August 1944- 21 May 1991	1985-91	Bombay
P.V. Narasimha Rao	28 June 1921- 23 December 2004	1992-96	Tirupati
Sitaram Kesri	November 1919- 24 October 2000	1997-98	Kolkata
Sonia Gandhi	9 December 1946-	1998-present	Kolkata

Index

S

T

U

V

W

Y